Surrealism and Women

C. Caulfield

Surrealism and Women

edited by
Mary Ann Caws
Rudolf E. Kuenzli
Gwen Raaberg

The MIT Press
Cambridge, Massachusetts
London, England

Third printing, 1993

First MIT Press Edition 1991

© 1990 Association for the Study of Dada and Surrealism

Originally published as the journal *Dada/Surrealism,* no. 18, by the Association for
the Study of Dada and Surrealism, The University of Iowa.

Printed and bound in the United States of America.

Library of Congress Cataloging in Publication Data

Surrealism and women / edited by Mary Ann Caws, Rudolf E. Kuenzli, Gwen
Raaberg.
     p.   cm.
    Includes bibliographical references.
    ISBN 0-262-53098-8
    1. Surrealism.   2. Feminism and the arts.   3. Arts, Modern – 20th century.
I. Caws, Mary Ann   II. Kuenzli, Rudolf E.   III. Raaberg, Gloria Gwen.
NX456.5.S8S87   1991
    700 – dc20
                                                90-15477
                                                  CIP

CONTENTS

I. INTRODUCTIONS

The Problematics of Women and Surrealism

Gwen Raaberg

The necessity for further investigation of the work of women Surrealists first became evident to me in the early 1970s when I came upon a painting by Remedios Varo in Mexico City's Museo de Arte Moderno. I recognized her work as that of a woman Surrealist and yet I was unfamiliar with it, although I was a student and teacher of Surrealism. The problem was obvious: exhibitions and scholarly texts examining the work of the Surrealists had not included the work of the women Surrealists except in a perfunctory manner (Meret Oppenheim's fur-lined teacup was a tiresomely repeated exception). Through a critical approach that focused on the male Surrealists and a historical practice that reiterated this exclusionary process, a membership role had been devised which was almost exclusively male and a canon established which excluded the major productions of women Surrealists.

Fortunately, since the 1970s the women writers and artists of Surrealism have increasingly attracted the attention of critics and historical scholars. One of the first investigations of women Surrealists appeared in the spring 1973 issue of the *Feminist Art Journal,* which featured a survey article by Gloria Feman Orenstein. *Obliques,* the French review, devoted a special issue in 1977 to "La Femme surréaliste" and compiled a listing of thirty-six women considered to be Surrealists. Jacqueline Chénieux included an important discussion of works by women surrealist writers in her *Le Surréalisme et le roman* (1983), and work by Renée Riese Hubert has furthered our understanding of both women surrealist writers and painters. Whitney Chadwick's *Women Artists and the Surrealist Movement* (1985) was a groundbreaking effort that has provided basic information invaluable to further research.[1]

But the issue of the women Surrealists has not been simply a matter of retrieving a history. It was not that the original generation of male Surrealists had ignored women. In fact, among twentieth-century artistic movements, the Surrealists undoubtedly had been most concerned with women. And the men were certainly aware of the work of these women writers and artists, for in many instances they were spouses and lovers. No women, though, had been listed as official members of the original

1

surrealist movement, nor had they signed the manifestoes. It was not until the 1930s and later that women began to be given a more significant role in the surrealist movement. Some of the women Surrealists, such as Meret Oppenheim and Gisèle Prassinos, were discovered by the males of the group. Others came to the movement through personal relationships with the male members, among them Leonora Carrington, partner of Max Ernst, and Remedios Varo, wife of Benjamin Péret. Many of the women writers and artists were younger than their male counterparts and often produced their most mature work after their relationships with the male Surrealists and the movement had ended. It is generally acknowledged, then, that the women belong more properly to a second generation of Surrealists. Moreover, some of these women distanced themselves from Breton and the movement as a whole, and have even refused the designation of Surrealist. Nevertheless, the women writers and artists discussed here had at some time in their career a direct connection to the surrealist movement, and they developed a large body of work within the context of surrealist principles.[2]

The women Surrealists, though, experienced a marginalization not only in male-dominated bourgeois culture but within the ranks of the avant-garde as well. André Breton was supportive of a number of the women Surrealists, promoting some writers, such as Joyce Mansour, and including some artists, such as Toyen, Frida Kahlo, and Judith Reigl, in exhibitions and critical evaluations of Surrealism. But even when the women were included by Breton and the male Surrealists, a full recognition of their conceptual and creative force seems lacking. Breton's evaluation of Judith Reigl (a Hungarian painter and illustrator of Lautréamont) in his brief essay included in *Surrealism and Painting* gives evidence of the problem:

It seems so unlikely that the ship sweeping forward could be steered by a woman's hand that some quite exceptional force must be assumed to be helping to drive it along. And it would appear, in fact, that, before casting off, her ship had drawn up an agreement with two hitherto inflexible powers. One of these is Lautréamont. . . . The other . . . is Csontvary, a titanic painter who is still almost unknown in France.[3]

Although the work is praised, the woman is not granted autonomous artistic powers.

The problem arises out of a situation in which the concepts and principles that focused Breton and other male Surrealists on the female also limited their capacity to view women as independent, active subjects. The Surrealists conceived of woman as man's mediator with nature and the unconscious, *femme-enfant,* muse, source and object of man's desire, embodiment of *amour fou,* and emblem of revolution. The concept of "woman" objectified by male needs was in direct conflict with the individ-

2

ual woman's subjective need for self-definition and free artistic expression. The women writers and artists who chose to work within the framework provided by surrealist principles thus found their situation marked by contradictions inherent in these very principles.

The articles included in this volume devoted to women and Surrealism enter into a critical discussion that proceeds out of a recognition of this fundamental problem. The analyses offer widely differing critical approaches and opinions, but all function within a critical discourse that acknowledges both the importance of the women Surrealists' contributions and the problematics of women writers and artists working within a surrealist context. The purpose of this collection of criticism is not to reject Surrealism but to rethink it, expanding our conception of the movement, its principles, and its artistic works to include the perspective of the women Surrealists. The goal is to develop our awareness of the full range of surrealist manifestations, by females as well as males, and to explore the complexity and problematical issues of surrealist vision(s): in short, to work toward a revision of Surrealism.

The contributors to this volume address issues in three areas of concern: (1) a further investigation of the historical context and the relationship of particular women writers and artists to the surrealist movement; (2) a consideration of the degree to which a woman writer/artist accepts or rejects surrealist principles, and an analysis of the particular characteristics of Surrealism in her work; and (3) an exploration of the problems women writers and artists experienced working within a surrealist context.

Within the parameters of these broad issues, a number of more specific problems and questions surface. A basic problem is the need for further clarification of the principles and practice of the male Surrealists. This issue, therefore, begins with editorial statements by Mary Ann Caws and Rudolf Kuenzli that are important in providing the ground for the critical discourses that follow. Responding to feminist critiques of the male Surrealists' conception of woman, some critics have attempted to redeem the surrealist enterprise by excluding works in certain genres. It has become a critical commonplace that although surrealist painting may be misogynist, surrealist poetry celebrates the female. Caws addresses this issue and concludes that the controversial attitudes of the male Surrealists toward women, although perhaps more subtle, are nevertheless present in the poetry.[4]

Kuenzli addresses similar attempts to defend Surrealism from charges of misogyny. He is particularly concerned with rejecting what he views as an attempt by Rosalind Krauss to make a special case for photography in *L'Amour fou: Photography and Surrealism*. Krauss's semiotic analysis focuses on surrealist photography as the Other of straight photography, positing the marginal as the metaphorical "feminine," as does contemporary French theory, and ignoring a historical critique of gender and power issues.[5] Kuenzli, however, argues for the necessity of an investigation of surrealist power relations and a certain line of interrogation: in the construction of surrealist images, "who has the power, who dominates, who is disfigured by whose power?" Caws and Kuenzli thus insist upon a fundamental critique of surrealist principles and practice, a reassessment which provides the critical context for the analyses of the women Surrealists that follow.

These critiques of male surrealist practice open directly onto the problematics of women writers and artists functioning as members of the surrealist movement and manipulating the language and images of surrealist discourse. As Robert Belton points out in his discussion of female and male surrealist discourse, we need to investigate the surrealist community of meaning and the "interpretive webs," the networks of verbal and visual signs that made surrealist writing and art intelligible to its members and audience. One set of critical issues addresses the historical and critical conception of the surrealist community: To what extent and in what ways are the women writers and artists part of the surrealist movement? Other issues focus on the discourse of that community: How have the women Surrealists been able to position themselves as creative subjects within this discourse? In what ways and to what extent have they accepted the male surrealist discourse, and how have they significantly changed – subverted, inverted, and extended – that discourse?

Gisèle Prassinos and Meret Oppenheim were among those women included as Surrealists by the original male members of the movement. Their works, therefore, provide a basis for investigating the surrealist "community of meaning" and the functioning of women writers and artists within that discourse. Prassinos was declared by the male Surrealists to be the embodiment of the *femme-enfant*. And although Oppenheim denies it in her interview with Belton, she undoubtedly functioned in this capacity for the Surrealists when, at the age of twenty, she was first included in their exhibitions. That Prassinos and Oppenheim (especially as figured in Man Ray's photograph of her, nude) also embodied for the Surrealists the principle of revolution does not mean that they were necessarily the active subjects of that revolution. Their works were inserted into a discourse already well established by Breton in the surrealist manifestoes and by the community of male members in their writings and art. As Inez Hedges points out in her article on Prassinos, the youthful female poet's rebellion was diverted to the purposes of the male Surrealists' revolt, effectively coopting her early writings. Similarly, Oppenheim's rebellious early work gained new meaning – and notoriety – by functioning within the discourse defined by the male Surrealists. Her fur-lined cup, as she notes in her interview, took on a meaning different from the one she had conceived when it was named and imbedded in a network of allusions by

Breton. It becomes significant in this context of cooptation and deflected meaning that both women, following their early discovery by the Surrealists, suffered prolonged periods of silence and inability to work creatively.

Oppenheim's work, though, often appears to establish its meaning well within the parameters of male surrealist discourse. It may even seem disingenuous of her to express surprise in her interview that the male Surrealists coopted the meaning of her "Spring Feast" on the nude body of a woman, recreated for the EROS exhibition in 1959, by assuming a male subject and power position in relation to the cannibalized woman. Renée Riese Hubert, however, analyzes Oppenheim's career in terms of a dialectic between "woman" and artist, and finds that the work opens a gap between woman as male object of desire and the female subject who assembled it. The contradictory status of a female in the subject position of surrealist discourse is thereby foregrounded and may be viewed by the critic as highly problematic.

Moreover, as Belton points out, it becomes incumbent upon the critic to open a gap between the work imbedded in its historical context and its reinterpretation from a later – and more consciously feminist – perspective. A recognition of the historical context, however, must inform any critique of these women as pro- or proto-feminists. We cannot expect them to exhibit a contemporary feminist perspective, although we can certainly observe (in Oppenheim's interview, for example) moments of precise definition of women's position in society and in the surrealist movement, as well as instances of denials and certain inconsistencies within the female artist's framework of meaning. It is in these moments of contradiction, as well as in moments of clarity and vision, that we can comprehend in the work of the women writers and artists the complexities of their relationship to Surrealism.

From this critical position grounded in a recognition of the basic problems women confronted in Surrealism, we must ask a crucial question: How did the women insert themselves into the male surrealist discourse and/or claim for themselves the subject position of a surrealist work? Orenstein has noted that some women set up in their works dialogues with their surrealist mates, presenting "a double-voiced discourse" that offers both a "dominant" and a "muted" perspective.[6] Susan Suleiman, expanding this idea through the theories of Mikhail Bakhtin, suggests that the women Surrealists' work may be seen as having a general strategy of "internal dialogism" in relation to the males' work.[7] Certainly, the attempt of these female writers and artists to work within the principles laid down by the male Surrealists commits them to a dialogic position. There are, however, a variety of specific strategies used by the women writers and artists. Their work often subtly subverts the male dialogue, as Orenstein points out in her analysis of Carrington, Dorothea Tanning, and Unica Zürn. Or it may pointedly reverse the male and female positions within the dialogue, as in some of Leonor Fini's paintings, such as *Chthonian Divinity Watching Over the Sleep of a Young Man* (1947), and in Valentine Penrose's poem-cycle/photocollage, *Dons des féminines* (1951).[8] Other literary and artistic works assert a more conscious presentation of difference, insisting upon the "feminine" as Other, marginal, or "ruined," as in Lee Miller's photograph, *Fallen Angel—London Blitz* (1940).[9] And there are those women Surrealists, such as Leonora Carrington and Remedios Varo, who seek to move the work beyond polemics and binary oppositions toward a discourse—a mythology and an iconography—based on women's own psychology and experiences.

In analyzing the issue of difference in surrealist discourse, Madeleine Cottenet-Hage focuses on female body imagery in the works of Carrington, Prassinos, and Mansour. This is an especially significant approach since female body imagery is one of the elements of surrealist discourse most emphasized by the male members of the movement and most criticized by contemporary feminists. She investigates the extent to which these three women were reacting against dominant male surrealist images of the female body and the extent to which they were successful in developing a corporeal imagery rooted in their own experiences. She finds that their works are not dominated, as those of the male Surrealists are, by the presence of the body of the Other through which they hope to gain access to surreality, but rather focus on themes which arise out of women's own bodily experiences. She concludes, though, that the movement toward surreality in the work of these women most often remains, as it does in work by the male Surrealists, problematical.

Joyce Mansour's work presents a particularly complex and enigmatic case of the relationship of the female writer to male surrealist discourse. Xavière Gauthier has declared that she finds little difference between sexual motifs in Mansour's work and in the male Surrealists' writings.[10] Hage points out that the detached presentation of sexual violence, female passivity, and victimization in Mansour's work is ambiguous and ambivalent, creating difficulties for the reader in locating the text's subject position, its perspective upon and distance from the narrative action. Judith Preckshot finds this very ambiguity significant, for although Mansour does not question authorship specifically in terms of gender, the shifting gender identities of her narrators reveal a crisis in textual authorial identity. Analyzing this problem through the writer's crucial relation to language, Preckshot points to the connection between Mansour's bilingualism and the necessary "self-translations" the woman writer makes in the process of inserting herself as Other into the male surrealist discourse.

The ambiguous status of the "I" in Mansour's narratives is acknowledged by Maryann De Julio, and she notes the disturbing effect of a split in the self that is produced textually by a female subjectivity reflecting on its own bodily objectification. Turning to an examination of Mansour's use of Egyptian mythology, De Julio argues that in her poems Mansour reclaims a female creation myth as a viable model for her activity as a writer and, therefore, her textual explorations of women's bodies serve to inscribe the female as creative subject. This approach offers a more positive reading of Mansour's textual presentation of female subjectivity and body imagery. Mansour's work remains problematic, however, for whether the intertextual dialogue is with male surrealist writings or with Egyptian mythology, the text reveals the struggle, the deeply ironic ambivalence of the female author who inserts herself into a prior discourse in which she functions neither simply as the one nor the other.

Kay Sage's work also reveals the struggle of a woman to assert herself as creative subject. Her experience of self as Other in relation to a dominant discourse is evident in a poem describing her multilingual voices as "translations": "I think in Chinese." Stephen Miller's investigation of Sage's artistic career presents the movement of the external life behind which we may view the search of the devoted wife and surrealist colleague to find within herself some more solid foundation for female identity. The development in her paintings of a characteristic iconography of scaffolding presents the metaphor of a structure that does not stand as a primary construct. The assertion of self in her paintings and poems is ironically accompanied by a denial: the scaffolding tower, she writes, is built "on despair," and there is nothing to hear or see in it. Sage's loss of creative energy, her depression and eventual suicide following the death of her husband, Yves Tanguy, suggest the internal conflicts that may beset the woman artist's search for autonomy.

It is significant, then, that in a consideration of the long and productive career of Leonora Carrington, Peter Christensen traces a movement in her writings and art from representations of heterosexual passion, to androgynous union, to the autonomy of women's communities. Carrington's "flight from passion" suggests that further questions need to be investigated regarding the surrealist conception of *amour fou*. In the context of Surrealism, love reactivates the libido and enlists it in the passionate overthrow of repressive and oppressive bourgeois existence. We must ask, though, to what extent the concept of surrealist passion was grounded in a premise of male activity and female passivity and a textual mode in which the male assumes the subject position and achieves liberation through the female as Other? This "liberation," as played out in the works of the male Surrealists, too often positions the female in the same passive and oppressed state that bourgeois culture has traditionally placed her. Carrington, in contrast, moves toward concepts of psychic androgyny, relationships that promote autonomy as well as union, and a spirituality ritualized through goddess worship, manifesting a world in which the female subject actively asserts herself in a discourse she shapes out of her own historical and experiential contexts.

7

The development in the work of Carrington, Remedios Varo, and Leonor Fini of an assertive female subject constructed out of her own mythology and values is precisely the characteristic that Georgiana Colvile finds essential in those women Surrealists whom she sees as able to move beyond a dependent, secondary position. She points out that these three artists draw on the associations among woman, nature, and beast made by the male Surrealists, but they move beyond the limitations of these concepts toward that point at which distinctions between external reality and inner self merge—the surrealist marvelous.

There is a discernible difference in those Surrealist works in which the artist assumes the subject position as a female. In the collages of Aube Elléouët, for example, the woman as authorial subject and as represented object is actively engaged in the process of her own transformation, even though the artist works within the boundaries of a conventional surrealist iconography.

Finally, we must ask, given the problems that arise out of their attempts to function within the context of Surrealism, what have the women Surrealists gained by their relationship to the movement and its principles? The most obvious attraction for them was simply that of companionship in a community of writers and artists—regardless of the difficulties inherent in the relationships. Perhaps the greatest advantage, though, is that within the context of the avant-garde, women writers and artists have been able actively to assert their marginality and their difference, and self-consciously to enlist their position as Other in Western culture in a direct confrontation of oppressive bourgeois society.[11] Certainly, too, surrealist techniques and strategies that provided means for getting at repressed areas of the psyche would be helpful to women attempting to assert aspects of the self unacceptable within traditionally prescribed roles for women. Moreover, surrealist principles were dedicated to breaking down the binary oppositions of mind/body, rational/irrational, and art/nature that had functioned to identify woman with the rejected terms—body, irrationality and nature—and situate her in an inferior position.

There are problems inherent in these very advantages, however. At the same time that Surrealism attacked some bourgeois concepts, it reinforced others. Surrealist strategies did not get at an "unconscious" free of socialization. The marginal roles assigned to women in society were often replicated within the movement. "Woman" functioned within male surrealist works at best as an idealized Other, at worst as an object for the projection of unresolved anxieties, and continued to be identified in traditional terms of body, irrationality, and nature. These works typically manifest a male subject seeking transformation through a female representational object, which paradoxically reinforces, especially for the female Surrealist and the female reader or viewer, the subject-object split that Surrealism was dedicated to overcoming. Most important, these works function to construct a surrealist discourse that presumes a dominant male subject and power position.

A number of the essays included here trace a pattern in which surrealist women writers and artists move through a stage of dialogic, sometimes polemical interaction with the male Surrealists' discourse toward a more independent and integrated female subject position. But it is at this point that some critics question whether these women are Surrealists. If they are, then their work would necessarily continue to function to some extent within surrealist discourse(s). At the same time, it is evident, as Hedges notes regarding Prassinos, that the works of these women cannot be completely contained by Surrealism—at least not by Surrealism as it has been defined by male surrealist works. The question here is, Do we as critics recognize surrealist discourses, including one arising primarily out of female experience, or do we accept as surrealist only that discourse established by the male members of the movement, a primary discourse which necessitates that women Surrealists must always participate secondarily and dialogically?

The relationship between women and Surrealism is essentially problematic. Nevertheless, the women Surrealists explored the challenges and contradictions of their situation with passion and courage, devising their own approaches to surrealist language, imagery, techniques, and principles, and experimenting with various translations of surrealist discourse. Ultimately, through their exploration of the female psyche and experiences, they developed new iconographies and mythologies, revising the premises of Surrealism and expanding the parameters of its discourse. Opening the surrealist canon to the works of these women enlarges the scope of Surrealism. And investigating the problems these writers and artists struggled to overcome in their works leads to a greater awareness of the complexity and the problematics of the surrealist undertaking.

We would like to thank Gail Zlatnik for her generous and superb editorial assistance, and Judith Pendleton for her great artistic sense and care.

Notes

1. Some of the most informative general investigations of women Surrealists are: Gloria Feman Orenstein, "Reclaiming the Great Mother: A Feminist Journey to Madness and Back in Search of a Goddess Heritage," *Symposium* 36.1 (Spring 1982), 45–70, and "Women of Surrealism," *Feminist Art Journal* 2.2 (Spring 1973), 1, 15–21; "La Femme surréaliste," special issue of *Obliques* 14–15 (1977); Jacqueline Chénieux, *Le Surréalisme et le roman* (Lausanne: L'Age d'Homme, 1983); Renée Riese Hubert, "Surrealist Women Painters, Feminist Portraits," *Dada/Surrealism* 13 (1984), 70–82; and Whitney Chadwick, *Women Artists and the Surrealist Movement* (Boston: Little, Brown, 1985).

2. Although not all of these women are discussed in this issue, a basic list of women Surrealists would at least include Eileen Agar, Leonora Carrington, Ithell Colquhoun, Leonor Fini, Valentine Hugo, Frida Kahlo, Joyce Mansour, Lee Miller, Meret Oppenheim, Valentine Penrose, Gisèle Prassinos, Kay Sage, Dorothea Tanning, Toyen, Remedios Varo, and Unica Zürn.

3. André Breton, *Le Surréalisme et la peinture* (Paris: Gallimard, 1965); English ed. trans. Simon Watson Taylor, *Surrealism and Painting* (New York: Harper and Row, 1972), 238.

4. See also Mary Ann Caws, "Ladies Shot and Painted: Female Embodiment in Surrealist Art," in *The Female Body in Western Culture,* ed. Susan R. Suleiman (Cambridge: Harvard University Press, 1986), 262–87.

5. Rosalind Krauss and Jane Livingston, *L'Amour fou: Photography and Surrealism* (New York: Abbeville Press, 1985). It should be noted, however, that a semiotic analysis could also provide a method for approaching the problematics of Surrealism. Krauss's analysis is based on notions of spacing which insert self-conscious signification into the artistic and critical process: the object photographed is acknowledged to be already object-as-sign. The methodology thus not only permits but indeed insists upon a deconstruction of the sign system.

6. Gloria Feman Orenstein, "Towards a Bifocal Vision in Surrealist Aesthetics," *Trivia* 3 (Fall 1983), 70–87.

7. Susan Rubin Suleiman, "A Double Margin: Reflections on Women Writers and the Avant-garde in France," *Yale French Studies* 75 (1988), 148–72.

8. Chadwick, 124, fig. 107. See also Hubert, "Surrealist Women Painters," 70–82.

9. Chadwick, 41, fig. 25.

10. Xavière Gauthier, *Surréalisme et sexualité* (Paris: Gallimard, 1971), 170–73. Gauthier's feminist critique of Surrealism therefore extended to Mansour as a female practitioner.

11. See Suleiman's discussion of the double margin of women and the avant-garde, 148–57. See also Hélène Cixous, "The Laugh of the Medusa," trans. Keith Cohen and Paula Cohen, in *New French Feminisms,* ed. Elaine Marks and Isabelle de Courtivron (New York: Schocken Books, 1981), 245–64. Cixous places women in a privileged position to write the insurgent text, although for Cixous, this text has yet to be written.

Seeing the Surrealist Woman: We Are a Problem

Mary Ann Caws

Nous porterons ailleurs le luxe de la peste
Nous un peu de gelée blanche sur les fagots humains
Et c'est tout . . .
Nous le pain sec et l'eau dans les prisons du ciel

(We'll carry the luxury of the plague elsewhere
We a bit of hoarfrost on human firewood
And that's all
We plain bread and water in the prisons of the sky)

André Breton, "Broken Line"[1]

Headless. And also footless. Often armless too; and always unarmed, except with poetry and passion. There they are, the surrealist women so shot and painted,[2] so stressed and dismembered, punctured and severed: is it any wonder she has (we have) gone to pieces? It is not just the dolls of Hans Bellmer, lying about, it is more. Worse, because more lustily appealing, as in Man Ray's images.

I am looking at one of the most problematic of them: to describe her (or the part of her that exists, confronting me), is already to feel nervous. She is posed like a challenge, wrapped like a dubious present in shimmering dark water-patterned and tight moire, glistening just about everywhere she is (no head, no feet, no anything but that body mesmerizing, arms akimbo), this dame Man Ray so severs and swaddles and stresses is none of us, exactly. But maybe is us all, as we are seen. Sure and strident, ready to do anything we can – except we can neither speak nor think nor see, nor walk and run, certainly not love and paint and write and be. Surrealist woman, problematic and imprisoned, for the other eyes.

Give them their head: they had one
The women we are presenting in, and saluting by, this volume *Women and Surrealism* are the contrary, each and all of them, of the dame wrapped up and shiny that Man Ray so shot. They, all of them, wrote or painted, saw and thought and were, not necessarily as the others of men, but not as

11

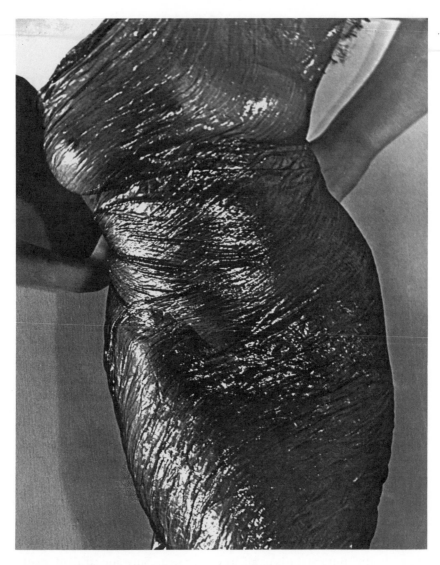

Man Ray, Untitled, 1929. Bibliothèque nationale, Paris.

their mothers either. We have wanted to give them their head, their eyes, and their hands, not just on their hips to provocate, but free, to use as they pleased and did.

Give them their voice: they had one

Sure, they spoke in differing accents, and their voice was not always pleasing. It was, from time to time, cruel, jesting, acerbic; and, from time to time (harder to take, for some of us), self-effacing. But we have wanted to give their multiple voices their due, so we could listen. And keep on listening.

Let them stand on their own two feet: they had two.

And were not necessarily the runners-around with or the runners-after their male companion, if they had or wanted one. They were capable of going, and of going fast and often first. We have wanted to let them choose and take their stride. Are they, then, strident women? Yes, sometimes, even frequently. And does that bother us? Nope.

Besides, Nadja knew how to draw.

And there she is, drawing away in those pages, with Breton looking on, only he gets bored.

Let him.

Now, I actually think Breton had some problem with the female gender. He really did.

The buildup was fine, and even glorious: In *Mad Love*,[3] he exclaims in horror about the conception of love burning itself out: "So Juliet, continuing to live, would no longer be always more Juliet for Romeo!" She should have been, of course, and in the innocence that love creates – and that he would have believed it possible to create – that would have been quite surely so. But Breton himself, and continually, is skeptical of the continuity of the sublime in the fact of love.

Look what happens to all his heroines: Nadja, fascinating because mad, is then disappointing, because she is not interesting enough; she reads the menu aloud and, says Breton, I was bored. Later, of course, when she has gone truly (therefore, for him, terrifyingly) mad, and been put away – after a pause ("They came to tell me Nadja was insane"), he can confess he was not up to loving her as he should have. But on the moment, boredom. In *The Communicating Vessels*,[4] Breton is enchanted at one moment by a woman who dangles her perfect legs sitting across from him, next to her dreadfully dull companion ("probably a teacher" – !), at another, by some lovely eyes walking along. He goes back to meet those eyes, but panics at the thought that actually, he wouldn't be able to recognize the girl were she not looking, because, well, of course, he had forgotten everything else. What matters, matters, and if you don't see it, the rest gets lost: "J'avais en effet, tout oublié de sa silhouette, de son maintien et, pour peu que ses yeux fussent baissés, je ne me sentais pas capable de l'identifier à trois pas" ("I had, in fact, forgotten everything about her silhouette and the way she carried herself, and if she were to lower her eyes, I would not have felt capable of identifying her three steps away").[5] Then the thing diminishes, and, although he is terribly grateful she was there that first Sunday, now when he meets her, and is not hoping to, her eyes may be still as lovely as before, but she has lost something of her, in fact all of her meaningfulness for him. The passage bears reading, with its impersonals: *"il* était donc vrai . . . *il* m'arrive . . . *il* faut bien reconnaître" – as if, through the impersonal expression, he as a person were to be let off the hook of caring, feeling, seeing more than the eyes, or of seeing at all. She has lost out, and lost him, whether she cared or not: she did break it off, but then, he somehow wins out in the expression. It is like the case of Nadja, however different. It is the problem of the surrealist woman, in these texts:

Il était donc vrai qu'elle n'avait à se trouver sur ma route que ce premier dimanche. Je lui sais encore un gré infini de s'y être trouvée. Maintenant que je ne la cherche plus, il m'arrive de la rencontrer quelquefois. Elle a toujours les yeux aussi beaux, mais il faut bien reconnaître qu'elle a perdu pour moi son prestige. (p. 98)

(It was true then that all she had to do was to be in my path that very first Sunday. I am still grateful to her for having been there. Now that I am no longer looking for her, I happen to run into her sometimes. She still has eyes just as beautiful, but it has to be admitted that she has lost her importance for me.)

And now, he says, she turns her head aside when they pass in the street. It somehow seems all very sad.

Ah, the seabirds

In *Mad Love*, there is a beach walk where everything goes wrong. All the presages are against the love, and it had no chance, that day: it was, says Breton, the nature of the site. "I remember, as I passed rather far from them, the singular irritation provoked in me by a bustling flock of seabirds squawking against a last ridge of foam. I even started throwing stones at them . . ." (102). Now they are walking not right by the water, because he hated taking off his shoes, and they are walking more and more distant from each other, this non-shoe-removal decision being the only definite thing about the situation. His mood is progressively worse, even with his shoes on, he longs to turn back – this is a constant in his love-walking, see the passage in Les Halles – and the mental distance between the lovers is suddenly immense: "The rift between us was deeper still, as if by all the height of the rock in which the stream we had crossed had been swallowed up. There was no point even in waiting for each other: impossible to exchange a word, to approach each other without turning aside and taking longer steps" (103). And then it turns out, it is indeed the site's problem, for they are walking near the House of the Hanged Man, painted by Cézanne (who, thinks Breton, painted other such things which are even more important than his apples). The *aura* around the house is, like the *aura* around the apples, what matters.

Now the issue is, in a sense, what has an aura and what does not. We know, from Walter Benjamin, how crucially important the aura is, and we know, from Breton, that the urgent thing is the mystery of it all – they are on the same frequency, the aura and the strangeness of woman, as long as she remains other. Or at least somewhat other.

According to Xavière Gauthier, in her *Surréalisme et sexualité,* everything in surrealist art is *"piégé"* or mined and trapped and undermined, because it is all highly ambivalent.[6] She studies several of the canvases of Magritte, such as *Le Chant d'amour* with its red shoes turning to feet, among others, and discusses the strong urges to violence and torture: in surrealist poetry, she says, women are loved, but in surrealist art, they are hated (331). And it is indeed the case that the images, even the ones seemingly the most loving, have an edge to them.

This is strangely true often, even in the poetry. Take the following examples from four different poems, two prose poems and two in verse: "Rendez-vous," about the sky ringed around by storms, ends with stifling, and with the cozy words: "la bague au châton vide que je t'ai donnée et qui te tuera" ("this ring with the empty setting that I gave you and that will kill you" [*Poems,* 21]). That is what happens with gifts.

Next, the dense and lyric "Forest in the Axe," full of oxymorons, ends with the opposite gender-murder, but the same feeling: "Il n'y a plus qu'une femme sur l'absence de pensée qui caractérise en noir pur cette époque maudite. Cette femme tient un bouquet d'immortelles de la forme de mon sang" ("No more than one woman out of the absence of thought which characterizes in pure black this damned age. That woman holds a bouquet of everlastings in the shape of my blood" [*Poems,* 58–59]). Something may indeed last, but in a very odd form: the violence of the setting, for that ring of emptiness and for this bouquet of blood, disconcerts, and tells what seems to be the truth. Bloody as it is.

One of the most moving verse poems, "Vigilance," ends with the statement of unity so often quoted: "Je ne touche plus que le coeur des choses / Je tiens le fil" ("I touch nothing but the heart of things / I hold the thread" [*Poems,* 78–79]), but it is preceded by a shell-shaped bit of lace from which, as in Botticelli's *Birth of Venus,* the woman emerges, here, just in the shape of one breast ("la forme parfaite d'un sein"). Of course two breasts have twice the same shape as one, usually, but all the same, the impression is less one of wholeness than one of partialness – less, I would say, partiality, in the positive sense – than partialness. It depends upon the way we read, of course, but in a certain angle, as Breton often said of his own vision, this is the way it looks.

Finally, in the poem of birth that begins "Il allait être cinq heures du matin" ("It was about to be five in the morning" [*Poems,* 102–3]), the ending, about a magic spell cast upon the narrator, takes effect again in the sort of violence that Gauthier has described for the art:

15

Tu avais gravé les signes infaillibles
De mon enchantement
Au moyen d'un poignard dont le manche de
corail bifurque à l'infini
Pour que ton sang et le mien
N'en fassent qu'un

(You had etched the unfailing signs
Of my enchantment
By means of a dagger whose coral handle
bifurcates to infinity
So that your blood and mine
Make but one [*Poems,* 103])

Now of course it is deeply erotic to be so joined, but one does wonder what the reader, so enjoined to participate in the sexual and emotional union here, however "free,"[7] is free to do and to read.

It is not so much that I want to begin reading Surrealism over, as that I see increasingly the problematics of the surrealist woman within that reading. We have wanted, here, to *make free* with the reading, and to let her creations make free. Let it not be taken as negative for Surrealism and its male leaders, but as a positive revisioning, rethinking, and call to re-reading.

Notes

1. Jean-Pierre Cauvin and Mary Ann Caws, trans. and eds. *Poems of André Breton* (Austin: University of Texas Press, 1982), 35.

2. I am taking a potshot at my own "Ladies Shot and Painted," in Susan Suleiman, ed., *The Female Body in Western Culture* (Cambridge: Harvard University Press, 1986), reprinted in longer form in Mary Ann Caws, *The Art of Interference: Stressed Readings in Visual and Verbal Texts* (Cambridge, England: Polity, 1989; Princeton: Princeton University Press, 1990). See also Susan Gubar, "Representing Pornography: Feminism, Criticism, and Depictions of Female Violation," in *Critical Inquiry* 13 (Summer 1987), 712–41.

3. Translated by Mary Ann Caws (Lincoln: University of Nebraska Press, 1988), 92.

4. Translated by Mary Ann Caws and Geoffrey Harris (Lincoln: University of Nebraska Press, 1990).

5. *Les Vases communicants* (Paris: Gallimard, 1955), 98.

6. Xavière Gauthier, *Surréalisme et sexualité* (Paris: Gallimard, coll. Idées, 1971), 25.

7. I am of course referring to Breton's great and famous poem, "L'Union libre" (*Poems,* 48–49).

Surrealism and Misogyny
Rudolf E. Kuenzli

Fig. 1 Surrealists around a painting by René Magritte. Published in *La Révolution surréaliste*, 1929.

A composite illustration published in *La Révolution surréaliste* in 1929 (Fig. 1), of photographs of the Surrealists arranged in a rectangle around Magritte's painting of a naked woman, has always seemed to me very telling. This work indicates that the surrealist movement, like so many other twentieth-century avant-garde movements (Futurism, Dada, Expression-

Fig. 2 Man Ray, *Waking Dream Séance*, 1924. Collection Lucien Treillard, Paris.

ism, etc.), was a men's club. The Surrealists lived in their own masculine world, with their eyes closed, the better to construct their male phantasms of the feminine. They did not see woman as a subject, but as a projection, an object of their own dreams of femininity. These masculine dreams play an active part in patriarchy's misogynistic positioning of women. It is precisely in Surrealism, with its emphasis on dreams, automatic writing, the unconscious, that we can expect to find some of the least inhibited renditions of male fantasies, and thus gain a good understanding of male desires and interests.

Surrealist art and poetry are addressed to men; women are only means to bring about these works. Woman is seen by the male Surrealists only in terms of what she can do for them. She is their muse – who also happens to know how to type, as in Man Ray's photograph of 1924 entitled *Waking*

Dream Séance (Fig. 2). The woman (here, actually Simone Breton) becomes the medium, the hands, through which the dreams of the Surrealists are preserved on paper. She is, so to speak, a recording machine. She of course has no dreams of her own, but faithfully encodes male dreams. Women are to the male Surrealists, as in the longstanding traditions of patriarchy, servants, helpers in the forms of child muse, virgin, *femme-enfant*, angel, celestial creature who is their salvation, or erotic object, model, doll – or she may be the threat of castration in the forms of the ubiquitous praying mantis and other devouring female animals.[1] Breton's relationship with the *femme-enfant* Nadja is illustrative: Nadja's mental distress is used by Breton as a way to the unconscious. She is a visionary; she can answer for him *his* questions, tell him who he is. Women, according to Freud's and Lacan's own misogynist stories, are closer to the unconscious than men, because they have not entirely entered the symbolic order. Lacan, who published his first texts in the surrealist magazine *Minotaure*, indicates in his *Seminaire livre XX* that the female subject neither succumbs to as complete an alienation from the real, the organic whole, nor enjoys as full an association with the symbolic as does the male subject.[2]

The Surrealists saw the actual demands of French women for social emancipation in 1924 as merely bourgeois. They preferred to celebrate female hysteria as *attitudes passionelles,* as *l'amour fou,* in the last issue of *La Révolution surréaliste.* When their attempted marriage with the French Communist Party failed, they turned in the *Second Surrealist Manifesto* of 1929 to erotic desire as their means of transforming human consciousness. Dali became for Breton the incorporation of this desire through his paranoiac-critical method, a technique of self-induced delirium in which the masculine ego molds the images and realities of the external world to correspond to his own inner needs and desires. Dali's *The Great Masturbator* of 1929 (Fig. 3) depicts Gala Eluard, soon to be Gala Dali, as his heroic savior, in a "psychodrama of frustration and mingled fear and desire in the presence of the loved one."[3] In this painting, a monstrous head bearing Dali's features is supported horizontally by its rigid nose. From the back of the head arises Gala's head, caressing the genitals of a male figure. An image of erotic desire and feared impotence, the painting, according to Whitney Chadwick, reveals Gala's dual roles as the stimulator of the erotic desire that initiates the delusional process, and the link between interior and exterior reality,[4] since she is emerging directly from Dali's own mind. *L'Age d'or* on which Dali collaborated with Buñuel, contains a scene not unlike that of *The Great Masturbator,* in which a woman sucks the toe of a statue.

In her book *Women Artists and the Surrealist Movement,* Chadwick has shown that only after having left the surrealist circle could women break out of the role of serving muse to become artists in their own right. Lee

Fig. 3   Salvador Dali, *The Geat Masturbator,* 1929–32. Oil on canvas. Private collection.

Miller, who first sought an aesthetic reality rather than a personal identity in Surrealism, played, acted out the male's object of desire, and her body became Man Ray's canvas for the play of shadowy lines. Miller's later insistence on her own freedom led to her refusal to be positioned as an erotic object for the male gaze, and thus to a break with Man Ray in 1932. She became a successful photographer herself. Jacqueline Lamba, whom Breton married in 1934 and who was an artist in her own right, had little time to involve herself in her own work while married to Breton. Chadwick writes: "The women closest to the Surrealists – among them Gala Dali, Nusch Eluard, Dora Maar, and Jacqueline Lamba – were beloved for the quality of their imaginations rather than for their artistic goals."[5] They *were* allowed to participate with the male Surrealists in making exquisite corpses, the surrealist parlor game.

The male Surrealists celebrated the Marquis de Sade, and none was more sadistic than Hans Bellmer, whose photographs of violated puppets and dolls were published in surrealist magazines. André Kertész's *Deformations* are another instance of the male Surrealists' disfiguring of the female figure, and Raoul Ubac's series entitled *The Battle of the Amazons* viciously hacks apart the arms, legs, and heads of female figures in his fear of castration.

20

Why belabor the obvious point that Surrealism, in celebrating the masculine unconscious, brings forth representations of the least-censored misogyny? These images of Ubac, Kertész, and Bellmer have recently been interpreted by Rosalind Krauss as being protofeminist in her exhibition catalogue entitled *L'Amour fou: Photography and Surrealism* of 1985.[6] Let me summarize her argument:

Her agenda in the two catalogue essays is to redeem Surrealism, which is generally seen as a formally regressive movement in art history, via the surrealist photograph. In order to redeem Surrealism one also has to clear it of misogynist charges. How does she do that? In her first essay, entitled "Photography in the Service of Surrealism," she analyzes the techniques through which the Surrealists modified, changed, and defamiliarized the straight image. These techniques include solarization, rayography, negative printing, multiple exposures, photomontage, collage, and doubling. The straight image is thus metamorphosed. The distortions that are thereby created serve to point out that even straight photography does not represent reality or nature, but social constructions. Fetishism is such a social construction, and the defamiliarizing techniques of the surrealist photographers reveal this. Krauss states, with regard to Kertész's *Distortions:* "Within surrealist photography, doubling also functions as the signifier of signification. It is this semiological, rather than stylistic, condition that unites the vast array of the movement's photographic production. . . . In this way the photographic medium is exploited to produce a paradox: the paradox of reality constituted as a sign – or presence transformed into absence, into representation, into spacing, into writing" (31).

In her second essay, "Corpus delicti," Krauss uses Bataille's notion of the *informe* to argue that surrealist photography collapses, undoes conceptional propositions. "Corpus delicti, " a juristic term meaning transgression, already alludes to Bataille. Again, through manipulations of straight photography, Surrealists transgress the familiar social constructions and produce a kind of formlessness, Bataille's *informe,* which Krauss connects with Freud's notion of the uncanny. This defamiliarization can be brought about not only by darkroom manipulation, but also by contrivance, such as in Brassaï's *Nude* of 1933 (Fig. 4). In this image sexual identity is collapsed: "The female body and the male organ have each become the sign for the other" (95).

Bellmer, Ubac, Kertész, and Brassaï, according to Krauss, foreground the social fetishization of reality: "It must be seen that in much of surrealist practice, woman, in being a fetish, is nowhere in nature. Having dissolved the natural in which 'normalcy' can be grounded, Surrealism was at least potentially open to the dissolving of distinctions that Bataille insisted was the job of the *informe*. Gender, at the heart of the surrealist project, was one of these catagories." Krauss continues: "If within surrealist poetry *woman* was constantly in construction, then at certain moments that project could at least prefigure a next step, in which a reading is opened onto deconstruction. It is for this reason," she states, "that the frequent characterizations of Surrealism as antifeminist seem to me to be mistaken" (95).

For Krauss it is precisely surrealist photography, rather than surrealist painting or writing, that presents this moment of deconstruction, the *informe* of gender categories: "Within surrealist photographic practice, too, *woman* was in construction, for she is the obsessional subject there as well. And since the vehicle through which she is figured is itself manifestly constructed (through darkroom manipulations and contrivances], *woman* and *photograph* become figures for each other's condition: ambivalent, blurred, indistinct, and lacking in, to use Edward Weston's word, 'authority'" (95).

Raoul Ubac's photomontages entitled *Battle of the Amazons* (Fig. 5) are seen by Krauss as producing the *informe* through the process of solarization: "These images are the result of successive attacks of solarization. In a first stage a montage would be produced, grouping together various shots of the same nude. This image would then be rephotographed and solarized, the resultant positive becoming a new element to be recombined, through montage, with other fragments and then to be rephotographed and resolarized. . . . A mode of producing a simultaneous positive/negative, solarization most frequently reads as the optical reorganization of the contours of the objects. Reversing and exaggerating the light/dark relationships at this precise registration of the envelope of form, solarization is a process that can obviously be put to the service of the *informe*" (70). This analysis describes Ubac as assaulting straight photography. However

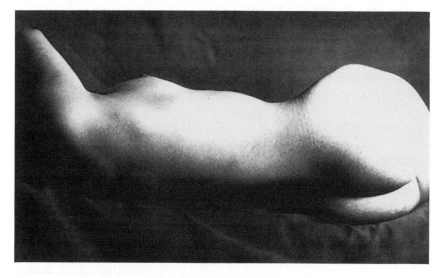

Fig. 4   Brassaï, Untitled, 1933. Collection Rosabianca Skira, Geneva.

Fig. 5   Raoul Ubac, *The Battle of the Amazons,* 1939. Galerie Adrien Maeght, Paris.

Krauss is completely silent about the violent, sadistic dismemberment of the female image.

In his introduction to André Kertész's *Distortions* (Fig. 6), Hilton Kramer at least senses that he has to forestall the viewer's perceptions of misogyny, and therefore explains these works in a "good old boy" way as just humor and fun: "They do not victimize but celebrate their subjects. . . . There is humor in these pictures, but it is the humor of love. They are sometimes funny, but they are never mean. . . . Kertész's transformations of the female anatomy are at once erotic and aesthetic – the love songs of a photographer.[7]

Krauss, however, does not sense the slightest hint of misogyny in these distortions. For her they are simply an instance of the surrealist technique of defamiliarization called doubling, here via the distorting mirrors. Hans Bellmer's dolls are for her another example of doubling "which produces the mark of the sign" (31). She mentions that Bellmer made his first doll upon having seen Jacques Offenbach's opera *The Tales of Hoffmann,* the first act of which focuses on the Olympia story derived from Hoffmann's "The Sandman." She links Bellmer's dolls to Freud's own analysis of Hoffman's story in his essay on the uncanny and sees these dolls as representing the fear of castration. In emphasizing Bellmer's construction of the desirable *informe,* Krauss is again silent about violations of the female figure.

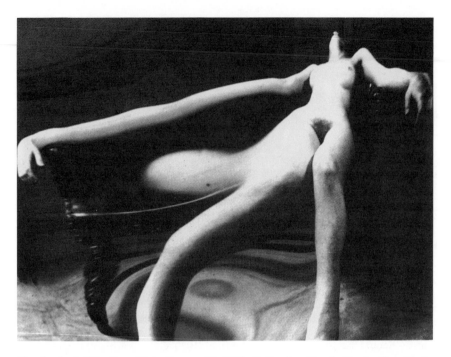

Fig. 6   André Kertész, *Distortion no. 79,* 1933. Collection Beady Davis, New York.

She seems to look at these dolls from the male point of view.

It is precisely Krauss's collusion with the male gaze that makes her unable to recognize the obvious misogyny in these works. The male Surrealists produced Bataille's *informe* only in regard to the female figure. Faced with the female figure, the male Surrealist fears castration, fears the dissolution of his ego. In order to overcome his fears, he fetishizes the female figure, he deforms, disfigures, manipulates her; he literally manhandles her in order to reestablish his own ego, and not his own *informe.* By consistently refusing to see these mangled bodies as female bodies, Krauss is unable to see the aggressive sexual-visual politics acted out in these photographs. In her description of the darkroom manipulations, she writes: "The variety of photographic methods has been exploited to produce . . . bodies dizzily yielding to the force of gravity [Bataille's *bassesse*]; of bodies in the grip of a distorting perspective; of bodies decapitated by the project of shadow; of bodies eaten away either by heat or light" (70). These are not just "bodies"; these are always female figures. Or she argues that surrealist photography explores a subjectivity "dispossessed of its [traditional Cartesian or humanist] privilege," "trapped in a cat's cradle of representation, caught in a hall of mirrors, lost in a labyrinth," a subjectivity linked to "concepts that at this moment combine and redefine the visual: Bataille's *in-*

24

forme, Caillois's mimicry, Lacan's 'picture' " (78). Again, the unformed subjectivity produced in surrealist photography is the female subjectivity only. In her attempt to develop a new approach to the visual in art criticism on the basis of these surrealist texts and photographs, Krauss consistently overlooks the gender-specific, sexist politics of these works.

The trapped, lost subjectivity constructed by the Surrealists is the *female* subjectivity – disfigured, reduced to an animal, to Bataille's *bassesse,* the result of the male's fear of castration and his fetishistic disavowals. Rather than exposing and deconstructing the patriarchal fetishization of women, as Krauss would have it, Surrealism seems to me to represent an intensification of that social fetishism, an intensification of patriarchy's misogyny. Krauss's belief in Freud's misogynistic stories, her basing her own theories on surrealist texts, her adoption of a male gaze blinds her. Her theorizing also indicates how much of our modern theory is caught in these surrealist male fantasies. In relying on these theories, Krauss buys into male misogyny and, in accord with Freud's story, into female misogyny as well. In his essay "Some Psychical Consequences of the Anatomical Distinction between the Sexes," Freud writes: "When she has passed beyond her first attempt at explaining her lack of a penis as being a punishment personal to herself and has realized that the sexual character is a universal one, she begins to share the contempt felt by men for a sex which is the lesser in so important a respect."[8]

Bataille's notions of the *informe,* of *bassesse,* serve the Surrealists and Krauss as means to dominate, colonize, dissolve, obliterate female subjectivity. Brassaï's female nude in the shape of a penis is straightforward colonization, occupation, a refusal to recognize difference. The questions in visual-sexual politics are: Who has the power? Who dominates? Who is disfigured by whose power? These power relations are not natural but *social* constructs, and the male Surrealists' blatant reinforcement of patriarchal power relations should not be theorized away in order to redeem Surrealism. They should be resisted, they should be rejected. "Rather than yielding our minds up with our modeled and remodeled bodies," Mary Ann Caws writes, "we must give our readings of our representations, and our opinions as to which deserve anger, and which, celebration."[9]

The first resistance to the Surrealists' manhandling of the female figure arose in the works of certain marginalized female artists and writers associated with this movement. The essays in this collection explore the complex strategies women Surrealists employed in order to construct and assert their own subjectivity in light of the male Surrealists' phantasms of women.

Notes

1. See Xavière Gauthier, *Surréalisme et sexualité* (Paris: Gallimard, 1971).

2. See Kaja Silverman, *The Subject of Semiotics* (New York and Oxford: Oxford University Press, 1983), 186.

3. Dawn Ades, *Salvador Dali* (New York: Harper and Row, 1982), 76.

4. Whitney Chadwick, *Women Artists and the Surrealist Movement* (Boston: Little, Brown, 1985), 37.

5. Ibid., 50.

6. Rosalind Krauss and Jane Livingston, *L'Amour fou: Photography and Surrealism* (Washington: Corcoran Gallery of Art, 1985).

7. André Kertész, *Distortions* (New York: Alfred Knopf, 1976), unp.

8. See Silverman, 142.

9. Mary Ann Caws, "Ladies Shot and Painted; Female Embodiment in Surrealist Art," in *The Female Body in Western Culture,* ed. Susan Suleiman (Cambridge: Harvard University Press, 1986), 285.

What Do Little Girls Dream Of:
The Insurgent Writing of
Gisèle Prassinos

Inez Hedges

> Where is the ebullient infinite woman
> who, immersed as she was in her naivete,
> kept in the dark about herself, led into self-
> disdain by the great arm of parental-
> conjugal phallocentrism, hasn't been
> ashamed of her strength? Who, surprised
> and horrified by the fantastic tumult of her
> drives . . . hasn't accused herself of being a
> monster?
>
> Hélène Cixous, "The Laugh of the Medusa"

Gisèle Prassinos was one of two women included in Breton's *Anthology of Black Humor*. In 1934, her brother Mario had introduced the fourteen-year-old schoolgirl to the Surrealists. As Madeleine Cottenet-Hage writes in a recently published book on Prassinos, Breton and the surrealist group regarded her writings as additional evidence that automatic writing proceeds from the unconscious (Cottenet-Hage 40–41). Breton would later write that her texts express "permanent revolution in the beautiful images of a five-cent coloring book" (Breton 432) and compare her to the surrealist ideal of the child-woman.

Prassinos's texts do have some similarities to automatic writing, yet they are distinctive in that the semantic incompatibilities occur mostly on the level of narrative and representation. She creates a strange universe in which little girls close their windows tightly at night to escape from butterflies ("A Young Persecuted Girl"), a bride with a potato-nose weds a man whose nose is a thimble ("Description of a Wedding"), and a jug of wine empties itself into a mirror, filling up the ocean reflected there ("Transformation"). Unlike Breton's and Eluard's texts in *Champs magnétiques,* where the rapid change of images leads to a kind of reader euphoria, Prassinos's would be more properly termed ecstatic – her reader ends up feeling that she is standing outside of herself, at least of her adult self.

Hélène Cixous, in the passage cited above, suggests that a woman awakened to her desires will in all probability brand herself as a monstrosity; the young Prassinos actually revels in being a little monster. Breton writes: "Sade withdraws his candy-dish" (432). Fathers are exposed, siblings murdered, the moral of fairy tales turned on its head, the literary canon made ridiculous.

In "Venda and the Parasite," Prassinos casts her story within a linear narrative structure, beginning with the child's birth and ending with her death. At her birth, her father places a glowworm in her hair that stays with her throughout her life, eating at her brain and burrowing into her neck. She is not allowed to remove it, even though its loud singing embarrasses her socially and prevents her from getting married. Eventually, she goes mad and dies, upon which the worm eats her up. There is something disturbing about this story, above and beyond its content (though the tale is no pleasant subject). The reader's uneasiness comes from the way that this text resonates with another well-known text of French literature: Charles Baudelaire's poem "La Chevelure." Baudelaire, as a canonical figure of French literature, is the "paternal text" against which this young writer rebels.

Rereading Baudelaire's poem, we see that the hair of the poet's mistress is associated with animals, plants, and phenomena of nature: a sheep ("o toison moutonnant"), a horse ("ta crinière lourde"), a forest ("forêt aromatique"), a gourd ("la gourde où je hume . . . le vin du souvenir"), a wave ("fortes tresses, soyez la houle"), a sea ("mer d'ébène," "noir ocean"), an oasis ("l'oasis où je rêve"). The poet immerses himself in the "aromatic forest" and discovers the worlds of Asia and Africa; he swims in the perfume of the hair and plunges into its dark sea which bears him away into a dream of tall ships.

In Prassinos's text as in Baudelaire's poem, the hair is vegetation where the worm can hide. But Venda finds her admirer bothersome, to say the least. It sings shrilly on her head, perhaps declaiming the admiratory stanzas of the famous poet. It digs deep into her scalp, without realizing that it's making her suffer. It capriciously takes a few bites from her brain, and then helps her learn to talk. Since the worm is the gift of her father, we might interpret this as meaning that little girls are not even free from being educated in the patriarchal system of values that oppresses them, and that turns them into admired objects. Like the poet of Baudelaire's poem, the worm gets to travel with the head of hair. And like the mistress celebrated by the poem, Venda is made special by the worm, singled out in society. Unlike the object of the poet's attention, however, she gets to talk back. She doesn't appreciate being special in this way. In the end the worm drives her mad. She begins to see herself as a white (sacrificial?) calf. When she dies, the worm is there to eat up every last trace of her. Because of the worm, she has never been allowed to live a normal life.

This is a savage scenario that taps the energy of the unconscious in the manner advocated by Breton in the *First Manifesto of Surrealism.* And there are many more. In a spectacular *mise-en-scène* of sibling rivalry, the girl in "My Sister" murders her sibling in order to steal the sweet smell of her breath. "Description of a Wedding" makes fun of male possessiveness—the father of the bride wears his wife buttoned to his vest, the groom is a dwarf. The bridal train sings a song featuring a chamberpot, a reminder that conjugal life means sharing the bathroom. As Breton realized, Prassinos has a fine ear for black humor. Her humor is a form of social criticism expressed in a style that approximates verbal collage; Max Ernst wrote in *Beyond Painting* that "collage is a hypersensitive and rigorously true instrument, like a seismograph, capable of registering the exact quantity of possibilities for human happiness in each epoch. The quantity of black humor contained in each authentic collage is found there in the inverse proportion of the possibilities for happiness" (17).

A comparison between Prassinos's images and Ernst's paintings reveals some striking similarities: the bride with her walnut eyes pierced by arrows echoes Ernst's 1922 painting *Oedipus Rex,* and the tale of the little girl persecuted by a butterfly brings to mind his *Two Children Threatened by a Nightingale* (1924). The most instructive comparison, however, is between his collage novel *A Young Girl Dreams of Taking the Veil* (a male artist's view of a young girl's unconscious) and Prassinos's texts. A whole section of Ernst's work deals with the hair of the little girl, which acts as a protagonist and interlocutor in her dream about becoming a nun. In one collage, the head of hair appears in the form of a sail. Like "Venda and the Parasite," this image recalls Baudelaire's lines:

Tu contiens, mer débène, un éblouissant rêve
De voiles, de rameurs, de flammes et de mâts.

The prospect of marriage is no more enticing in Ernst's depiction: in the little girl's dream, as recreated by Ernst, the girl's hair makes fun of her. The heroine says: "My place is at the feet of a merciful husband." To which the hair replies: "To dream, to dream, to babble on sick Friday" ("le vendredi malsain").

Despite these similarities, Prassinos's texts have their own distinctive character; in no sense could they be called derivative of Surrealism. Unlike Breton's and Eluard's attempts at automatic writing, unlike Ernst's collages, her tales emphasize narrative. Whitney Chadwick, in her compelling analysis of women painters and writers associated with the men of the surrealist movement, explains that personal narrative dominates in the works of the women artists: "The self-referential nature of the work of these women, isolated as it is in most cases from the shared theoretical positions and commitments of the surrealist group, almost guarantees an art in which personal reality dominates and narrative flow, rather than abrupt dislocation and juxtaposition, provides structure" (221).

29

I hesitate to describe the writings of a fourteen-year-old schoolgirl as "feminist," but I do think that they tap an energy that could be useful to feminism. Kristeva has warned that feminism risks falling into a romantic idea of the subject:

A woman cannot "be"; it is something which does not even belong to the order of being. It follows that a feminist practice can only be negative, at odds with what already exists so that we may say "that's not it" and "that's still not it." In "woman" I see something that cannot be represented, something that is still not said, something above and beyond nomenclatures and ideologies. . . . it is what some modern texts never stop signifying: testing the limits of language and sociality—the law and its transgression, mastery and (sexual) pleasure—without reserving one for males and the other for females, on the condition that it is never mentioned. From this point of view, it seems that certain feminist demands revive a kind of romanticism, a belief in identity (the reverse of phallocratism). (Kristeva 137–38)

Prassinos's texts, unlike those that Kristeva warns against, explore the plural identity of their subjects and inscribe themselves within the modernist project. They are transgressive or, to use Cixous's word, "insurgent." Prassinos breaks through the worn scripts for what little girls are supposed to dream of (the happy endings of fairy tales) and gives us, instead, some real dreams from the unconscious, that place where, Cixous writes, "the repressed manage to survive" (250). By humorously parodying the (male) fragmentation of the female body, Prassinos assertively takes back control of her body, which then becomes the battleground for the fight against the patriarchal order.

In the short piece that furnishes the title for the collection of Prassinos's writings of her surrealist period (republished in 1976), the feminine voice is treated as a dissociated part that can be separated from the body. "Trouver sans chercher" ("Finding what you're not looking for") is an inversion of a familiar French locution; it could stand as a paraphrase of Breton's definition of automatic writing. Here the speaker is the girl's mother, a figure as submissive as the mother in the story "Venda and the Parasite." Disturbed by her daughter's "masculine" voice which scares away clients, she proposes a visit to the surgeon so that the girl can get "the real voice of a woman." But luckily a young man passes by who has the opposite problem: his voice is too feminine. Unhesitatingly this mother offers him her daughter's voice.

Although I do not agree with Cottenet-Hage that the common thread running through all of Prassinos's work is that of submissiveness (13), this short piece shows ambivalence. The masculine voice, which I would identify with the young writer's sense of her own notoriety in the predominantly male world of Surrealism, causes some maladjustment. The voice is said to chase away the "clients" (suitors? seen as tricks?) and this disturbs the mother. The mother is so concerned that she doesn't even arrange for an exchange of voices—for all we know, the girl loses her voice entirely. Better that a woman have no voice at all than a masculine voice.

It is tempting to relate this brief story to Prassinos's own ten-year silence between the writings of her surrealist period and her subsequent books of poetry and novels—works that, despite their merits, no longer continue the rebellious path of Prassinos's younger self. The ambivalent attitude toward the mother who sacrifices her daughter's voice leaves some doubts, however, as to whether this piece is really an expression of Prassinos's "abdication."

The common thread in these early writings is one that does provide a guiding metaphor for feminism. Over and over again the narrative persona is described as a thief, an appropriator. The theme is mirrored in the discursive strategy of the texts, which are animated by a truly Promethean urge to steal power from its jealously guarded source—be that canonical texts, discourses of authority (of school, of parents, of the state), or patriarchal controls. Once seized, that power is exposed and demystified. The ultimate theft of course is to steal one's own body back from those who have ex- and appropriated it. Prassinos's turning away from Surrealism might be seen as a resistance against that famous picture of her by Man Ray (in Chadwick 48 and on the cover of Cottenet-Hage) in which she embodies the child-woman reading to the assembled (male) Surrealists. It is an image of her made by males, truly "found without looking for it." Mary Ann Caws has traced a similar problematic in many surrealist renderings of the female body (Caws 1985).

Though Prassinos's early writings were coopted by Surrealism, which deflected her revolt into theirs, contemporary readers may recognize the impossibility of completely subsuming these texts within that movement. They should be read for their own sheer firepower.

References

Breton, André, 1970. *Anthologie de l'humour noir.* Paris: Jean-Jacques Pauvert.

Caws, Mary Ann, 1985. "Ladies Shot and Painted: Female Embodiment in Surrealist Art," in Susan Rubin Suleiman, ed., *The Female Body in Western Culture.* Cambridge: Harvard University Press.

Chadwick, Whitney, 1985. *Women Artists and the Surrealist Movement.* Boston: Little, Brown.

Chénieux, Jacqueline, 1977. "Gisèle Prassinos disqualifiée disqualifiante." *Obliques* 14–15, 207–15.

Cixous, Hélène, 1981. "The Laugh of the Medusa," in *New French Feminisms,* ed. Elaine Marks and Isabelle de Courtivron. New York: Schocken.

Ernst, Max, 1948. *Beyond Painting and Other Writings by the Artist and His Friends.* New York: Wittenborn, Schultz.

———, 1982. *A Little Girl Dreams of Taking the Veil.* Trans. Dorothea Tanning. New York: George Braziller.

Kristeva, Julia, 1981. "La femme, ce n'est jamais ça," in *New French Feminisms.*

Prassinos, Gisèle, 1976. *Trouver sans chercher.* Paris: Flammarion.

Finding What You Are Not Looking For

Gisèle Prassinos

Venda and the Parasite

When Venda was born, her father placed a glowworm on her blond hair. The worm sniffed the pink skin of her little skull, raised its antennae to avoid hurting her, and began its quiet life in the midst of the bush. It spent its time climbing on the long spiral threads. But when it got to the top, its weight made it sway and it fell down unconscious. All the while Venda slept.

At night it sang and when people came to see Venda in her cradle it transferred the entire electrical force of its body into its carapace so that they could see it better. Its song became more shrill, and when the visitors saw the luminous thing jumping they thought that Venda was the child of the devil. The worm dug deep holes into her soft skin and made itself at home there, without thinking that it might make the child suffer.

One day it got to the brain. It liked the gluey and unctuous substance and started to eat it slowly, a piece each morning. But it got tired of it and closed up the wound with its sticky saliva.

Soon Venda started to walk. The glowworm was thrown off-balance and lost itself in the baby's neck. It learned to talk at the same time or sooner than she did, and it helped her practice the sentences of her lesson. This got her the reputation of being an intelligent girl.

Once Venda's hair was long enough to be rolled around her head into a nicely twisted little bun, the animal felt out of its element. This orderly mountain, unpleasant to the sight, obliged it to climb very high and to rummage to the point of exhaustion in order to regain its place. But it quickly adapted; this made it lose weight so that it shone less at night when Venda put the light out to sleep. That made the little girl feel better. She didn't like people pointing at her when she went by houses at night with the glowworm jumping for joy and crying with all its might for attention. She would try to hide it under her curls or catch its legs under the corner of her barrette, but the animal always succeeded in escaping and starting up its antics all over again.

One day Venda explained to her father that she suffered a lot from the way people looked down on her because of the glowworm. She volunteered that she was in love with a young man who had made an offer of marriage providing that she get rid of the animal.

"This third party must not come between us," he sobbed. "It bothers us and cools our passionate embraces." But her father was inflexible.

"You are so beautiful with this light in your golden locks!" He became sentimental and kissed Venda on her neck in the place where the animal had built the principal entrance to its lair.

Venda's mother was as capricious as her spouse when the young girl threw herself at her feet in despair, begging for permission to kill her persecutor. She embraced her child and told her a story about a cricket, so sad and so slow that it made them both cry, thus permanently avoiding the real issue.

Venda bravely resigned herself. Before he died, her father made her swear always to keep on her head the animal he had set to abide there. In the throes of death, even as he expressed his pity for her, he caressed Venda's ever-immobile bun and felt with his burning fingers the sweet electrical casing of the glowworm.

Soon after, with sighs and tears, her mother went to join her husband, not without forgetting her eternal admonishments.

Venda got older. Her hair was turning white and the worm was still glowing; it jumped and whistled gaily, hurting the now sensitive head of its hostess.

After a few years, she lost her reason. Singing, she danced on the road in her fine white undershirt, raising her arms and legs up high.

"I am a white calf," she said laughing. And the worm answered: "I too am a white calf," and, after thinking a while, "We are two white calves."

Venda died.

In the grave was found her alluring body that the glowworm had just finished devouring.

My Sister

I know that my sister smells of bananas. Her large hair, when it rubs my nose, has the ordinary smell of missed dessert. But when she turns toward me and her mouth opens to smile at me, I like the new smell so much that I feel like biting her lips and her tongue. Underneath there is something that cracks and carries you away.

Soon my sister will fall asleep. I take her pointed arms and cross them over her eyes so that the last light will close them altogether. But she keeps smiling triumphantly at me and the strong odor rises, so strong that I suddenly think of killing my sister in order to take it from her.

I sink my knife in, cutting through her pretty gown. Under the sheets her hands are cold and white. Mine, too alive, have no strength, but I see, nestled in her hand, a little puckered fruit made of shiny rosy fragments that I melt between my fingers.

Description of a Wedding

The procession is composed of thirty persons. The bride precedes it, holding her recent husband by the arm. She has a huge round head furnished with a superb potato that fulfills the function of a nose. Her eyes are pierced walnuts dotted with the points of red pencils. Her mouth is very blue and she has a row of black pasty teeth. Since she is naked, you can see her body strewn with woolen tumors and her bellybutton from which hangs a little flowering dandelion. On the whole, she gives the impression of a wounded dove.

Next to her, her recent husband reaches only to her knee. He has a poor face broadened into a large smile that comes from his nose (which is in the form of a thimble and is tipped by a little navy blue button). He is clothed in a sack of green cloth that covers the top of his knees. His aluminum legs get cavities whenever he laughs. Instead of eyes he has two wilted violets. His arms are so short that in order to hold his wife he has to stop in the middle of the road. She looks at him sadly while he sings the first couplet of a song from his native land:

Diffuse Kashmir prairie
my beautiful and tender Palmyra
in your heart of vine
have a furrow of bravery.

Behind them you can see the honor attendants who sing a hymn to the bride:

Wildflower
Spring rose bower
Chamberpot
Clatter.

Then comes the father of the bride with his wife buttoned to his vest.

The Young Persecuted Girl

A young girl who was in bed was afraid lest a butterfly she saw that morning come to wake her. Before going to bed, she put on a necklace of fresh chervil and little dull glass ladybirds, striped with yellow waxed cloth. She was very proud of it and thought that the butterfly wouldn't dare touch her when it saw that she was not alone.

But it came anyway: on the windowpane you could see the reflection of a ball of lead, topped with two long horns of bronzed celluloid. Then the pane moved and you couldn't see anything. So the young girl went to sleep.

When she awakened (because of one of her curls that came unrolled), the pane was back in its original place. This time, she saw a little hollowed-out cube of glass, full of water, in which a number of balls of string soaked in gasoline were swimming. She wanted to get up in order to destroy this horrible vision, but the window closed violently in her face without making any noise.

Laughing uproariously, she went back to bed. She was happy because she thought the butterfly had been crushed between the two panels of the window. She pulled the bedcover over her with the soul of a pigeon to protect her.

After an hour, she awoke again because the pigeon's soul had fled. She followed it to the window but there she stopped because the wind was raising up her hair. She looked at the pane and saw a sickly little leek whose outer leaves were ragged and full of desiccated tips. Amazed, she slid onto the marble floor and closed her eyes.

She didn't open them again until three days later.

Transformation

A herd of soldiers looked into the mirror while passing by. They saw a large bed of white wood behind which an embroidered curtain held up rows of glass bottle stoppers. This bed was covered with a pelisse full of holes made of interlacing feathers. It all floated slowly on a white sea stocked with accessories.

One of the soldiers stepped out of line and posted himself in front of the mirror which swayed. He took a silk pompon stuck to his hat and watched it open like a flower whose petals evaporate in the light. When everything had disappeared, the stem changed into an enormous pitcher of wine which spilled into the mirror and augmented the volume of the sea. At once, the large bed was lifted up and tossed aside while he pushed with undulating arms full of nervous calluses that followed the movements of the water. Thus the big bed went away, carrying with it the soldier who made a sign to his friends to accompany him. Soon they all followed and the mirror reflected another image.

Finding What You're Not Looking For

My daughter has the poor voice of a man, a male filament that has introduced itself into her throat.

"In my pocket," she says, "I have some nice countenances of assassins that are just what you require."

And she rummages around in the spot, poor valiant hardworking girl, while our clients flee, terrified, with troubled and already worn-out ears.

Then my daughter moans and grows despondent.

"Cease your lamentations, my poor girl," I say while I caress her. "We'll go to the surgeon so that he can give you the real voice of a woman."

At this moment a handsome young man passes by and greets us. He stops and asks something. His voice is frail and soft, we can't hear him.

"Serene, ingenuous, perfidious countenances," says my poor girl, trying to belittle herself. And she conceals her tears so as not to have on her conscience the flight of this new client.

From his tiny lips, he murmurs an unexpected wish: "I want a voice," he says.

"I'll give you my poor daughter's," I said, smiling with joy.

Translated by Inez Hedges from
Gisèle Prassinos, *Trouver sans
chercher* (Paris: Flammarion, 1976)

From *Déjeuner en fourrure* to *Caroline:* Meret Oppenheim's Chronicle of Surrealism

Renée Riese Hubert

In 1936, a surrealist object, first exhibited in Paris, was bought by the Museum of Modern Art. *Le Déjeuner en fourrure* gave immediate notoriety to its creator, Meret Oppenheim. Although startled by the daring invention, worthy incarnation of Lautréamont's metaphor, the public seemed somewhat unconcerned about the artist and her other creations. It would have been easy to find out that the same artist had participated in group exhibits, had had a one-woman show in Basel, and, three years earlier, had served as a photographic model for Man Ray. Contrary to the discretion about the gender of *Le Déjeuner*'s creator, the photographs provided an unmistakable monument to her femininity and a testimony to her willingness to expose it. In the former, displayed in the show entitled "Dada, Surrealism, and Fantastic Art" among predominantly male creations, Oppenheim proved herself to be an active creator, while in the photographs she appeared to be the object of male creativity rather than the basis of her own. From the beginning, Oppenheim's career can be viewed in terms of the dialectical relationship between woman and practicing artist.

Posing in 1933 as Man Ray's model, producing in 1936 *Le Déjeuner en fourrure*, an object selected to represent surrealist practice most pointedly – how can these earlier manifestations be linked to her 1975 speech, where she stresses the woman artist's responsibility, her necessary independence, her need to produce work which would not limit her to a female audience. The woman, the artist, the Surrealist, to what extent are they present at each stage of her career, to what extent are they compatible? In the 1980s, Oppenheim's poetry, written over a thirty-year period, was for the first time published in a volume entitled *Husch, husch, der schönste Vokal entleert sich* (1985) (Hush, hush, the most beautiful vowel empties itself) as well as in two *livres d'artiste, Sansibar* (1981) and *Caroline* (1985), where she strongly manifests her double talent.[1] Does this artist in her final works deviate, as it seems, from her previous polemical productions?

I shall briefly discuss two of Oppenheim's objects: *Ma gouvernante*

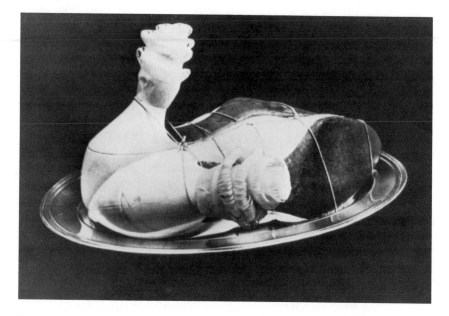

Fig. 1 Oppenheim, *Ma gouvernante*, 1936. Moderna Museet, Stockholm.

Fig. 2 Oppenheim, *Le Couple*, 1957.

38

(1936) (Fig. 1) and *Le Couple* (1957) (Fig. 2), as they will enable me to enter into a problematic central to her as well as to other Surrealists. In both these works, the viewer confronts a pair of lady's footgear. Both a unity and duality, each pair ironically personifies the couple. As one shoe or half-boot provides a mirror image of the other, the notion of the original and the copy is subverted. In both objects, the footgear is defunctionalized: it does not cover feet; it does not serve for walking. It is through this process of defunctionalization that Oppenheim turns footwear into a work of art. The roast made of two shoes, rather than one leg, is presented with strings and paper frills; it is made of four elements borrowed from everyday life, which the artist assembles and displaces without putting their identity in jeopardy. The analogy between *Ma gouvernante* and *Le Déjeuner en fourrure* is striking. In the latter, a cup, a saucer, and a spoon, dressed up in fur, retain their shape as they hide their porcelain skeleton. Both the breakfast set and the shoes are disguised and defunctionalized. The disguised objects are at once themselves and not themselves. In both *Ma gouvernante* and *Le Déjeuner en fourrure*, Oppenheim alludes to the feminine. The fur suggests an expensively decked-out woman; the cup, hollow yet round, can evoke female genitalia; the spoon with its phallic shape further eroticizes the hairy object. The artist problematizes the feminine without referring directly to a body and even less to a face. Her shoes on a platter belong to feminine apparel: high-heeled, they expose their full curvature. The frills and the strings contribute both to cannibalization and feminization.

Why does Oppenheim show a pair rather than a single shoe? Allusions to gender, displacement, and cannibalism could have been made by presenting a single shoe. The shoes, tied together, have lost their independence. Diminished or elevated to the role of a roast fresh out of the oven, these lady's shoes are ready to be devoured by consumers. Through the strings they are turned into a mutual and common imprisonment. Hypothetical movement is transmuted into a single immobile package. Oppenheim, eager in real life to avoid partnership, here warns against the perils of the couple.

In *Le Couple*, dark, heavy, old-fashioned lady's half-boots face the viewer at a disquieting angle. Half laced, folded over, they produce an air of casualness. But these half-boots refrain from matching and forming a pair simply by refusing to submit to the expected parallel positions dictated by the human feet. They seem to have collided with one another, for they have become imbedded in one another at the toes. Worse still, one boot, by exposing its lining, sticks out its tongue at its sidekick; it assumes an aggressive posture as the other makes ready to lean over. Can we consider them male and female, sexually interacting companions? Has the artist maliciously outlined a situation that actually reverses the one in *Ma gouvernante?* In one work, the partners belong together, while in the other

39

they assert their individuality. Two critics, Helfenstein and Legrand, suggest that the half-boots of *Le Couple* form one rather than two objects, that they have overcome such perpetrators of division as the one and the other, male and female.[2] The everyday object, with its ready-made appearance worthy of Duchamp, assumes a questionably spiritual meaning. *Le Couple,* parodying Platonic allegory, might well be one of her earliest works relevant to a concern with androgyny. *Boîte alerte* (1959), which served as a catalogue for an art show entitled "EROS," includes another version of *Le Couple* entitled *A délacer.* The boots, still affixed to one another but laced to the very top, stand stiffly erect. The title suggests various physical activities having moral implications, such as unknotting, freeing, relaxing. But the act of untying the laces will not suffice to emancipate the toes. The artist has transformed a dialectical stance into an ironic trap.

Boîte alerte also includes a reproduction of Oppenheim's *Festin,* an often-photographed installation displaying hunger for food and sex. In one of these photographs the female nude, a papier-mâché mannequin stretched out on a tablecloth, is surrounded by candles and male onlookers. This particular version of the installation suggests that the viewer participates in a wake. Mannequins by Masson, Paalen, Dali, Ernst, Matta, and Dominguez in the important 1939 surrealist exhibit emphasized the erotization of women and the enthronement of male desire. These mannequins, each one assuming an upright position next to a street sign with a provocative name, alternatively reveal and conceal their genitals. They reduce fashion, regarded as the epitome of bourgeois convention, to prostitution. Oppenheim's mannequin, recumbent on a white cloth, seems to have moved one step further than her male companions to mercenary surrender. Surrounded by knives, forks, nuts, and apples, and somewhat reminiscent of Dali's *Maldoror* illustrations, this mannequin cannot escape cannibalization. Her body has become the domain of both order and disorder, invaded as it is by food, which occupies and almost eclipses her genitals. Oppenheim practices surrealist displacement insofar as the white cloth serves at once as a sheet, as a shroud, and as table linen. Whereas her well-rounded breasts surpass the accompanying fruit, her pubic hair appears to cover her forehead. Having abdicated her upright stance, the mannequin resembles, even more than the platter of shoes in *Ma gouvernante,* a gastronomic *pièce montée.* By means of this cornucopia, where sex and food become interchangeable, the 1936 *Déjeuner en fourrure* evolves into *Le Dîner sur la femme nue,* as *Le Festin* is sometimes entitled. By means of this object, Oppenheim opens a gap between the male object of desire and the woman artist who assembled it.

Contrary to Leonora Carrington or Unica Zürn, Oppenheim did not have to overcome a strait-laced social and religious upbringing. When in 1933 she became Man Ray's model, she was certainly in full possession of her independence. On the surface, he was the artist, she his chosen model, but would she have consented at that date to serve as a mere object for contemplation, a woman immobilized for, and mesmerized by, phallic scrutiny? Her nudity was not to be exclusively a product for consumption. Man Ray put every possible photographic technique into action to realize in Oppenheim's presence the full potential of experimental portraiture under the aegis of both dream and reality.

Throughout her life, Oppenheim has been willing to pose for photographers. Catalogues devoted to her abound in portraits. Many belong to the later years, when she was to a certain extent lionized by a younger generation. In what manner can this photographic record be linked to her own quest for identity, to her own representation of self? She portrayed herself making faces or, long before she had reached old age, as an elderly woman. Passivity and narcissism were never her goal. By pointedly avoiding any coincidence between her own self and her portraits, she succeeded in undermining the standard clichés of portraiture. Her departure from ordinary practice suggests an early preoccupation with the dialectics of the couple. Man Ray, I presume, could not have dictated appealing poses to his model even if he had so wished. She participated in the unconventional *mises en scène* in such a way that she became his partner. Some of the sets include Marcoussis wearing a carnival beard, others a lithographic printing press. Oppenheim's nude body relates to the position of the wheel, to the shadows that the spokes cast on her, extending some contours, restricting others (Fig. 3). Mary Ann Caws shows in "Ladies Shot and Painted" that wheel and woman, mechanic and organic interact. Rather than display her body in conventional isolation, Oppenheim participates in a process of remodeling by means of the press's teeth, curve, and handle.[3] Caws discusses two versions of one photograph: in the uncropped version, the handle protrudes horizontally just above the model's pubic hair, further eroticizing the relationship between the *machine célibataire* and the female body. Caws suggests that Oppenheim becomes a partner in the printmaking process; and indeed, the nude with ink on her arm turns herself into a textile canvas. Man Ray and Oppenheim become an interacting couple playing radically different parts. Marcoussis appears in two of the photos. As she stands next to the painter, her body magically elongates. Among the dark objects of the room and the dark clothes of the painter, her white body radiates. When Marcoussis with her consent wipes off the text she has inscribed on her hand, she incarnates a radiant work of art that does not fit into a frame. Like Oppenheim's objects, the photographs suggest transgressions.

The title *Husch, husch, der schönste Vokal entleert sich* again reveals her taste for playfulness and paradox. The link between the verbal and the visual, apparent in the titling of many of the artist's works, reaches a high point in two *livres d'artiste: Sansibar,* illustrated with serigraphs, and *Caro-*

Fig. 3 Man Ray, *Erotique-voilée*, 1933. Musée National d'Art Moderne, Centre Georges Pompidou, Paris.

line, adorned with colored etchings, a new and challenging medium for her. Verbal humor based on intertextuality, either by parody or inverted proverbs, occurs frequently in the poems and corresponds to the technique of disguise and displacement detected in the objects. She plays substitution games with numbers by making them take on unexpected grammatical functions; for instance, "Wer einmal pfeift, gehört nicht her. / Er wird gesiebt, geachtet . . ." (He who whistles once is not listened to – does not belong. / He will be strained, respected – he will be 'sevened,' 'eighted') (p. 27). The grammatical structure and hortatory tone of the first line link it to the proverb "Wer einmal lügt dem glaubt man nicht." Compared to lying, whistling causes only a slight disturbance. In the short title poem, "Husch, husch . . . ," sounds play an even more central role: "Von Beeren nährt man sich / Mit dem Schuh verehrt man sich / Husch, husch, der schönste Vokal entleert sich" (We feed ourselves with berries / We honor ourselves with a shoe / Hush, hush, the most beautiful vowel empties itself). Two drawings included in the volume are relevant to this text: *Modeentwurf für Ohrschmuck* (Fashion Sketch for Ear Jewelry) (p. 97) and *Ohren-Geschichte* (p. 104). The former presents the ear with its semicircular or spiral pattern, its enclosures, its tunnels adorned with jewels which eroticize the act of listening. As in her sculpture *The Ear of Giacometti* (1933) allusions to the ear, its passages and patterns recur in *Ohren-Geschichte* – meaning both tales about ears and nuisances caused by ears. Sound and silence, openings and closures are all comprised within the meanderings of the tales. "Husch, husch . . . ," like the ear, the sound, the story, refuses linear development. The norms stated in the first two lines quickly turn into paradox.

The poem that bears the rather mysterious title of "Sansibar," borrowed perhaps from a Bernese tavern, focuses on the problem of identity and creation in a reverse or negative way through loss and eventual destruction: "Weil er sich den Rücken kehrt" (Because he turns his back to himself) (p. 19). Facing one's own back, humorously aporic as the line appears, suggests a double disruption from the self to the self and the self to the other. Isolation, loss of orientation are logical consequences of the anonymity that has emerged. In the final stages, the poet turns once more to cannibalism, the act of self-devouring: "Sie essen ihren Pelz" (They are eating their fur). Animals cannot be distinguished from humans; communication is disrupted. In this 1933 poem, Oppenheim has already created verbally the image which she will embody three years later in *Le Déjeuner en fourrure*. The "Sansibar" poem marks the beginning of a series of references relevant to the problem of identity, to the act of devouring and to artistic creation. Man Ray's photograph of the 1936 object was serigraphed by Oppenheim in the 1950s, as though she wished to recover the interaction of the 1933 photographs and the problematics of posing as a model. By letting an art object be transformed into a photograph only to have it finally materialize as a graphic work, Oppenheim seems to have deliberately blurred distinctions. A 1970 avatar entitled *Souvenir du déjeuner en fourrure,* an adaptation of poster art and keepsakes, typically reveals the deviations which successful surrealist art works can undergo, for it perversely subverts the romantic notion of memory.

The opening lines of Oppenheim's poem "La Rosée sur la rose" prepare the reader for a lyric, even a romantic conventionality, a self-reflexive venture, a glimpse of an ideal, only to surprise him or her by a sudden reversal from plenitude to emptiness, an eruption of humor and a definitive displacement from what she had led one to expect. The poem, written in French, results in an unmatching duality rather than in a progressive unfolding. Allusions to dew and roses seem to echo an intimate lyricism. And poetic rite forbids that the rose's pure beauty be approached before a given hour. But suddenly the rose welcomes artificiality in turning into blackness and wax. Resurrected in the clouds, it consumes marzipan. The rose is no longer a rose even by its own name. A similar principle governs *Why, Why?* (1968), a still life consisting of five constellated roses. Each of the flowers distances itself from nature and conventional floral representation. A white porcelain rose surmounted by sketches of two other roses in the process of fabrication, by a red cloth flower in the clutches of a reptilian stem, and by a construct of wooden fragments produces a *mise en abîme* summarizing the conflict, so often repeated in modern art, between two-dimensional and three-dimensional representation. The multiplication of dissimilar roses also undermines poetic analogy. As in "La Rosée sur la rose," it is not only once again the object itself which is problematized, but the literary or plastic genre in subservience to which roses are only too frequently represented. Moreover, the Man Ray photographs, by foregrounding interaction, had alluded to stages of creation, a process undeniably present in *Why, Why?*

To the highly varied texts produced at different times a certain unity is restored by presenting them on pages facing serigraphs or etchings, printed on convexly embossed paper. The text of *Sansibar* is enclosed in a concave semicircle, while that of *Caroline* is printed on an open rectangular page. An attempt to match while upholding, if not emphasizing, distinctions seems to be a common feature of the two books. The highly stylized designs, acknowledged as interpretations by Oppenheim herself, avoid any attempt to duplicate or imitate the text. In spite of the distinct otherness of the graphics in relation to textual identity, Oppenheim deviates from other surrealist approaches to illustration, dominated as they are by tension – for instance, André Masson's *Saison en enfer* and Salvador Dali's *Chants de Maldoror*. Oppenheim's streamlined plates adapt spatial contexts so as to emphasize affinities with typographical inscriptions.

Text and illustration cannot be considered equal partners in the production of *Sansibar* and *Caroline*. With one or two exceptions, the graphic illustrations comment on texts written much earlier. The illustrations exclude narrative and dramatic elements. In the absence of conflicts and reversals pertaining to the serigraphs and etchings, Oppenheim lifts the confrontation between text and image to a poetic and spiritual level. The text necessarily becomes other. The inner struggle that Oppenheim waged against duality, beginning with her refusal to throw in her lot permanently with a "genius," a refusal restated in such works as *Le Couple* and explained in her polemical speech at Basel, is aesthetically resolved in her illustrated books. We should look at the two *livres d'artiste* in light of the artist's reflections on androgyny in *Aufzeichnungen* as well as her preoccupation with Bettina Brentano and Caroline von Günderode, to whom she devoted paintings.[4] In an interview with Christiane Meyer-Thoss, Oppenheim states in regard to the correspondence between the two women:

Ich möchte, dass man weiss, dass ich diesen Briefwechsel als dichterisches Werk an sich begreife; als Bezeichnung für diesen Briefwechsel ist mir wichtig "Hymnische Gespräche." Damit möchte ich den Finger drauf legen, dass es sich nicht um einen gewöhnlichen Briefwechsel handelt, sondern um ein Kunstwerk. . . .

Christiane Meyer-Thoss replies:

Ich habe beim Lesen stark den Eindruck gehabt, dass es im Grunde eine einzige Person ist, die sich hier auseinandersetzt in diesem Briefwechsel, obwohl natürlich zwei Personen agieren. (*Meret Oppenheim, 39*)

(I would like it to be known that I consider this correspondence a poetic work. It matters to me that I designate it as "Hymnic Dialogues." I insist that we are not dealing with an ordinary exchange of letters, but a work of art. . . .

As I read I had the strong impression that basically it is one person who argues in this correspondence although two people play a role.)

Among Oppenheim's poems, texts without a declared narrator alternate with more personal ones overtly linked to her autobiographical enterprise. In her persistent self-representation both in word and image, she goes beyond other women artists involved with surrealist art and ideology: Fini, Tanning, Carrington, Zürn. Unlike Carrington and Zürn, Oppenheim refused even temporarily to assert herself with or against another artist. First-person narrative, references to an inner life characterize "Dort oben in jenem Garten" (Yonder in That Garden). The poetic voice is at once one and multiple. The shadows that are beheld, seen both as a burden and as a solace, provide images of self-awareness. The poet pledges her solidarity with their arboriform and statuesque images and with the distant part of herself. In the illustration just as in the text, Oppenheim solicits the past (Fig. 4). Her serigraph is based on her sculpture entitled *Sechs Wolken auf einer Brücke* (1963) (Six Clouds on a Bridge). Clouds, like the shapes in the poem, differing in outlines, form rich constellations evoking stars, flowers, trees, statues, which, transcribed from copper onto paper, suggest a landscape mysteriously concretizing inner life. The illustration, echoing the artist's past, implicitly evokes memories inscribed in the poem. *Sechs Wolken auf einer Brücke,* combined with the poetic text "Dort oben in jenem Garten," even if it ends in irony, points to Oppenheim's aim to build bridges between figments of her self.

In *Caroline*, "Une Dame dans la quarantaine" (A Forty-year-old Lady)

Dort oben in jenem Garten
Dort stehen meine Schatten
Die mir den Rücken kühlen.

Sie stehen in dem Garten
Sie streiten um ein altes Brot
Und krähen wie die Hähne.

Heut will ich sie besuchen
Heut will ich sie begrüssen
Und ihre Nasen zählen.

Fig. 4   Oppenheim, *Sansibar*, no. 11, 1943. Kunstmuseum Bern.

ends with a capital R in quotation marks. This same letter isolated in a semicircle and serving as an illustration merely inscribes the conclusion of the text, a conclusion that the text itself had prepared for the illustration. The unassuming forty-year-old woman in the process of fabricating objects and words turns out to be an artist. Art provides the middle-aged woman with an identity. She practices, like Oppenheim, the technique of disguise, for her coins are made of chocolate and her mice are shaped like the letter R. This letter, covered with delicate lines and spots, emblematizes writing and drawing so as to display the transformatory process characteristic of art.

The last poem that Oppenheim wrote is about self-portraits: "Selbstportrait seit 50,000 v. Chr. bis X." In both her poetic texts and her visual portraits, Oppenheim refuses to idealize herself or to escape to imaginary settings in the manner of Fini, Carrington, Hugo, or Tanning. Oppenheim isolates her face without situating herself in any given context. The 1964 *X-Ray,* with its gigantic skull, jewels, and hand, may be read as an ironic

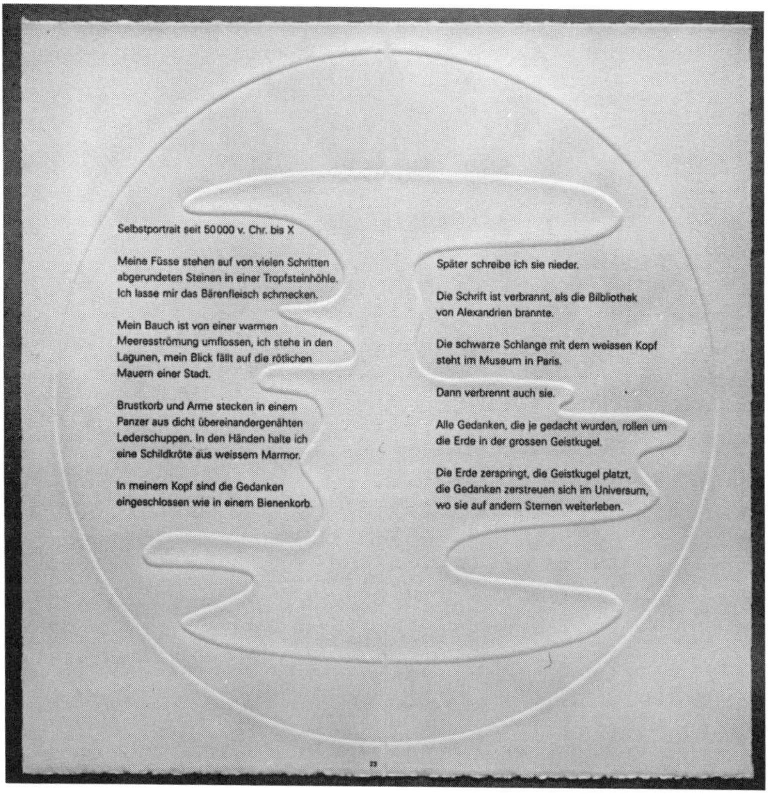

Fig. 5 Oppenheim, *Selbstportrait seit 50,000 v. Chr. bis X, Caroline,* no. 23, 1980. Kunstmuseum Bern.

counterpart of Man Ray's solarized portraits of the young model. Here portraiture is neither a way of seduction nor of revelation.

In the *Selbstportrait,* she explores both the space of her body and the creative activity of her mind (Fig. 5). The reader of the text moves upwards from the feet to the belly and the chest, the arms, the eyes, and the head; simultaneously s/he passes from the prehistory of the stone age to medieval times and the modern world. As the intellectual process is set into motion to salvage all stages of experience, irony emerges: "In meinem Kopf sind die Gedanken eingeschlossen wie in einem Bienenkorb" (In my head, ideas are enclosed as in a beehive) (p. 87). The portrait, extending from primitive signs to modern writing, does not need consolidation, as dispersion and regeneration alternate. The first person disappears, conflagration arises: "Die Schrift ist verbrannt. . . . Dann verbrennt auch sie [die Schlange]. . . . Die Erde zerspringt, die Geisteskugel platzt, die Gedanken zerstreuen sich im Universum, wo sie auf andern Sternen weiterleben" (The writing is burnt, then the snake also burns, the earth splits, the mental sphere bursts, ideas disperse in the universe in order to continue to live on other planets). Displacement and discrimination, equivalent to planting and uprooting, establish constant contact and exchange between the brain and the globe, a self subject to inner changes and the universe.

In *Selbstportrait,* as in one other text of *Caroline,* the space of the poem and illustration coincide. The embossing of the page creates an interplay with the black letterpress. As Hans Christoph von Tavel has pointed out, the poem ends with "Aufgehen in All" (Dissolution in the universe), which is not alien to her androgynous dream.[5] The two facing pages are united instead of contrasted, forming a circle which suggests a cloud with its fluctuations, retreats, and advances, altering, in harmony with the poetic text, its shape and itinerary, its serpentine inscriptions. By means of these *Prägedrucke* the page restores the image of a face on which the poet inscribes her own thoughts, her own wrinkles, her own fluctuations. Is this page with its concavities and convexities, where black notations, no longer as confining as the brain, interact, radically different from the 1980 *Portrait mit Tätowierung (Portrait with Tattoo)*? Has she turned her photograph into a page and the page with the poem into a photograph? Oppenheim has found a mask which combines avant-garde posture with primitive rites. She has finally transferred the dialectics of the couple into an image where the self and its creation come close to fusion.

In 1975, when Oppenheim accepted the prize offered to her by the city of Basel, she asserted her position on identity, feminism, partnership, and creation, a position which had already surfaced, at least obliquely, in the Man Ray photographs, her objects, her *livres de peintre,* and her self-portraits. In her speech, she comments on the social isolation of women. She separates the social issue from art. Granting freedom to women pertains to society, but there is no masculine or feminine art. Moreover, she urges men to recognize the feminine spirit in themselves, and she advises women to affirm their masculinity. Androgyny lifts creation to a higher level. Her refusal of partnership resulted in the recognition of the couple within herself. By this allegiance she joins other Surrealists, such as the Breton of *Arcane 17* or the Brauner of *Nombre.* In her final works, *Sansibar* and *Caroline,* Oppenheim also aimed at attaining a higher reality, leaving behind the incongruous juxtapositions grounded in Lautréamont's metaphor, which undoubtedly had led to the great success of *Le Déjeuner en fourrure.*

Notes

1. *Husch, husch, der schönste Vokal entleert sich* (Frankfurt: Suhrkamp, 1984); *Sansibar,* with 15 colored silkscreen and blind stampings and 16 texts (Basel: Edition Fanal, 1981); *Caroline,* 21 colored etchings, 2 blind stampings and 23 poems (Basel: Edition Fanal, 1985).

2. Joseph Helfenstein, "Androgynität als Bildthema und Persönlichkeitsmodell" in *Meret Oppenheim* (Bern: Kunstmuseum Bern, 1987), 13–36; Gérard Legrand, "Le Dilemme de l'androgynat" in *Boîte alerte,* catalogue of L'Exposition Internationale du Surréalisme, 1959–60 (Paris: Galerie Daniel Cordier, 1959), 102–9.

3. Mary Ann Caws, "Ladies Shot and Painted: Female Embodient in Surrealist Art," in Susan Rubin Suleiman, ed., *The Female Body in Western Culture* (Cambridge: Harvard University Press, 1986), 262–87.

4. *Aufzeichnungen, 1925–85* (Bern and Berlin: Verlag Gachnang und Springer, 1986), 18.

5. Hans Christoph von Tavel, "Das Vermächtnis von Meret Oppenheim im Kunstmuseum," in *Meret Oppenheim,* 9.

6. Extracts reprinted in *La Femme surréaliste, Obliques* 14–15 (1977), 193–94.

I wish to express my gratitude to Joseph Helfenstein, Kunstmuseum Bern, and to André Schweizer, Edition Fanal, for their generous help. This article was written during my residence as a fellow of the Camargo Foundation.

Speaking with Forked Tongues: "Male" Discourse in "Female" Surrealism?

Robert J. Belton

Surrealism is popularly understood as an unreflective indulgence in sub-conscious material, and to some extent it was. However, the corollary of this notion – that the content thus unearthed was in some way a psychic constant, unchanging in time or place – is entirely untrue. Surrealism, like any other cultural phenomenon, was the product of an enormously com-plicated network of sources and influences. Some of these were expressly social and political, and only secondarily were they "aesthetic."

Much has recently been made of the contributions of women artists to Surrealism, but little or no attention has been paid to a fundamental ques-tion: given that (male) surrealist art presented a biased image of Woman, is it not possible that the works of female Surrealists are similarly compro-mised, especially if one can determine that the Surrealists' "interpretive webs" – that is, networks of allusions which made the content of surrealist art intelligible to other members – undermine descriptions of Surrealism as pro- or proto-feminist? A further question then arises: to what extent does "objective" cultural and contextual description – especially in cases where a patriarchal order is so obviously manifest – actually *prohibit* the generation of new readings in a contemporary feminist mode? In other words, where do our priorities lie: in reconstructing and attributing historically "true" intentions to female artists or in deconstructing the very hypothesis that such a thing can be done? This paper wrangles with these issues and others chiefly to examine the ways in which "unilingual" patriarchy construes itself as the norm. The conclusion is that there *can* be no conclusion and that we must simply learn what it is to "speak with forked tongues."

In her inventorial survey *Women Artists and the Surrealist Movement*, Whitney Chadwick notes time and again that "almost without exception, women artists viewed themselves as having functioned independently of . . . surrealist doctrine."[1] Despite a rapidly growing body of research on these women artists, however, a number of fundamental questions must be asked. For example, the commentaries of several writers have made the endeavors of these women seem wholly proto- or at least pro-feminist. The situation is a good deal more involved than this, since it is clear that surrealist doctrine was ideologically patriarchal, and I submit that the work of female artists requires a double interpretation – what my title designates as a forked tongue. This tongue is both that of the artists involved and that of the interpretive community. But as we shall see, this complicates rather than clarifies the issues.

To establish the maleness of the surrealist rhetoric with simple sweeps of the brush is, of course, extremely difficult. Interested parties could refer to my article in *Woman's Art Journal* and to Xavière Gauthier's *Surréalisme et sexualité*.[2] For the moment, let it suffice to acknowledge that the image of "Woman" was the most frequently used tactic in the Surrealists' revolutionary strategy of articulating desire in order to reshape the world. Of course, the image of "Woman" underwent various treatments which made it clear that it (she?) was more a metaphor of language than a flesh-and-blood entity. As such, she could be more easily manipulated with devices like surrealist juxtaposition – the most basic form of which is the collage, which every undergraduate should now recognize as absolutely central to the surrealist project. What is not so clear is that the principle of juxtaposition, exemplified most tellingly by the proto-surrealist Isidore Ducasse in his oft-quoted phrase "as beautiful as the chance encounter of an umbrella and a sewing machine on a dissection table," was interpreted by the surrealist mentality in directly Freudian terms. The coincidence of a man's phallic accessory and an unthinking domestic instrument on a "bed" designed for bloodletting was simply too potently, aggressively, and violently sexual to be avoided. Since we cannot afford the space to explore this further, let us note in passing that Ducasse's simile, as the archetypal act of collage, virtually ensured that other juxtapositions would connote sexual violence for the male Surrealist. If there were not such a buried deep structure in this means of defamiliarizing the world in order to reconstruct it in the image of desire, then collage would not have had its compelling power for male Surrealists.

Surrealism, having not long ago been dismissed as a decadent, self-indulgent art, has recently been undergoing a reevaluation. The defamiliarization of which I speak is now considered by some to be a forerunner of the postmodernist mentality, particularly as it addresses questions of linguistic shifts, figurative language, and the like. However, to lionize Surrealism only in this regard would be to do a grave disservice to ourselves, for Surrealism's iconography and historical mentality are often not worthy of our admiration, even while some of its methods might be. This is not to say that there is something inherently wrong with the expression of desire in and of itself. (That would be prudish, as well as morally, ethically and theoretically naïve.) But in the surrealist lexicon – which was the result of an admittedly elastic, but still limited, repertory of interpretive webs – the practice of tearing something from its original context in order to associate it with some other, similarly decontextualized image was metaphorically realized as brutally sexual defloration, plain and simple.[3]

I have explained elsewhere how André Masson's famous images of earth goddesses are cultural "fibs" made up of meanings and implications torn from their original literary, mythological and psychological contexts.[4] Not the least of these meanings is hidden in the fact that they are usually headless, which Masson explicitly linked to the loss of virginity in brutal drawings like *Naissance de la femme (1943)*.[5] The further association of violent sexual initiation with maternity was very powerful in the patriarchal French mentality between the world wars. In 1939, for example, new legislation made it illegal for women to use contraceptives or to obtain an abortion, because women's role was to repopulate a decimated country. Of course, headlessness also connotes the loss of intelligence, which is particularly interesting in this context since French pro-natalist policy was one of the principal reasons that women did not get the right to vote for another half-decade. It was "natural," then, for women to lose their heads: their biological creativity would not be hindered, and their powers of reason were of no use since women had no political position. Far from being a vindication of matriarchal rights and principles, Masson's reclining, maternal terramorphs were icons of a historically specific antifeminism.

In point of fact, the male Surrealists were almost totally indifferent to the work of women artists as art, even though they exhibited alongside them from time to time. Their writings on art typically ignored the contribution of female artists, and individual women were mentioned chiefly as the wife or companion of a respected male. One looks in vain through their prolific writings for the same intensive level of discussion that is revealed in dozens of pages on Max Ernst or Giorgio de Chirico. Paul Eluard was a bit of an exception because he was a regular collaborator with Valentine Hugo, at least insofar as he had her illustrate his works – usually previously published ones, at that. But setting Breton a little to one side because of the notes on female artists in his *Le Surréalisme et la peinture* would be a profound error. What he wrote there is of extraordinarily little value as an appraisal of their production. Instead, we find poetically effusive meditations: the virtually unknown Mimi Parent, for instance, is commemorated only with "In Mimi's thistled eyes shine the gardens of Armide [a celebrated enchantress] at midnight." When a woman's paintings are mentioned, they are never treated with the same perspicuity as those of a man. For example, the art of Frida Kahlo, whose likeness to a sort of seductive butterfly was Breton's primary concern, is summarized quickly as "a ribbon around a bomb."[6] It is a sad fact that a great many of the women who participated in surrealist exhibitions seem to have been allowed to do so precisely because they too were nicely packaged explosives. Of course, this meant that women's works were included to exploit some residual shock, outside of the artists' intentions, like embodiments of Breton's famous conception of the marvelous as convulsive beauty.

This is what brings us to our first female illustration of the male discourse of which I speak: Meret Oppenheim's famous fur-covered cup, saucer, and spoon of 1936. Known only as *Object* in the permanent collection of New York's Museum of Modern Art—a situation which has undoubtedly contributed to its status as one of the more important surrealist objects—the work's true title is *Déjeuner en fourrure*. It is particularly crucial to note this because the way the male Surrealists understood the work is very much an elaboration of its title. But it was *not* Oppenheim's choice. She wanted only to explore the implications of a conversation with Picasso about decorative, if unusual, fur-covered jewelry.[7] Breton, on the other hand, wanted to exploit the aura of scandalous female sexuality that he took for granted in Edouard Manet's celebrated *Déjeuner sur l'herbe* (1863) and the blatant sexual fetishism of Leopold von Sacher-Masoch's *Venus im Pelz* (*Venus in Furs*, 1870), known in France as *Vénus en fourrures*. The concavity of Oppenheim's cup then punned with the rigidity of the spoon which would be inserted into it, while the hairy gustatory sensation that accompanied the act resonated with the sophomoric humor that the male Surrealists found so endearing. Here, the compromised character of the principle of juxtaposition is once again clearly male. In fact, we are justified in asking whether the work is truly Oppenheim's at all, for in a conversation that took place only shortly before she died, she implied to me that it was not her "creation" apart from the actual manufacture.[8] Clearly, then, some of the works of women involved in Surrealism were simply overcome by association with male meanings.

This cannot be said of Leonora Carrington, who seems to have been willing to borrow one of the models of male surrealist endeavor. Chadwick has linked Carrington's *Autoportrait: à l'auberge du cheval d'Aube* (1937–38)[9] to "childhood worlds of fantasy and magic . . . capable of creative transformation through mental rather than sexual power" (79). Only the repudiation of the obviously sexual redeems what is otherwise still compromised by adherence to the male modernist models of regression and metamorphosis, for there is nothing intrinsically good about the toys of childhood. Moreover, this *femme-enfant's* toys provide a clear escape from the enclosing walls only by a transformation begun by a man: the white rocking horse comes alive in the window in the distance, giving a release which Carrington herself explicitly associated with the shamanistic activities of Ernst (79). The implication is that without the intervention of this male element, the central figure would remain trapped, like the female arms and feet of the chair on which she sits, itself so reminiscent of contemporary fetishizing works by Masson and Kurt Seligmann. If Carrington was truly exploring herself in this work, then she seems to have concluded that she was genuinely creative, but chiefly because her ability to regress had been awakened by Ernst. One could say much the same thing of the ostensibly feminist reclamation of sorcery and the intuitive control of nature signaled by the figure's devil-horned gesture and the mammiferous hyena it invokes.

Gloria Feman Orenstein has argued that Carrington constantly liberated the fundamental animal nature of women as a metaphor of originary female creativity, implying that such a regression was in fact a forward step towards freedom. On the other hand, Renée Riese Hubert has proposed exactly the opposite – that the painting emblematizes female imprisonment.[10] What are we to make of this interpretive contradiction? Is it just a matter of opinion or differences in the respective authors' horizons of expectations? To what extent does specific cultural analysis of the period in which the work was made support or deny one of the interpretations?

Perhaps the real strength of the picture is in its fusion of biological creativity, represented by the hyena, and artistic creativity, represented by the sorceress-hysteric. Nevertheless, even if this is the picture's strength, then it is a force imparted by the corrupted vocabulary of male Surrealism: let us not forget that hysteria (of which sorcery was an early manifestation) was a supreme means of expression outside of the control of the hysteric herself, at least as far as Surrealism was concerned. To sum up, then, Carrington's *Autoportrait* can be understood as toeing the party line, so to speak, accepting the dependent role of the prelogical entity. It does so, however, without the usual erotic overtones.

Many other women artists exploited the childhood metaphor, of course – one thinks especially of Dorothea Tanning's ostensibly autobiographical *Children's Games* of 1942, in which playtime amounts to a demolition and disordering of the world analogous to the surrealist revolution.[11] Still, it would be quite incorrect to assume that there is no depiction of adult sexual experience in the work of women. Fini's graphic works include illustrations of a woman fondling a man's erect penis, oral sex, a man with an erection subduing a woman, and a number of other such things.[12] One of Valentine Hugo's illustrations for the Marquis de Sade's *Eugénie de Franval* (1948) is a fragment of an explicit copulation, with a female hand guiding a phallus into a vagina. Black and white stars twinkle around the lovers, suggesting the cosmos during sex, yet another way to disorder the world.[13]

It may be, however, that the sense of disarray is an illusion, for one often uncovers evocations of the same "natural order" – that is, female dependence and subordination – that marks the works of male artists. Hugo's untitled "object of symbolic function" (Fig. 1) is a thinly veiled allegory of the sexual chase and the psychological games employed by both sexes in the eternal round: on a gaming board which clearly indicates chance and risk, Hugo placed two gloves, one of which penetrates the other by slipping a finger just under the cuff. It is the female that is penetrated, for Hugo has coded the sexes through color (virginal white versus carnal red)

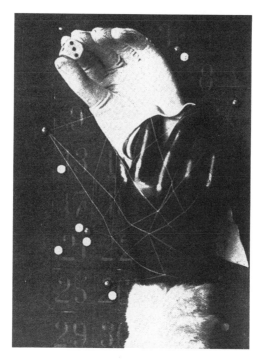

Fig. 1 Valentine Hugo, Untitled (Object of symbolic function), 1931. Assemblage. Whereabouts unknown.

and position (male convexity versus female concavity). Moreover, the female fingers hold a die which is not only another sign of chance but may also be a characteristic surrealist pun. Man Ray's 1929 film *Le Mystère du chateau de dés* (*The Mystery of the Chateau of Dice*) was inspired by a line of Stéphane Mallarmé's poetry: "un coup de dés n'abolira jamais le hasard" ("a throw of the dice will never abolish chance"). Hugo's object may have been intended to play off the same phrase by roughly reversing *coup de dés* to *dé à coudre*, "thimble." The resonance of a thimble in this context is once again sexual, involving penetrating fingers, an overtone of domestic subordination, and a fashionably Lautréamontesque allusion to a sewing machine. And for those who miss the association, Hugo has literally pinned it down: red and white thumbtacks entrap the gloves in a net of sorts, which may relate to the types of "black widow" representations that one finds in the photographic works of Man Ray.[14] But who can say if this is a condemnation or a desire, for the work can be interpreted as autobiography: it was fabricated in the middle of a short period of eighteen months during which Hugo and Breton were extremely close. The artist loved the suitor of the *femme-enfant* to the point of distraction, but at forty-four years of age she

55

was simply too old to divert him for long. She was also too sophisticated, presumably, and too capable; unlike Tanning, she did not exploit the imagery of childhood in her art. Of course, it is also quite probable that Hugo was consciously manipulating, tongue in cheek, the same quasi-Freudian clichés that the male artists exploited.

There were other alternatives. Instead of regressive escapism or adult conformism, one could select the mythic origins of the world and the goddess that created it. There is no doubt that many of the women artists knew Robert Graves's *The White Goddess,* an attempt to retrieve matriarchal traditions from a vague past obscured by patriarchal suppression and out-and-out corruption. For example, Carrington certainly knew of the great goddess Danu (Chadwick 198), whom Graves described as a universal Mother existing prior to the Judaeo-Christian Father. Greek myths deprived her of her divinity and made her Danaë, the mortal who was impregnated by Zeus's shower of gold – a dim reflection of the earth-mother fructified by rain. Carrington's restoration of the goddess to her former omnipotent stature leads some to conclude that the artist was making feminist headway, but such observations ignore the multiplicity of ideologies that contribute to feminism. For instance, a feminist could easily ask what purpose is really served if one forgets that all such deities began as allegorizations or personifications of natural processes and rudimentary biology. Add to this the specifically antifeminist mind-set of a postwar France that forbade contraception, and we realize that women's myths of Woman as nature are as culturally determined as men's myths of Woman as nature.

The fundamental ambiguity of goddess-reclamation is reflected in the comments of the artists themselves. Carrington asserted in 1976:

[Women's rights] must be Taken Back
Again, including the mysteries
which were ours and which were violated,
stolen or destroyed. . . .

Tanning, on the other hand, ridiculed the idea of women's mysteries like Mother Nature: "Can't you see her, tentacles waving in the void, her body dragging its track of slime . . . ?"[15] Historians of art are equally divided: Estella Lauter has argued that a uniquely feminine reality is exposed through such salvage operations, whereas Linda Nochlin seems convinced that a return to the mythic nature-woman is the very antithesis of historical action.[16]

Regardless of the goddess, a concern primarily with the self links some of the women artists to the surrealist movement as clearly as any individual motif or technical device. With the exceptions of Grace Pailthorpe, whose psychological concerns with genuine expression led her to describe male surrealist art as unreliable (Chadwick 222), and Lee Miller and

Toyen, both of whom turned from themselves to comment on World War II (Chadwick 232–33), the women Surrealists can be described in the same terms of narcissism and abrogation of social responsibility that are applicable to the men. None of them, for example, appeared to have been involved with the women's movement until the 1970s, when it became yet another fashion to retrieve women artists. Only one of them, Eileen Agar, read the writings of Thomas Malthus (Chadwick 130), whose economically and demographically based principles of population control were imperative to some of the more outspoken French feminists' demands for birth control. It is thus not incidental that the artists themselves were quite at odds with the subject of motherhood; they all dealt with it as a personal issue, rather than as a social one. Carrington and Miller both have children, but Agar, Fini, and Oppenheim were indifferent or actively opposed. Tanning depicted reproduction as violent and alienating in her *Maternity* (1946), while her *Maternity II* (1953) shows it as animalistic at best. Where the former painting reveals physical isolation and torn clothing, the latter has a wide-eyed, disheveled woman on all fours, surrounded by a litter of anthropoid pups reminiscent of her famous dog, Katchina.[17] In complete contrast, Kahlo's paintings on the subject are the most intensely moving of any produced by an artist even loosely affiliated with Surrealism; hers are genuine cries of psychological and physical distress, chiefly because of her damaged spine, her broken marriage, and her miscarriages. However, the very authenticity of her self-exploration marks her pictures as well beyond the artificial interlacings of Surrealism, despite their superficial likenesses.[18]

Kahlo's undeniable sincerity marked her as an artist of deeper importance than any other woman with links to Surrealism. Those others may have been more talented – Hugo's draughtsmanship is excellent, if a little mannered. Others were certainly more confrontational – Bona de Mandiargue's nipple-exposing evening dress is provocation through subordination par excellence.[19] But no one was more brutally immediate and deeply personal while, paradoxically, seeming so universal. Because of this, Kahlo's work really should not be discussed here. Nor should those works executed by other women artists after they had escaped the immediate circle of Surrealism, by which time French women had finally received the right to vote – that is, when social and ideological circumstances intervene less in the act of interpretation, ensuring that we can read metaphors more elastically and with less historical specificity. Works of the later periods seem less "spoiled," as it were, when they are chronologically and geographically remote. Unfortunately, there is no way to assess the sincerity of any of these artists (male or female, I suppose it need not be said). Presumably, they all were true to themselves, but their adherence to surrealist routine colored their work.

We can only conclude that the participation of living women in a movement which disdained them in favor of a number of abstractions is problematic in the extreme. Moreover, the accounts of the women themselves are often contradictory: for every Fini, who sought a degree of independence from her male associates – although it should be noted that there is at least a rumor that Breton prevented Fini from any participation in the movement on personal grounds – there was a Kay Sage, who said it was "natural" that she took more interest in the work of her husband Yves Tanguy than he did in hers, or a Leonora Carrington, seated like a disciple at the feet of Max Ernst (Chadwick 81, 98, and 80, respectively). So why did women participate? The answer is quite unclear: on one side are the women who have freely admitted that it was only because of their attachments to men; on the other are those who participated because Surrealism itself had become a new cultural fashion. With this in mind, it is important to note that the vast majority of women appeared on the horizon just as Surrealism became increasingly preoccupied with advertising, haute couture, and jewelry (see Chadwick 55, 119, 122). That this is so has nothing whatsoever to do with the artists' integrity or with their gender; it shows only that the historical moment of major innovation had passed. Surrealism's basic tenets were thoroughly entrenched and its productions, most notably in the visual arts, were rapidly degenerating into easily consumable mannerisms.

The great majority of the women artists were thus pressed into service as reinforcements, as it were. Many of them perpetuated some aspects of the negative iconography of Woman, perhaps unwittingly or in spite of attempts to subvert them. Ithell Colquhoun, Fini, Oppenheim, and Toyen, for instance, all made images that continued to exploit male castration anxiety and/or the femme fatale.[20] Some of those who chose not to draw directly from the stagnant pool of surrealist ideas were nevertheless influenced by it, even if only through their relationships with men. The most productive periods of several women were precipitated by the loss of their painter-mates (Chadwick 84, 92, 102), which suggests such a high degree of dependence that it is no surprise their works became synonymous with self-exploration: they had nowhere else to look.

The most fundamental aporia now comes into view: if spiritual self-exploration – at least as it surfaces in the frequently appearing motif of the spiritual quest (Chadwick 214, 218) – indicates a heartfelt desire to find oneself without adherence to Freudian clichés, as well as to establish or to renew old metaphors of women's (nonreproductive) creativity, then certain notions of creativity, even talent, were approved by women, while spirituality was understood at face value, not as metaphor. Since such a defense would therefore reverse two basic surrealist tenets – the repudiation of talent, authorial motivation, or creativity, and spirituality taken strictly as metaphor – it would appear that some of these women artists were not really Surrealists at all. Accordingly, Chadwick herself notes that it might be more profitable to describe these artists as Magic Realists or Neo-Romantics (220). Considering Fini's work, Marcel Brion has suggested "fantastic realism."[21] Whatever they are called, some of the works of the women artists with connections to Surrealism redefine it in such a way that they actually leave the movement's "pioneering exploration of creative waters" behind.[22] It is for this reason that I quite arbitrarily decide not to follow them here.

For the moment, it is imperative to explore further the nature of the contradiction itself, especially since the female iconographies cannot absolutely be distinguished from those of the male artists. Of course, it is now becoming commonplace to assert that men and women may use the same vocabularies, but that they speak fundamentally different dialects.[23] Another, less flattering explanation is that some of the women were making a special effort to "speak," as it were, the tongue of those who oppressed them. In the current social psychology of language, this phenomenon is studied under the rubric "speech accommodation theory," which alleges, among other things, that "people are more likely to converge towards the speech patterns of their recipients when they desire their approval and when the perceived costs for doing so are proportionally lower than the anticipated rewards."[24] Unfortunately, the empirical findings of this discipline are not of much help in the present context, because most experiments have dealt with interacting people of apparently equal status, which certainly is not the case for us. On a theoretical level, however, it is not difficult to imagine why an empowered gender would refuse to listen to a subordinated one unless the latter linguistically accommodated the former. This, in turn, would further ensure that the subordinated group would be perceived as powerless on its own. (Oppenheim spoke most succinctly to this in her *Geneviève*, whose broken arms signal a plaintive cry of despair in the face of creative paralysis).

Some will say that the brevity of this consideration of women artists gives them short shrift. This is true, but it is defensible on the grounds that this essay is built on the deconstructed ruins of the ideology behind Surrealism, which was entirely the contribution of males. The women who merely subscribed to it deserve no more and no less attention than any other third- or fourth-generation Surrealists, who are also given short shrift. Those women who heroically rose above it – the better part of those whose names are mentioned above – are gradually being more profitably examined in contexts which correctly downplay or elide the surrealist connections. In any case, the women's Woman was founded to a certain degree on the actual experience of womanhood, even when tinted by male preoccupations. In contrast, the men's Woman was fabricated from patriarchal habits of mind, sexual proclivities, and even unconscious political attitudes.

With the last point in mind, it is interesting to speculate why none of the

Surrealists, male or female, were interested in the vote for women in the 1930s. The biggest fear of the French Senate was that women, statistically proven to attend church in larger numbers than men, would vote for the clerical parties, thereby threatening the security of the lay republic. The church was anathema to the Surrealists as well. Breton, for one, even threatened his daughter with Mass as a form of punishment (Chadwick 61). In failing to support universal suffrage vocally, the Surrealists were thus in step with the very bourgeoisie they had hoped to overthrow. It follows that the Surrealist Woman would have virtually no power of self-determination.

Here, the thicket of problems becomes denser yet. If we consider the specific case of the iconography of female powerlessness in Surrealism, it becomes impossible to determine the intentions of a particular artist. An image of a bound woman, for example, could be either a fetishistic indulgence for antifeminist reasons or an outcry against the oppression of women. This situation is unresolvable, unless we reorient ourselves and the terms of the discourse entirely. To this end, we note the words of Susanne Kappeler, who considers the iconography of powerlessness to be a pornography of representation, by which she means not sex or morality, but a new perspective on the very function of representation itself in contemporary society: "We have a cultural discourse that is monologic, a self-representation of a dominant group, and a distribution of roles that reflects the inequality of the subject and the object."[25] As much could be said of Surrealism. The women who did speak up during that particular monologue were drowned out by male voices because their historical moment – which was not that of political representation but of insights and values – had not yet come.

Where do we end vis-à-vis the interpretability of the women's works? If we end by describing them as having objective meaning relating only to the social codes created by men, the works suffer and we seem to be blaming the victims for their own oppression. Besides, we must begin to think of all artists as "reactive beings . . . capable of selecting their own input and negotiating their status . . . ," at least to some extent.[26] If, on the other hand, we say it is up to our own interpretive ingenuity to see the works as locales for the proliferation of pro- or proto-feminist meaning, then we may be giving our own horizon of expectations priority over the historical and material conditions which inflected the work to begin with. The long and the short of the story, then, is that we have discovered the issue of methodology itself to be deeply problematic in such a socially crucial area. It is necessary, in a word, to learn to speak with forked tongues. And since we have no metalanguage with which to characterize absolutely where the female Surrealists stand, what we must do is remain eternally vigilant to *our own* psychological, social, ideological, and methodological preoccupations. Only when *they* are exposed and examined can we begin the great interpretive endeavor Kappeler calls the "dialectic of inter-subjectivity." What this means for the layman is that we must keep our minds open and share, or at the very least intervene with, each other's monologues.

Isn't this what most feminists always wanted anyway?

Notes

1. (London: Thames and Hudson, 1985), 11. Subsequent references will be retained in the text.

2. Robert Belton, "Edgar Allen Poe and the Surrealists' Image of Woman," *Woman's Art Journal* 8:1 (Spring–Summer 1987), 8–12; Xavière Gauthier, *Surréalisme et sexualité* (Paris: Gallimard, 1971).

3. I have discussed the work of André Masson and Alberto Giacometti in this regard in "On the Image of Woman in Surrealist Art" (Ph.D. diss., University of Toronto, 1988).

4. "André Masson's Earth-Mothers in Their Cultural Context," *Revue d'art canadien/Canadian Art Review* 15:1 (1988), 51–57.

5. Reproduced in Carmine Benincasa, *Dalla bestemmia all'invocazione: il cammino di André Masson* (Parma: Centro studi e archivio della communicazione, dipartimento arte, Università di Parma, 1981), cat. no. 55.

6. Breton, *Le Surréalisme et la peinture,* rev. ed. (Paris: Gallimard, 1979), 391 and 144, respectively. Curiously, Parent is not mentioned in Chadwick, nor are almost two dozen other women who have equal claim to be included in a book purporting to deal with female artists associated with Surrealism, whether they accepted or rejected the label of "Surrealist" (p. 10). Fortunately, they are represented in *La Femme surréaliste: Obliques* 14–15 (1977), 1–321.

7. For the origins of the piece, see Nicolas Calas, "Meret Oppenheim: Confrontations," *Artforum* 16:10 (Summer 1978), 24.

8. Oppenheim confirmed Breton's "collaboration" in conversation, Paris, 7 November 1984. An excerpt of our conversation appears in this collection of essays.

9. Perhaps the most frequently reproduced of Carrington's paintings, the *Autoportrait* has most recently been fruitfully discussed in Janice Helland, "Surrealism and Esoteric Feminism in the Paintings of Leonora Carrington," *RACAR* 16:1 (1989), 53–61 and fig. 98. (One wonders if the *Aube* of the title is just the metaphorical dawn or an allusion to André Breton's daughter, who would then have been between eight and twenty-four months old.)

10. Gloria Feman Orenstein, "La Nature animale et divine de la femme dans les oeuvres de Leonora Carrington," *Mélusine* 2 (1981), 130–37; Renée Riese Hubert, "Surrealist Women Painters, Feminist Portraits," *Dada/Surrealism* 13 (1983), 80.

11. Reproduced in Hubert, 76.

12. Jean-Paul Guibbert, *Leonor Fini, graphique,* 2d ed. (Lausanne: Clairefontaine, 1976), 58, 151, 107.

13. An excellent reproduction is in Anne de Margerie, *Valentine Hugo, 1887–1968, étude documentaire* (Paris: Damase, 1983), 113.

14. One such is reproduced in Robert Benayoun, *L'Erotique du surréalisme,* rev. ed. (Paris: Pauvert, 1978), 68.

15. Carrington, untitled statement, in *Leonora Carrington: A Retrospective Exhibition* (New York: Center for Inter-American Relations, 1976), unpaginated; Tanning, "Dorothea Her Lights and Shadows," *Dorothea Tanning* (New York: Gimpel-Weitzenhoffer Gallery, 16 October–15 November 1979), unpaginated.

16. Estella Lauter, *Women as Mythmakers: Poetry and Visual Art by Twentieth-Century Women* (Bloomington: Indiana University Press, 1984), 20; Ann Sutherland Harris and Linda Nochlin, *Women Artists, 1550–1950* (Los Angeles: Los Angeles County Museum, 21 December 1976–13 March 1977), 67 and note 243.

17. Reproduced in Alain Bosquet, *Dorothea Tanning* (Paris: Pauvert, 1966), 34 and 72, respectively.

18. Hayden Herrera, *Frida: A Biography of Frida Kahlo* (New York: Harper and Row, 1983), 133–60, 258, and elsewhere.

19. Reproduced in *La Femme surréaliste: Obliques,* 72.

20. See Colquhoun's *Pine Family* (1941) and Fini's *Chthonian Divinity Watching Over the Sleep of a Young Man* (1947), reproduced in Chadwick, figs. 106 and 107. An untitled and undated drawing by Oppenheim features a crucified penis; reproduced in *La Femme surréaliste: Obliques,* 192. Toyen's *Dessin érotique* (1936) is a drawing of a woman's gloved hands manipulating severed male genitals bleeding from the urethra; reproduced in *Styrsky, Toyen, Heisler* (Paris: Centre Georges Pompidou, 1982), 65.

21. Marcel Brion, *Leonor Fini* (Paris: Pauvert, 1955), unpaginated.

22. With this final phrase, Chadwick, 237, leaves the reader with the impression that Surrealism was a harmless investigation of aesthetic originality and productivity. This is precisely the impression that we are here trying to avoid.

23. The sources are far too numerous to list here. A useful introduction with a comprehensive bibliography is Mary Ritchie Key, *Male/Female Language* (Metuchen, N.J.: Scarecrow, 1975).

24. Jitendra N. Thakerar et al., "Psychological and Linguistic Parameters of Speech Accommodation Theory," in Colin Fraser and Klaus R. Scherer, eds., *Advances in the Social Psychology of Language* (Cambridge: Cambridge University Press, 1982), 218.

25. Susanne Kappeler, *The Pornography of Representation* (Cambridge, England: Polity, 1986), 215.

26. Howard Giles and Philip Smith, "Accommodation Theory: Optimal Levels of Convergence," in Howard Giles and Robert N. St. Clair, eds., *Language and Social Psychology* (Oxford: Basil Blackwell, 1979), 64. The authors are speaking of the field of developmental psychology, but their words seem oddly appropriate here.

Androgyny: Interview with Meret Oppenheim

Robert J. Belton

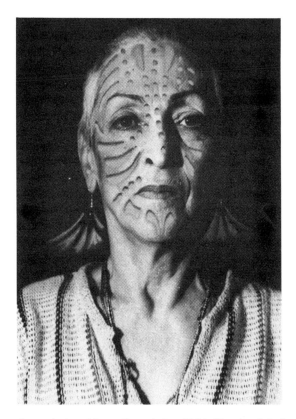

Oppenheim, *Meret Oppenheim,* 1984. Hand-painted photograph. Courtesy Galerie Farideh Cadot, Paris.

In the spring of 1986, I received a telephone call informing me that Meret Oppenheim had died at the age of seventy-two. I felt a peculiar sense of loss, though I had only met the Swiss artist once.[1] When I communicated this emotion to a colleague, I was surprised to discover that he knew little of her aside from her most famous work, a fur-covered cup, saucer, and

Fig. 1   Oppenheim, *Object (Déjeuner en fourrure)*, 1936. Fur-covered cup, saucer, and spoon. Museum of Modern Art, New York.

spoon in the Museum of Modern Art in New York.[2] Too many people know Oppenheim only through this object – known in France as the *Déjeuner en fourrure* of 1936 (Fig. 1) – yet the artist herself considered it one of her less important works. I resolved to publish a small portion of our meandering conversation, not originally intended as an interview, in the hopes that fewer people would see her only as the maker of the quintessential surrealist object.[3]

Oppenheim was born in Berlin-Charlottenburg in 1913 to a German father and a Swiss mother. She spent the war with her grandparents in Switzerland. Although she may have received some inspiration from her maternal grandmother, who had earlier been a printer and subsequently a writer, she did not begin to paint and draw until 1920 or 1921. Her exposure to modernism began with the onset of adolescence in the later 1920s. She collected reproductions of expressionist, fauve, and cubist works. By 1930, she had begun to think of herself as an artist with modernist leanings, and in a school notebook she made drawings with some collage elements. After leaving the school she attended a few weeks of classes in Basel's Ecole des Arts et Métiers. There she met two artists, obscure to us today, Walter Kurtwiemkin and Irene Zurkinden, who inspired her to go to Paris.

Oppenheim arrived in the French capital in May of 1932. She took a small hotel room in the rue d'Odessa, a very short walk from the Académie de la Grande Chaumière, where she sporadically attended open drawing classes. Much more important to her development were her discovery of the work of Max Ernst and her acquaintance with Alberto Giacometti, then still in league with the Surrealists. In 1933, Giacometti brought Hans Arp to her studio, a visit which led to an invitation to exhibit with the surrealist group. This marked the beginning of a new phase of Surrealism, for the French movement had formerly restricted the participation of women to the subordinate role of the *femme-enfant,* a manipulable, fairylike muse, enchanting in her innocence, youth, and purity. Oppenheim was very much seen as a *femme-enfant* – she was just twenty years old – but the participation in the same exhibition of the older, much less fairylike Valentine Hugo[4] may have helped the young Swiss woman's reputation as an artist. Nevertheless, Man Ray took delight in manipulating her image. He photographed her in the nude, standing beside a printing press so that the press's handle formed a false phallus.[5]

Oppenheim's greatest *succès de scandale,* however, was the *Déjeuner en fourrure,* which Alfred H. Barr, Jr., bought for the Museum of Modern Art in 1936. Despite this, the artist soon entered a prolonged period of artistic crisis and emotional despondency. She began to reexamine her life and her career in 1937. Although she maintained contact with artists' groups and participated in collective exhibitions nearly annually, she slipped into a period of total negativity which lasted seventeen years. She made little, destroying much of her output. Though she had visited Paris in 1939 and 1950, it was not until 1954 that she felt her self-exile come to a definitive end. This was marked by her decision to take a studio once again, this time in Bern, where she had moved in 1949 with her new husband, Wolfgang La Roche. In 1959 she achieved another *succès de scandale* with her famous inaugural feast served on the nude body of a woman at the EROS exhibition of surealist art.[6]

The number of her exhibitions increased regularly, and in 1967 the Moderna Museet of Stockholm assembled a retrospective of her work. In 1972 she took a studio in Paris, while retaining her studio in Bern. In 1975 she was honored with the art prize of the city of Basel. In 1984–85 a final retrospective toured Paris, Bern, Frankfurt, and Berlin. She died in late 1985.

RB I'll put my first question in terms of cartoonlike simplicity: André Breton believed women were like goddesses, whereas Xavière Gauthier says Woman is often trampled, destroyed for a perverse delight.[7] Which is closer to the truth?

MO Neither is right. The problem is that men have always *had* women. Women are not goddesses, not fairies, not sphinxes. All these are the projections of men. Neither are men the projections of women. They are not heroes, not brigands, soldiers, what-have-you. Love always leads to overestimations of others, in both directions, men to women, women to men. In fact, I discovered the wonderful poetesses Bettina Brentano and Karoline von Günderode very late in life, later than I should have, because all the men around me said you must read Rimbaud, you must read Novalis, and so on. The women were loved, but only as women. Now, I am not a feminist, but this situation does no justice to two writers of very high poetic quality.

RB So gender identity plays no role in the character of art in your view?

MO There is no difference between man and woman; there is only artist or poet. Sex plays no role whatsoever. That's why I refuse to participate in exhibitions of women only.

RB What then is the role of love? What is the function, the effect of these overestimates? Has it anything to do with sensuality?

MO Friendship is the most satisfying criterion for marriage and other relations between men and women. Pure sensuality is much less worthy of confidence.

RB Especially where sensuality is a screen for some dominance or other.

MO Yes.

RB This is sometimes the case in the treatment of the *image* of women in surrealist art, is it not?

MO Certainly Woman has been mistreated, which makes this Gauthier seem correct – I have the book but I confess I haven't read it. Bellmer and Molinier, for example, mistreated the bodies of their women.[8] But they are cases, psychological cases, perverts. Crazies, you know.

RB Patrick Waldberg told me the same thing, and Marcel Jean refused to talk about them at all.

MO I am not surprised.

RB Let's talk about *your* career a little. What was it that brought you to Paris? Surely it wasn't Surrealism?

MO Not at all. One day when I was ill my father asked me what I wanted to do with my life. I said I wanted to be a painter. I was eighteen. He said, "A painter? In Paris or Munich?" I chose Paris, because Irene Zurkinden, a Neo-Impressionist from Basel, could introduce me to the Montparnasse crowd. I didn't know Surrealism, but I had a collection of reproductions of expressionist work and some of the French school. It wasn't long before I met the Surrealists, though. I was very bored with my studies at the Grande Chaumière and I met Alberto Giacometti at the Café du Dôme just up the street. I drew his ear and made a little wax version too.[9] I went to his studio and saw his sculptures of the surrealist period. I admired him and I invited him to my first studio in the fall of 1933. It was in the rue d'Alésia.

RB   Isn't that rather far to the south?

MO Not at all. A few blocks only.

RB   And it was Giacometti who introduced you to the Surrealists?

MO Yes. He came to see my work in the new studio and came back later with Hans Arp. They invited me to show with the Surrealists in the Salon des Surindépendants.

RB   That was in 1933. Do you think that the presence of Valentine Hugo in the exhibition helped your reception by the group? She was much older and, unlike the surrealist woman of the 1920s, she had been long recognized as an artist.

MO I don't really remember. I don't even remember what was in the show, though I still have the catalogue. It's not important to me anymore. I was definitely the youngest person in Breton's circle.

RB   How did you become a member of the circle?

MO André Breton asked me to come to the café in the Place Blanche. He asked me at the opening of the Salon. I was young and impressed. We met there nearly every day. Most of them were much older, as much as two decades.

RB   Did you find yourself alienated by this difference?

MO I was not a *femme-enfant,* if that is what you mean. I was sexually active at the age of seventeen. No, any distance I may have felt was more a matter of language. I didn't have a good grasp of French then. Besides, I didn't really understand their political talk.

RB   They didn't specifically discuss political roles for women, by any chance?

MO Politics in the abstract only.

RB   How were you understood by them? You say you were not a *femme-enfant.* What was your role?

MO It was not political. In fact, when I returned to Paris in 1950 I saw little of the Surrealists precisely because of their dogmatism, political and otherwise. Yet, there is a part of my nature which is, how could I put it, surreal or surrealistic. I was doing Surrealism before the letter. I have become known as a maker of surrealist objects, but they were the least of my endeavors. I thought of myself as a picture-maker.

RB   It's ironic, then, that the *Déjeuner en fourrure* is considered your masterpiece.

MO   That's the Museum of Modern Art for you! But to return to the dogmatism of Breton and others—it was he who named it *Déjeuner en fourrure*, playing on the associations with queer sexuality in Manet's *Déjeuner sur l'herbe* and Sacher-Masoch's *Vénus en fourrures*.[10] The word-games of critics, the power struggles of men! So part of its scandalous appeal was not invented by me. It was a fluke. I had been making bits of fur-covered jewelry to make a little money in 1936. I showed a piece to Picasso and Dora Maar and they joked that anything could be covered with fur—the chairs, the door. I added the cups and saucers on the table. I was thinking only of the contrast of material textures. Later, Breton asked me to participate in the Ratton show.[11] I simply made up the object according to the idea. I didn't care about any title at all. I don't really care that it is now known by Breton's title.

RB   So there wasn't any sense of being exploited by Breton?

MO   No.

RB   And it wasn't due to this that you left Paris a year later?

MO   Well, no. I ran out of money and my parents couldn't send any. My father was in Switzerland, where he couldn't work.

RB   There was also your crisis of conscience. Depression?

MO   It is difficult to talk about.

RB   You worked very sporadically.

MO   I did no work at all for eighteen months. Then I went back to the Ecole des Arts et Métiers in Basel. I always had something in the works, though it was years before I felt anything positive or optimistic about it. It was mechanical, like the academic drawing I did at the Ecole.

RB   It didn't bore you like at the Grande Chaumière?

MO   Yes. Terribly boring. But it was very useful.

RB   How so? (Oppenheim then waved her hand through the air and made no reply.) How did your crisis period end?

MO   Suddenly. I recovered my pleasure in making pictures very suddenly in late 1954. I just walked out the door and rented a studio.

RB In Basel?

MO In Bern.

RB Yes, of course. With your husband. Did he help you out of your crisis?

MO Let's not talk about this any longer. Just remember what I said about friendship.

RB Yes, of course. You said that sexuality is less important than friendship.

MO More or less. But sometimes I find it difficult to put into words. It took me a month to write my little speech accepting the artistic prize at Basel in 1975.[12] I was still rewriting it three years later.

RB You take quite a strong position in that text, especially concerning the female artist.

MO Yes. I thanked the city for the award and went on to say how difficult it is for a woman to receive such attention.

RB And yet you say you are not a feminist.

MO Not in the usual sense. You see, any great artist expresses the whole being. In a man, a feminine part helps in the creation of this expression. In a woman, there is a corresponding masculine component. I added a note to my speech which clears this up.

RB Your terminology sounds Jungian.

MO Terminology? We don't yet have proper terms for these ideas. But Jungian, yes. I started to read him in the crisis period. My father brought him to my attention. Jung went far beyond Freud's obsession with sexuality. Woman's problem is not her sexuality but her relations with society.

RB This sounds like conventional feminism.

MO There is a difference. I don't believe that women should become like men or adopt a male lifestyle. I believe that women *are* like men. Man is a genius who needs a muse. Woman is a muse who needs a genius. It's a kind of androgyny.

RB Speaking of androgyny, how do you feel about the photograph that Man Ray made of you? The one with the printing press handle mimicking a phallus.

MO I don't know. That was Man Ray's work.

RB You don't recognize this as your work in any way?

MO Not at all. He was the boss.

RB Then *your* nudity was *his* statement?

MO Yes, except insofar as I was of a rebellious nature.

RB   Then your notion of a mental androgyny of sorts has little to do with Man Ray's physical androgyny?

MO   It happens that way. The feast at the EROS exhibition in 1960 started out as a spring festival for friends in Bern. Breton heard that I had served a meal on a nude woman and asked that I recreate it for the EROS show. But the original intention was misunderstood. Instead of a simple spring festival, it was yet another woman taken as a source of male pleasure. There's always a gap between aims and public comprehension.

RB   It's like dreams. A different interpretation for every person.

MO   Perhaps the only one of value is that of the dreamer.

RB   So only you can interpret your dreams and your work?

MO   Perhaps dreams. But they are analyzed in a Jungian way, not a Freudian one. Jung placed more emphasis on the collective unconscious and on archetypal images. Jung taught me that some people just need someone else to talk to. But my father didn't understand what Jung had to say about the feminine part of a man. None of the men understood women.

Fig. 2 Oppenheim, *Femme-pierre*, 1938. Oil on cardboard. Private collection, Switzerland.

Fig. 3   Oppenheim, *Geneviève,* 1971, after a drawing of 1942. Wood and oil-based paint.

RB   So your works are not analogous to dreams?

MO   As a matter of principle, I absolutely did not illustrate my dreams in my work. They were strictly part of my interior development. Now, as analogies . . . , I don't know.

RB Your *Femme-pierre* of 1938 (Fig. 2), which shows a sleeping woman lying by a stream – on closer examination, she becomes a pile of stones. Is this an archetypal woman?

MO Yes and no. A stone woman is prevented from action but her legs are immersed in the stream. Which is to say it is a picture of contraries: sleeping stone and living waters. But she is not some ideal woman. It's the same for my *Geneviève* (Fig. 3). Neither represents Woman in general. They are both very . . .

RB Specific?

MO Specific to my case. Both were made during my crisis period. The stone is my inability to do any work, and the only really positive thing is the feet, which represent a connection with the unconscious.

RB Is this related to Joan Miró's *The Farmer's Wife,*[13] in which her large feet put her fertile nature in contact with the fertile ground?

MO Not at all. A man could make exactly the same statement using identical plastic elements. It's the same with *Geneviève.* My arms were broken like the sculpture's oars. I could do nothing. My arms weren't actually broken, you understand, but the point I am making is that the idea is not Woman but me, myself. It could just as easily have been a man.

RB And so we return to the Jungian androgyny.

MO Let's put it this way: I am ready to believe now that men and women are absolutely equal in their brains. Of course, women are generally less strong, slower than men in physical terms. Still, it's like dogs that are bred in a certain way. So too are women. Now this is just a crazy idea of my own but suppose that in primitive societies, the slower women were the ones who were caught by men, then raped and impregnated. The fast ones never had any children, so the slow were effectively "bred" by men so they would be subordinate. So that men could wield the power, whether it be the power of the arm, the tool, the weapon, the bomb, money, whatever.

RB But now we live in an enlightened era and things are beginning to change.

MO Slowly. The French Revolution occurred during an enlightened era and look what happened then. During, they signed equal rights amendments; after, they annulled them with the guillotine.

RB Must women take power?

MO It is always a question of taking, as I said in my speech at Basel. But don't ever forget that women can be as evil as men. We must see behind our projections, you know. Woman as an abstract thing is no more perfect than Man.

Fig. 4 Oppenheim, Untitled painting, after an exquisite corpse by the artist with Robert Lupo and Anna Boetti. Whereabouts unknown.

RB Is that why one of your paintings shows a crucified phallus (Fig. 4)?

MO That started as an exquisite corpse.[14] It's not supposed to be any sort of feminist revenge.

RB It makes me think of the serpent lifted up by Moses, like a prophecy of the crucifixion.[15] And the serpent is like a phallus.

MO People say I make a lot of serpents. (She opens a copy of Bice Curiger's monograph,[16] counting reproductions.) Seven or eight. Some say the serpent equals the male. Breton was fascinated by this kind of thing. That recalls paradise and the fall of man. The woman is always blamed. But what is actually happening is not a fall but an ascent, away from the world of animals. One sees these serpents in representations of the goddesses of Crete. The serpent means a spiritual ascent into the universe. And the universe has a bad enough reputation already without blaming women for the fall of man. (Laughter)

RB Some of the Surrealists seemed to think that being more than animal is not so good.

MO Humankind is the only thing that gives value to life. Not animals, not television, not soccer. We are part of a grand spiral,[17] and we are on a point on that spiral that is seeing a beginning to the end of the – Jewish? – tradition that women are second-class citizens.

RB Possessions, too.

MO We must be good friends, men and women.

RB Finally, can art play a role in a social revolution for women?

MO Well, yes, inasmuch as art can produce a spiritual state. After everything else is destroyed, art and philosophy remain.

Madame Oppenheim escorted me back down the stairs and stepped outside with me to mail some letters. "It's so tranquil," she said, "but the light is not good." As we shook hands, she invited me to call again anytime. I had hoped to do so before that light finally failed.

Notes

1. This was during a lengthy stay in Paris funded by the Social Sciences and Humanities Research Council of Canada. I am indebted to the Council for its support.

2. See *The Museum of Modern Art, New York: The History and the Collection* (New York: Abrams, 1984), catalogue no. 191, pp. 146–47.

3. Unfortunately, this is very much the impression of the obituary in *Art in America* 74:1 (January, 1986), 166, 168, as well as in the entries of most general reference works.

4. Hugo was then forty-six years old. She had first exhibited in 1909. See Anne de Margerie, *Valentine Hugo, 1887–1968* (Paris: Damase, 1983).

5. Entitled *Erotique-voilée,* the photograph was reproduced with the phallic portion cropped out in *Minotaure* 5 (February 1934), 15. The full version is available in Mary Ann Caws, "Ladies Shot and Painted: Female Embodiment in Surrealist Art," in Susan Suleiman, ed., *The Female Body in Western Culture: Contemporary Perspectives* (Cambridge: Harvard, 1986), 262–87.

6. So called because of the central theme. The usual orthography is *Exposition inteRnatiOnale du Surréalisme* (Paris: Galerie Daniel Cordier, 1959–60).

7. The reference is to Xavière Gauthier's *Surréalisme et sexualité* (Paris: Gallimard, 1971). Breton's position is outlined therein.

8. Hans Bellmer (1902–75), German-born but associated with Surrealism from 1934, when his famous distorted *Doll* first appeared in *Minotaure* 6 (5 December 1934), 30–31. Pierre Molinier (1900–76), obscure French painter and maker of nar-

cissistic photographs of himself as a woman. Both artists were given to extreme manipulations of the female form. Both are discussed by Gauthier, *Surréalisme et sexualité*.

9. See the reproduction in *Meret Oppenheim* (Paris: ARC Musée d'art moderne de la ville de Paris, 27 October–10 December 1984), 11.

10. The reference is to Leopold von Sacher-Masoch (1836–95), whose *Venus in Furs* led Richard von Krafft-Ebing (1840–1902) to describe sexual submission as masochism.

11. *L'Exposition d'objets surréalistes* (Paris: Galerie Ratton, 22–29 May 1936).

12. This is the "Allocution à Bâle" reprinted with revisions of 1978 in the ARC catalogue (n. 9), 32–33.

13. Reproduced and discussed in James Thrall Soby, *Joan Miró* (New York: Museum of Modern Art, 1959), 34–36.

14. The famous Surrealist game in which each person draws a portion of a figure without seeing what others have done. Oppenheim practiced it with Roberto Lupo and Anna Boetti.

15. John 3:14–15.

16. Bice Curiger, *Meret Oppenheim,* second edition (Zürich: ABC-Verlag, 1984).

17. A large tower-fountain has been erected by Oppenheim in Bern with a spiral motif. Unfortunately, the work did not come up in conversation. See the reproduction in the ARC catalogue (n. 9), 70.

The Body Subversive: Corporeal Imagery in Carrington, Prassinos and Mansour

Madeleine Cottenet-Hage

How "to connect what has been so cruelly disorganized?" asks Adrienne Rich, pondering over women's lost sense of physical wholeness (Gallop 1). This question may have taken on a special urgency for surrealist women-artists. How were they to respond to images of the female body dismantled, dismembered, aggressed, turned inside out, recomposed to please men's wildest erotic fantasies? And, when not pulled apart, portrayed nude and coy as in Magritte's famous collage *Je ne vois pas . . . dans la forêt,* in which a female icon stands in lieu of the word *femme.* Undoubtedly, though in varying degrees, the three artists who will be the focus of my essay were familiar with the paintings and writings of their male contemporaries. Carrington (born in 1918), also a painter, was Ernst's companion in the early forties and, later in Mexico, a close friend of Remedios Varo and Benjamin Péret. Mansour (1928–86) was associated with surrealist artists and dedicated several of her works to André Breton. Though only ten years younger than Carrington, she could be said to belong to the second generation of surrealist writers, all her works having been published after the Second World War. Finally, Prassinos (born in 1920), discovered by Breton and his friends when she was fourteen and introduced as the muse of *l'écriture automatique* (in the Winter 1935 issue of *Minotaure*), published frequently in surrealist publications between 1934 and 1938. Yet of the three she may have been the one writer with the least personal exposure to male surrealist art and the one who cultivated Surrealism the least consciously. She was, as she would say later, "born a Surrealist," and after 1947 pursued her artistic career on the sidelines, so to speak. To what extent did these writers create a corporeal imagery rooted in their own experiences, and to what extent were they reacting to/against the dominant male surrealist imagery? Upon what different basis did their own body imagery, which at times seems so similar, so disorganized and often subjected to so much violence, rest? These are questions which underlie the following discussion.

Unlike the works of male surrealist writers, those of the women are not dominated by the ubiquitous presence of a mythical sexual Other upon whom their hopes of acceding to surreality would be pinned. They do not present us with a male counterpart to the *femme-enfant* or the *femme-sorcière*. Even when erotic fantasies are directly, rather than obliquely, expressed, as is the case with Joyce Mansour, the female reality lies at the very center of the picture. Beyond their differences, their writings share a common trait: a self-directed, narcissistic (?) movement keeps drawing them back to their own selves mirrored in textual images.[1] Furthermore, an underlying concern about the body's integrity comes to light in all three writers and manifests itself in a variety of motifs, all hinging upon a central problematic: the inside/outside opposition. If we accept the model of female psychic development proposed by object relation psychologists such as Nancy Chodorov, this central concern could be seen as a paradigm of female writing. For fusion is a greater risk for a woman than a man, and defining boundaries as separate from those of the Mother more difficult for the former than for the latter. In the pages which follow I shall explore some of the motifs which highlight these problematics. I shall then examine how the recurrent images of senility and decay, while harking back to a similar anxiety about the Self, shift the center of concern from the spatial to the temporal. I shall suggest that they be considered as a revenge and an attempt to negotiate new relationships – through a reappropriation of the aging, deformed body – with the Self. Finally, I shall examine how the overdetermination – in Mansour – and the occultation of the sexual body – in Carrington and Prassinos – lead me to conclude that in this domain the liberation of Eros advocated by the male Surrealists was not achieved by women. Or, if it was, it was not without malaise.

Inside/Outside

The nine variations on the hand-and-glove drawing which are found in the margins of Leonora Carrington's *Down Below* – an autobiographical account of the artist's experience of insanity in 1941 – may serve as an emblem of a surrealist woman's preoccupation with the definition of an inner versus an outer space.

Besides the esoteric significance of these drawings (Carrington's interest in esoteric traditions is well known) their fascination resides in the multiple, chiastic figures of inner/outer surfaces they offer. Not only does the inside become the outside but the inside (the hand) now comes into contact with, now is separated from the outside (the glove). These games are all the more intriguing as the glove, turned inside out, will be worn on the other hand, suggesting the existence of yet another figure: exchanges between the One and the Other (alterity). In addition, unveiling takes place in the process of putting on/taking off the glove. Not only is the naked flesh revealed but the glove once removed undergoes a transformation: it loses its rigidity. The glove-and-hand variations can therefore be seen as a mise-en-scène, a playing or acting out of a loss of substance, an emptying out of one's inside. In a story dating from the thirties, *La Débutante* (in which one may discern surrealist echoes of *Little Red Riding Hood*), Leonora Carrington had already woven a tale around the notion of inside/outside surfaces and of boundaries. In it a young girl, wishing to stay away from a "debutante" party given in her honor, asks a hyena to stand in for her. The latter, after killing a young servant, uses the skin of her face as a disguise and joins the guests. The hyena, however, will be betrayed by its smell, for the skin, the visible sign of differentiation among individuals as well as the boundary marker between the inside and the outside of the body, cannot, alone, create one's identity.

But what is identity, anyway, Carrington asks, via one of her characters in *The Stone Door*? Personality transfers, disguises, hybrid characters abound in her writings as the question of separateness, frontiers between genders and species, keeps generating fantastic characters in no less fantastic tales. Perhaps one of the most arresting images of the fusion process occurs in *The Neutral Man.* In the following scene, a woman is making her face up before going to a costume ball:

I buttered my face thickly with an electric green phosphorescent pomade. On this base, I spread tiny imitation diamonds, so as to sprinkle myself with stars like a night sky, with no other pretensions. (42)

Not only does a night sky suggest the presence of infinite depth (which makes the notion of surface meaningless) but if, as we know, the night symbolizes the realm of the indeterminate, of the unconscious, then Carrington's facial mask strongly suggests abandoning the possibility of distinct, analytical knowledge of the self and of the universe and enacting a desire to be One with – diffused in – an undifferentiated cosmos (in which distinctions between gender, among other things, become irrelevant; hence the interesting title of "The Neutral Man"). As we shall later see, the desire for fusion, though strong, is nevertheless coexistent with its fear. But I shall return to this.

Questions of differentiation, of inside/outside and of boundaries are no less pressing in Prassinos, but they tend to be articulated in terms of the preservation or protection of an inner self often threatened by invasion from the outside. The surfaces are weak, porous, easily penetrated. In her early texts (examples of automatic writing), the bodies are full of holes: mentions of eye sockets, nostrils, mouths, ears, navels are constant. Yet the gaze never ventures lower than the abdomen, and the pubic area will remain undisclosed until 1975, when in *Brelin le Frou,* a short humorous treatise on the mores of the inhabitants of an imaginary Frubie, stylized drawings of male characters will suddenly be adorned with penises. But until then, Prassinos's bodies are strangely desexualized.

78

The natural bodily orifices are generally supplemented with others resulting from some biological freak occurrence or aggressive external intervention. Thus, in "Sondue," "a large opening reveals the inside of her body" (*TSC* 101). Acts of perforation (driving sharp objects into or pushing needles through holes, digging holes into a protagonist's body) are frequent occupations for Prassinos's imaginary characters. Similarly evisceration (emptying out, digging out the bowels, draining liquids, enucleating the eye) are common pastimes. In both cases, the lexicon highlights a preoccupation with the inside/outside distinction, a distinction humorously (or tragically) negated by the use of the oxymoron "entrailles extérieures" (outer bowels) in a text with an equally oxymoronic title, "Journoir" (*TSC* 43).

Such images point to a fundamentally ambivalent fear-cum-desire of not only seeing what is concealed but being seen and, subsequently, being invaded (penetrated), an ambivalence possibly colored by guilt as a fantastic tale, "L'Index fou," indicates (*ME* 84–85). A narrator (whose sex is unspecified, as is so often the case with Prassinos) experiences unpleasant itching sensations in the stomach area and begins scratching. But when he/she decides to stop, the finger rebels and boldly pursues, tearing muscles, nerves and blood vessels. The finger will eventually be punished for its audacity: it will be severed. Several meanings can be read into this "oneiric" fable. The sexual one seems the most obvious. Either masturbation must be punished or penetration is dangerous. But the imagery may also symbolize the artist's desire for the inner reality, for the world of imagination, and at the same time a fear of what this reality contains and at what cost it may be revealed. The index finger may be interpreted as an image of the writer's "pen" which is eventually discarded in a self-censuring and self-mutilating act. Such prudent withdrawal, such renunciation in the face of possible tumultuous revelations is not uncommon in Prassinos's writings of the adult period, often serving as textual closure (in particular in her novel *La Voyageuse*). Yet another reading would uncover in this text an ontological fear of a loss of being, an empty inner space revealed through an inward journey.

Such fear is further manifested in the numerous instances in which the life substance – the bodily fluids, blood and water – are shown flowing outside while bodies, gradually becoming limp and flabby, collapse. Skins shrivel, the protagonists are miniaturized, as is the case of an infant left in the charge of a young woman in "La Nourrice" (*ME*); or the lovely grocer's wife in *Le Grand repas*. (Miniaturization may reflect a secret desire to reintegrate the maternal body in order to patch it up or recover a lost symbiosis between mother and child.) Finally, one must consider the probable role of seizures, experienced by Prassinos until she was seventeen, in the production of images of loss (of consciousness), of split (between body and mind), of physical changes (dwindling or expanding). Whatever the direct

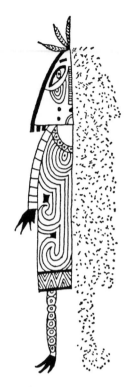

Fig. 1   Prassinos, *La Gomme. (MCE,* 64.)

source of imagery, experience is transformed by its infusion with a larger, more complex meaning. Woman viewing herself as threatened in her very existence, owning a body which is denied its due space, will become one of the core images in Prassinos's mature writings. In 1982, using the surrealist technique of literal exploration of a linguistic image, she tells the story of a young female character whom everyone describes as "self-effacing" ("effacée," *MCE* 64–66; Fig. 1). In her mature age, unable to endure any longer the neglect to which she feels subjected, she decides to erase herself literally. Little by little she removes the contours of her own body. The holes have now become so large that Woman is reduced finally to one large, blank space.

The obsession of the "open" body is no less pervasive in Mansour's work. But while the sexual connotations are lost to view in Prassinos because of a transfer of the gaze from the lower to the upper parts of the body, in Mansour the gaze is redirected toward the lower part, out of which erogeneity radiates to the whole body. (Significantly, one of her collections of poems bears the title of *The Erogenous Hour.*) If any woman writer did heed the surrealist call for erotic subversion, she was the one. But the Mansourian eros raises disturbing questions. It appears profoundly ambivalent,

80

riddled with anxieties, impulses to life and death; a devouring monster calling to be devoured. In Mansour, the body lies open, ceaselessly waiting, hungering for penetration. There is a sense of an inner empty space which can only be filled/reassured by the violent appropriation or absorption of the body of the Other. Unlike Prassinos, for whom penetration implies a threat of loss, loss in Mansour is associated with the absence of penetration. There is no more desolate image in Mansour than that of the senile female body condemned to emptiness.

Mansour's texts bristle with the same obsessive images of body holes: there is hardly a page which does not mention mouths, eardrums (pierced), anuses, vulvae, vaginas, navels, buttocks lusting for phallic penetration (Mansour's lexical range in naming erogenous parts is unusually broad). Their obsessive presence is not only a factor of their being mentioned frequently but of their duplication or multiplication in a single space. In the doubly paradoxical environment of a Swiss hospital in "Iles flottantes," Mansour's vision reaches paroxysmic proportions. Her world has been transformed into an immense, grotesque carnival of collective fornication and masturbation in which the young and the old, the sane and the sick, become demonic participants in a "purée lubrique" (71). Georges Bataille's definition of eroticism as "l'approbation de la vie jusque dans la mort" (*L'Erotisme* 15) could hardly be more fitting. Mansour's characters are inhabited by a nostalgia for a lost continuity, to which only death can restore them by ridding them of their separate identities. Their necrophilia points to an intimate, though assuredly deviant, sense of the connection between eros and thanatos. One may not like Mansour's world but it has undeniable power in its desperate, violent search for a final appeasement of the kind which serves as closure to her story *Jules César*. Jules César, who has nursed twins, is lying on a raft.

Couchée sur le dos, trempée jusqu'à l'os par ces longues et déchirantes giclées qui viennent tout droit de l'extrémité de la colonne vertébrale, les jambes largement ouvertes, elle hurlait, jet sur jet, son orgasme à la nuit. Et juste avant la décomposition finale, quand tomba la dernière pelure de son ventre, les fourmis sortirent des vagues de sa blessure. . . . Elles cherchaient sur l'horizon la terre promise, mais la saleté des flots négatifs s'étalait partout, inerte et monstrueuse, indivisible unité. Alors le sexe de Jules César, enfin assouvi, sourit bêtement vers le ciel et son âme impatiente bâilla. (*Histoires nocives* 54)

(Lying on her back, soaked to the bone by these long, harrowing spurts spouting directly from the tip of her spine, with her legs wide apart, she howled with each new gush her orgasm into the night. And just before the final coming apart, when the last remnant of her belly peeled off, the ants crawled out of her wavelike wound. . . . They were looking for the promised land over the horizon, but everywhere the foul, negative waters lay, lifeless and monstrous, indivisible oneness. Then Jules César's genitals, satiated at last, smiled inanely to the sky and her eager soul yawned.)

The connection between images of "holes," the actualization of "jouissance" and the quest for "unity" is made evident by the very textual proximity in which they are held and by the use of "alors," which underlines the causal relationship.

In Mansour, the rage with which her characters seek pleasure in coital fusion directly linked to the "opaqueness" of the body, its dense materiality. The body cannot be "traversed" to achieve a union of minds or spirits. Nothing extends beyond the purely physical. Matter can be distorted, it develops curves or hollows according to whether and how much it is being nourished, it experiences sexual pleasure and rots in a world indifferent to its presence and its absence alike.

The body in Carrington is completely different. Here, it is amenable to limitless possibilities of exchange with the outside. At the same time these exchanges must always be read as a victory over the dangers of excess: excessive fusion or irreparable split between the inside and the outside, the Self and the Other, both of which Carrington experienced dramatically during her temporary insanity. In *Down Below*, Carrington recounts how, in the early years of the war, she had come to see her stomach as "the seat of society" which needed cleansing if the world were to be healed and her body to be restored to its essential function, that of mirroring the earth "faithfully." Through this mirroring, osmosis had opened the Self to the outside, and the bad, as well as the good, was introjected, literally "jamming" the psychic processes and robbing her of rational control. However, though the pain of disorganization was great, it was to be matched by a sense of exhilaration, of feeling completely one with the world of animals and nature. Both the anxiety and the joy associated with the memory are reflected in Carrington's fiction. Her characters fear being robbed of their identities at the same time as they desire not to be confined to them. The many hybrid creatures (the androgynous Maude in *The Hearing Trumpet*), the women-wolves (Anubeth in *The Hearing Trumpet* and Helvalino in *The Seventh House*), the women-horses (in *The Oval Lady*), and the women-birds (in *Soeurs*) can be seen as an attempt to balance polarities while transcending the normal, rational boundaries of reality; rather than fusion, they symbolize the juxtaposition of two distinct identities. Their double origin marks a surplus rather than a subtraction of being.

The Mutant Body

The importance of defining surfaces, the fear of invasion, rift, loss, the desire for penetration, fusion, are different modes of a central ontological questioning about the place of the subject in space. The transformations of that subject over time are reflected in the many representations of the aging or diseased female body which create yet another link among the three women artists.

Once again, Carrington will provide us with our opening. In *The Hearing Trumpet,* the narrator recalls an exchange with one of her young suitors who has been taunting her for reading fairy tales "at her age." "Qu'est-ce que l'âge, après tout?" she asks rhetorically. "What is age, after all? Something which you do not understand, my love." Certainly the feeling of being, as Breton once put it, "très mal avec le temps" is neither a female nor a male prerogative. We are all at odds with the passing of time, although – and one almost hates to repeat an all too evident truth – time is more visibly and tangibly inscribed in the female biology. Hence the urgency with which representations of the aging body impinge upon the imaginary and impose themselves on the female texts. One of Prassinos's earliest texts – selected by Breton for publication in *Minotaure* in 1935 – opens with the following verbless mise en scène: "Un trou noir, une petite vieille, des animaux" ("A black hole, a little old woman, animals"). Following this is a description of the old woman in which realism gradually gives way to surrealistic visions:

Ses cheveux rares sont ramassés trois par trois et attachés par un petit cordon vert. Son visage est tout ratatiné et de forme triangulaire. Son front, tellement ridé et ramassé qu'il n'a pas plus d'un centimètre de haut. . . . Sa bouche est dépourvue de lèvres et sa mâchoire inférieure tellement enfoncée qu'on ne voit plus ses dents. . . . De son cou pendent des morceaux de choir qui ont voulu être retenus par des épingles de nourrice. Ses oreilles sont couronnées de gros grains de beauté à poils. (*TSC* 74–75)[2]

(Her sparse hair is tied, three by three, and attached with a small green string. Her face is all shriveled up and triangular-shaped. Her forehead, so wrinkled and contracted that it is no more than half an inch high. . . . Her mouth has no lips and her lower jaw recedes so far back that her teeth cannot be seen. . . . From her neck, pieces of flesh, which one has tried to hold together with safety pins, hang loose. Her ears are crowned with large hairy moles.)

As images of old women reappear throughout Prassinos's works they get stripped of their darkly humorous contours and take on either more nostalgic and softer or more directly probing and menacing tones, probably because with time they change from being spectacles to being mirrors of the self.

Carrington, too, stages old women, in particular in *The Hearing Trumpet,* whose heroine is a jaunty ninety-nine-year-old with a frame that has been gnarled by rheumatisms. Though toothless, she is not excessively troubled by the fact that she cannot wear dentures. For, she says, "je n'ai personne à mordre" ("I have no one to bite"), suggesting, as is often the case in Carrington, the existence of a violent substratum always likely to erupt. But it may also suggest that with age there is no longer any need to "devour" the external world; that "inner" fullness has been reached. If so, both the fear of an interior vacuum and of penetration are assuaged.

In Mansour, representations of the senile female body take on a much more violent, disturbing quality. "L'enfer des femmes," she writes, "prend naissance dans leur corps / Et finit sans maquillage à la morgue" ("Women's hell is born in their bodies / And ends unadorned in the mortuary") (*Faire signe au machiniste* 11). Her old women are terrifying with their "pubis de rats aux dents carriées" ("their ratty pubes with decayed teeth") (*Faire signe* 21). They have introjected death itself and turned into cannibalistic hags whose shriveled mouths, leaden breasts and useless, gaping pelves make interior emptiness gruesomely manifest.

Undoubtedly, Mansour's cruel representations are offered in defiance, as a revenge, against the inevitable pain which accompanies "l'âpre lutte amoureuse de l'homme et de la femme qu'un 'millénaire de coits burinés' sépare" ("the bitter love fight of man and woman whom a thousand years of coital burrowing has kept apart") (Gauthier 1977, 273). It is against men that the poetic voice can say to a woman friend, "J'aime . . . / Tes rides tes seins ballants / Ta vieillesse contre mon corps tendu" ("I love . . . / Your wrinkles your sagging breasts / Your senility against my taut body") (*Cris* 7). But Mansour's rage is more broadly directed at the pain of endless desire of *Damnations* and of unmet desire, the pain of disease and death, in short, the pain of living.

In Mansour the anguish experienced in the very "déchirures" of her body and/or her "cris" (two of her titles) can only be exorcised through the cruel exposure of the very images that are feared. There is nowhere to turn, no appeasement, no youthful serene vision of beauty. Only bodies contorted by violent desire, rotting flesh the more violently exposed because it belongs to one who is loved. Mansour has chosen a deliberately antiromantic, antisentimental "combat" strategy. Her work is sustained by a determination to journey to the end of the night, to paraphrase Céline, to go to the end of horror and disgust, to reject all notions of decency and expose the body at the very center of life's drama. Not surprisingly, deadly disease becomes the "hero" of one of her more macabre stories, "Le Cancer," written after the death of her friend, the pianist Clara Haskill. In it, a young mute servant is obsessed by the enormous hump which has grown on his mistress's back. "It stood up, pink, overshadowing the body on its spidery legs, enthroned above the oblong breasts and the hollow buttocks: a fortress" (J. H. Matthews's translation, 190). He desires it but her death will deny him possession. In a gesture of revenge, he will stab it with a knife.

The anarchical proliferation of cells—the onslaught of chaos—has disorganized the bodily contours; it is as though the vaginal cavity had suddenly been projected outside, leaving the lower area "hollow" and weak, creating a (phallic) grotesque excrescence which, furthermore, suggests a mammary displacement from front to back. The woman's body has become a monstrosity, and it is this very monstrosity after which the young man lusts. Mansour's story could read like an inversion or a subversion of

Hans Bellmer's well-known re-compositions of prenubile anatomies and, more widely, of the efforts of surrealist erotic art in general. Not only has a "witch" been substituted for a nymph as the object of desire but the ending of the story denies any "positive, if desperate, effort to reintegrate mind and body, to possess the loved one more completely than physical love allows" (Short 1980, 166). The violence done to the body (both by the writer and her mute protagonist, to whom she lends her voice) is a vain attempt to keep thanatos at bay by performing a textual excision, by temporarily investing the hump, singled out among the various bodily parts, with erogenous, hence life-affirming, power. But we know from the ending what fate such efforts will meet.

Leonora Carrington's short story "A Man in Love" (in *The Oval Lady*), in a lighter humorous vein, entertains a somewhat analogous hope that life could be kept germinating from a deathly soil. Here a fruit grocer has been trying to keep his young wife's deceased body alive by watering it. "I think," he says, "that it is my love that keeps her so warm nowadays; she is probably dead, but the warmth remains" (this is my translation from the French text, which shows slight variations from the English text).

More akin to Mansour's darkly fantastic tale is Prassinos's opening text in *Mon Coeur les écoute*. A narrator tells how he has discovered parasitic membranes growing on his body and how, on a voyage around the world, he has witnessed the sudden death of two young brothers overcome by the same disease.

Ils titubaient, se contorsionnaient avec une étrange lenteur, le plus fort soutenant le plus las, s'enlaçant, s'étreignant en silence. . . . On eût dit deux danseurs costumés mimant la frayeur et le désespoir le plus intense. Quand l'ambulance arriva enfin, épuisés les enfants s'abattirent. Un instant après, je vis se révulser leurs yeux que la prompte végétation n'avait pas eu le temps d'atteindre. (9–10)

(They were staggering, with eerie slow contortions, the stronger supporting the weaker one, their arms around each other, embracing silently. . . . They looked like two costumed dancers miming fright and uttermost despair. When the ambulance came at last, the children collapsed, worn out. A moment later, I saw the revulsion in their eyes, which the fast-growing vegetation had not yet reached.)

From a similar image, that of the proliferation of deadly cells—an intimation of life reverting to chaos—Prassinos draws effects that are profoundly different from Mansour's. The violent spectacle is not matched with a violent response. On the contrary, the description is punctuated with emotive lexemae or syntagms such as "s'étreignent," "épuisés," "le désespoir le plus intense," which connote empathy, a movement of identification with the Other, whereby body and spirit are kept together as a constant. Furthermore the experience draws from Prassinos's narrator a wise though melancholy acceptance of life as both life and death. The title appropriately states it: "Ce que je sais" ("What I know"). He has acquired a knowledge or awareness of the human condition which he believes is shared by his fellow wo/men. This theme is developed in another text, "Les Germes" (*MCE*), based upon a similar image. This time, a woman narrator has had parasitic membranes removed from her body. But she is seized with remorse. She has paid for her life with the death of a part of herself. For life, no matter how deviant, abnormal, chaotic, is still life. Hence the need for all to live in good intelligence with a body (and spirit) in which time inscribes changes. This positive or humanistic message, however, is articulated *a contrario*, that is, in the regretful mode of the past conditional: "Depuis, j'essaie d'imaginer ce qu'elle, la vie, serait devenue plus tard, je rêve aux liens d'amitié et d'amour qui nous auraient unies immanquablement" ("Since then, I have tried to imagine what life would have been later, I dream of the friendship and love ties which would necessarily have bound us") (53). Again, Prassinos's text closes on a double note: loss and regret. Rebelliousness is definitely out of her range in her mature age.

Alone of the three writers, Carrington moves from an anguished awareness of the fragility of the body and the self to a joyous affirmation of the possibilities of regeneration through a mythical rewriting of the human story. *The Stone Door* and *The Hearing Trumpet* are both surrealistic versions of the quest for the grail or, as J. Chénieux-Gendron writes in her introduction to *The Hearing Trumpet*, of a quest for rules of good living ("règle du bien vivre," 12). In the tale, old "silly" women, full of imagination and a great sense of fun, wreck an institution in which they have been placed to make way for a new era marked, among other things, by a spirit of sisterhood and the embracing of change as an existential principle. (One of the wondrous far-reaching effects of their mini-revolution is the reversal of the earth's poles, with the north moving downward towards the south.) As a condition for personal renewal, however, they must descend into the bowels of the earth (a tower) and undergo a trial: they must jump into a bubbling carrot and onion soup (to which they will contribute the meaty part!) which their ageless double has been cooking up. Needless to say, the soup euphemizes a highly comical and feminist version of the lustral waters of the new birth. After the forced bath, the women find themselves reunited with their previously disassembled egos; they are once more full and whole, infused with a new energy (wherein mythical truth is joyously grounded in psychological truth, which teaches us that progress in psychic integration, hence well-being, is accompanied by the liberation of vital energy). Here is the heroine speaking:

Never before had I experienced the joy of rhythmic dance, even in the days of foxtrot in the arms of some eligible young man. We seemed inspired by some marvelous power, which poured energy into our decrepit carcasses. (117)

In Carrington the female body, once reunited, becomes the focal point of cosmic forces. Just as the world axis has pivoted, the time axis has been reversed, and the old women become the instigators of a new age in which the frontiers between species will be transgressed and the planet will be peopled with werewolves, cats, bees and goats, as well as humans.

The Relational Body: Sexual and Maternal

In Carrington a reorganization of the female body is therefore accomplished, but only thanks to the jump into a mythical broth, both literally and figuratively. This jump or displacement of the story into the imaginary sphere is accompanied, on the other hand, by a near blacking-out of whole areas of the female experience, namely, the sexual and the life-bearing experiences, or at best by an oblique approach to them.

To be sure, sexuality and maternity can be found in Carrington's as well as Prassinos's works but almost always in disguise, shrouded in polysemic symbols, thus confirming Whitney Chadwick's own observations about the pictorial art of women artists associated with Surrealism. For one thing, we are struck by the absence, or very blurry representations, of the nude body, female as well as male. In Carrington, women are often richly adorned in costumes reminiscent of the Renaissance (again suggesting that the woman's reaffirmation can be expressed only via a mythopoetic or mythohistorical translation). Sometimes slender feminine figures are silhouetted against a background but the specific traits of their femininity are missing. In *The Hearing Trumpet,* there is almost an intimation of violation connected with the unveiling of the nude body of one of the old pensioners, believed to be a woman until death exposed "him." It is not clear whether the scandal is in the lie or in the exposure of the lie linked with the sexual identity. In the latter case, we might conclude that one's sexual identity is a matter of personal choice and should be left at that.

Similarly elliptical is Prassinos's work in its representation of the erotic body. It was not until the early eighties that she dared cut out, for one of her felt tapestries, a young naked virgin, whom she placed on old King David's lap. Undeniably, an often conflictual sado-masochistic sexual substratum can be read into her automatic writing, but in her later work there is great reluctance to deal head-on with matters of sexuality and erotic desire. Even in a novel like *La Confidente,* with its many hints at the dark forces of eros and the attending pain of nonfulfillment, the narrative discourse conceals the issues in a Dionysian subtext which is anything but apparent to the uninformed reader.

In neither Carrington nor Prassinos does one find narratives of sexual encounters other than by inference. Lovemaking is glossed over by textual silence or actual blanks in the page, as is the case in *Pigeon vole,* where we surmise that a young woman mates with a wild boar (39). Passionate love does not often figure prominently in either of these writers' works. When it does, its intensity is defused by a humorous treatment. In "A Man in

Love" Carrington deconstructs the *amour fou* paradigm in part through the literalization of a typical male surrealist image of "la femme végétale" (the body of the "beloved" lies on a bed overgrown with grass). If passion for a man (or for a woman) exists, it is in the form of a memory or a dream, never a present reality and in any case never the subject of textual representation. Men are on the whole inessential to women and women pursue their quest independently, obstinately, despite the fact that, in *The Stone Door*, one of Carrington's characters declares that woman needs man to open the door for her, an admission she later shrugs off as a youthful fiction (see her interview with Germaine Rouvre in *Obliques*, 91).

Mansour is situated at the opposite pole. Not only is the naked body, male or female, constantly being held up to our gaze but it is subjected to constant naming, part after part. The result is a fragmentation of the body. There is no whole. Nothing suggests that one can ever have access to something beyond the parts. Hence the impossibility for coitus to transcend its own limitation: orgasmic violence and intense but temporary pleasure. Mansour's representations of sexual encounters are disturbing, as the following lines from *Jules César*, a tale placed under the sign of Sodom, attest:

Il força sa femme à genoux, la tenant fermement par les cheveux, il ouvrit ses cuisses brutalement et enfonça sa langue dans le nombril tout en la courbant en arrière jusqu'à ce que sa tête touchât terre. Longtemps, il nettoya ainsi le corps de sa femme de ses démons familiers; enfin, ému par la nudité flasque de l'épouse soumise qui, langue pendante, semblait dormir, il la coucha sur l'herbe broutée par la lune et bondit sur elle sans même se déshabiller. (16)

(He forced his wife down to her knees, holding her tightly by her hair. With a brutal gesture, he opened her legs and pushed his tongue into her navel while bending her backwards until her head touched the ground. For a long time, he cleansed his wife's body of its [her?] familiar demons; at last, moved by the limp nakedness of his docile spouse asleep, or so she seemed, with her tongue hanging out, he laid her on the moon-grazed grass and threw himself over her without even undressing.)

Thereupon he sinks his teeth into her neck, covers her with mud and spits bile into her eyes before his frenzy subsides. The sado-masochistic relationship – the sole relationship ever to bind couples in Mansour's stories – is all the more disquieting as the actors' roles are clearly distinguished. The female body is the one that is taken, rejected, sodomized, passively opening and closing.

Mansour's writing functions like a mirror held up to the violence which pervades her tales of erotic encounters. It is difficult to decide where the writer positions her gaze and whether she partakes in the pleasure or the pain, whether she submits or inflicts. The ambiguous use of the possessive "ses" with "démons familiers" is revealing. Whose "familiar demons" are being appeased? The man's, the woman's, the body's as distinct from the person? And is the author relishing the cruel telling or is she denouncing the man's abuse? Are we witnessing nothing but a representation of her fantasies, to which she acquiesces? Or do we, in the images, detect a glimmer of hope at the end of the story that language ("la langue/tongue") will be able to cleanse the "damned" body to its very core, and restore it to the purity of its very beginning (the navel, i.e., the centermost physical part, through which it is connected to its maternal origin)?

Ambiguity turns into straightforward ambivalence in the treatment of images of childbearing. One of a few texts to deal with this theme, *Jules César*, opens with an account of the birth of twins amidst libations of beer (an appropriate word of double entendre in French, meaning both "beer" and "coffin"):

Comme toute mère qui a abrité des enfants neuf mois sous son corset avec amour, la mère ne pensait plus qu'à sa taille retrouvée et aux robes presque remettables qu'elle porterait dès que ses muscles relâchés répondraient à l'appel. Elle qui avait caressé ce ventre toujours grandissant, qui l'avait montré avec fierté aux parents, qui l'avait dissimulé avec adresse aux amants, elle qui avait nourri cette tumeur mouvante de graisse, qui l'avait aérée, masquée, barbouillée de rouge les jours de fête, elle ne songeait plus qu'à le faire totalement disparaître, jusqu'à se priver de toute nourriture avant le petit déjeuner. (10–11)

(Like any mother who has, for nine months, sheltered her children with love under her corset, the mother was only thinking of her thinner waistline and the dresses which could almost fit again and which she would wear as soon as her limp muscles would respond to the call. She, who had stroked this always growing belly, who had exhibited it with so much pride in front of parents, who had skillfully concealed it from lovers, she who had fed this tumor alive with fat, who had aired it, masked it, daubed it with red on feast days, harbored but one thought: to have it disappear totally, to the point of depriving herself of food before breakfast.)

Thus, once the child has been expelled, the maternal body turns away from the body which it has engendered, back upon itself. It cuts off this growth – appropriately named "tumor," a word whose death associations are reinforced by Mansour's own intertextual references to "Le Cancer" and "Îles flottantes." The twins will be entrusted to a nurse, the titulary "Jules César." The refusal of food may signify a refusal to be at the same time mother to another and one's own mother. A refusal of the mothering/ mothered female self with hints of a possible death – "faire disparaître *le ventre*" and not just the signs of pregnancy. Yet this very same mother, like "any [expectant] mother" has been proud, she has caressed the "tumor," she has fed and bathed it; but she has also hidden it, masked it, and dabbed it with red. Red, the color of fire and blood, is as symbolically ambivalent as these two elements expressing both the male and female, the diurnal and the nocturnal, life and death (cf. Jean Chevalier and Alain Gheerbrant, *Dictionnaire des symboles*). Covering the body with blood is a common ritual in various initiation rites but, to the extent that blood is associated with what is most intimate, its exposure to the outside – as is the case here – takes on a transgressive, ominous and impure connotation. Hence Mansour's representation of the procreative body is caught in the same supremely ambivalent flux of desires and fears which are characteristic of her imaginary universe.

Neither Carrington nor Prassinos deals with the maternal body as directly as does Mansour. Literal birth is always a past event or one placed in a mythical future. In Carrington's case, it is all the more remarkable as, alone among the three artists, she gave birth to two children. In addition, she held very strong views – not necessarily in line with her feminist allegiance in recent years – as to the importance of maternity as a specific female experience: "We, women, are animals conditioned by maternity. . . . For female animals love-making, which is followed by the great drama of the birth of a new animal, pushes us into the depths of the biological cave [*souterrain*]" (*Obliques* 91). Yet in her own writings, the cave, of which she offers many versions, is the setting for a symbolic coming to life, not of actual birth-giving.

Similarly, in Prassinos the biological reality is obfuscated, and giving life is translated into symbolic births, either psychological (rebirth of the Self) or textual (begetting a new text). Two texts, however, one in *La Confidente* and the other in *Mon Coeur les écoute,* introduce an interesting corrective. In both cases, we are presented with birth or pre-birth scenes in which the concreteness of the details sets up expectations that a real delivery will take place. Yet, at one point something happens to the text and the literal shifts over to the metaphorical, as though unable to move beyond some unformulated interdiction. In the short piece "Qui?" ("Who?") (*MCE* 54–55), the shift is straightforward and very much in line with the textual strategies used in the collection, namely, the moving back and forth between the literal and metaphorical meanings of a word or a phrase (always linked to the physical or biological reality) from which tight logical developments take a premise to absurd and/or fantastic conclusions. In "Qui?" Prassinos sets the stage very adroitly by describing what we think are the pains of pregnancy only to have us understand at the end that she was describing the artist in the throes of creation. Yet, to add another twist to these pages, a drawing below the final lines (Fig. 2), done by Prassinos herself, represents a strange creature with a baby in her womb, thus deconstructing her own symbolic construction and reimposing the literal over the metaphoric level. Noticeable, though, in the drawing is the fact that the child is not connected to a "life cord" which descends from what seems to be the heart-lung combination down to the rectal area. The latter, on the other hand, is adorned with two small, round appendices shaped like testicles, which confer upon this maternal representation an androgynous character.

In *La Confidente,* the ambiguity is far greater, the deferring of meaning sustained much longer, and eventually three different interpretations can be argued concurrently. To add to the complexity, the same birth scene is inserted *twice* in exactly the same terms in two different places in the novel, once at the beginning and once at the end. The first time, there is an abrupt shift in the narrative, preceded by a statement attributed to the narrator, that she "was not Nicholas's mother" (Nicholas is a friend whom she had hoped to save from a failing marriage). Then four paragraphs set in quotation marks interrupt the story line, much like a flashback scene in a film, suggesting the intrusion of a strong mental picture. Two scenes are superimposed: a postdelivery scene and a double loss-of-consciousness episode, framing the bringing to life of a son. The second time the scene is repeated as the narrator, taking her friend's son with her on the train to Paris, has fallen asleep. It can therefore be interpreted as a dream sequence precipitated by her mental perception that two births, not just one, have been taking place at the conclusion of the novel: she has acquired a child. Not her own biological child but an adopted son who will fulfill her maternal desires. At the same time a new self has been delivered, as the last, very lyrical page indicates:

Fig. 2   Prassinos, *Qui?* (*MCE,* 64.)

Je m'allonge d'un siècle. Une maison se construit pour moi dont les murs sauront absorber ma voix et la redire, où les choses apprendront à me raconter. Je suis effigie familière à des millions de mains, je suis statue de parc au tournant d'une allée, et, malgré les rousses et vertes souillures de saisons sur mes épaules, l'on me reconnaît. (236-37)

(I am longer by a century. A house is being built for me whose walls will be able to absorb my voice and broadcast it, where things will learn how to tell about me. I am an effigy known by millions of hands, I am a statue in the park at the end of a path, and, despite the rust and green stains of seasons upon my shoulders, I am recognized.)

If being born signifies taking possession of one's space in the world and being acknowledged (recognized) as a person in one's own right, then this is exactly what the "confidente" set out to find in this 1962 novel, and the birth motif becomes an appropriate metaphor for it. To these two symbolical meanings, the already mentioned Dionysian motif adds yet another dimension and may account for the doubling of the birth scene; for the young Greek god was the god "twice born." *La Confidente* may then be read as a disguised appeal to seek rebirth through a descent into the subterranean regions of the unformed, uncontrolled physical forces.

Conclusion

What, then, are the broad lines which have emerged from our reading? First, a shared anxiety about the boundaries of the self is defined in terms of physical images. Whether dreaded or desired, invasion from the outside threatens the inner space, either by taking away from it or exposing its own emptiness. Second, we see a redesigning of the traditional body representations. In place of the symmetrical body, free of excesses (of flesh, of movement, of color, of expression), a new body is brushed onto the canvas: an unstable body, made of parts that can be disassembled and recombined in fanciful ways: an asymmetrical body – as Prassinos's illustration for *Mon Coeur les écoute* visually exemplifies: a hybrid body, half-human, half-animal or nature. In sum, all are depictions of a grotesque body which call into question canonic representations, particularly those of the female body.[3] Beyond their differences, the bodies in Mansour, Carrington and Prassinos alike occupy either too much space or not enough, never just the right space. Their very disorganization defies the laws of anatomy and physics (the order of male or rational knowledge). To that extent, the images of the body which we are offered are subversive: they point to an absent image, that of the harmonious female body, young and chastely naked, which stood in the name of Woman in Magritte's collage.

But subversion does not necessarily mean reorganization or victory. In a somewhat reductive way, one could argue that in Mansour excess – be it excess of violence, eroticism, repetitiveness, crudity or obscenity – is born from her powerlessness to transcend her experience of emptiness and death. Her laughter, her "rire jaune," is a brave put-on. Her text, with its sado-masochistic brutality and the use of a lexicon to which we are more accustomed in male than in female writings, strikes an ambiguous chord. Is Mansour merely attempting to outdo the male by beating him on his own terrain or is she developing a new language for women by tearing down the barriers that separate not only the genders but the decent from the indecent, the private from the public, the poetic from the gruesome, the perverse from the normal, and so forth? I see in Mansour a failure to re-write the body from a new perspective. Hers is a vision of a private hell in which the female body cannot transgress its own division between pleasure (*jouissance*) and pain, desiring and hating itself for it.

With Prassinos, according to the various periods of her creative life, different ludic combinations may be interpreted as constituting attempts at reorganizing. Yet we are always left with surplus parts . . . a body in want of a whole continues to haunt her works. The link between her unfinished or erased bodies and the early death of her mother is one of the many hermeneutic avenues which should be explored.

In addition, inasmuch as Gisèle Prassinos's literary beginnings took place under the aegis of *écriture automatique* – which can be summarily described as a writing "from the inside" – it is not unlikely that her sense of loss and mourning for the once abundant outpouring of language and images, which she expressed in her mature works, may also have reinforced mental images of the body both as a cherished yet incompletely accessible inner space (to be defended against intrusion) and a surface to be traversed in order to reach meaning. It would account for her recurrent use of the anatomical metaphor to articulate an abstract message (as in the fifty-one texts of *Mon Coeur les écoute*). Using the body qua metaphor is tantamount to traversing it for the purposes of reaching a meaning situated beyond it, thereby reducing it once more to a porous surface. We have then come full circle to our initial discussion about the unreliability of the bodily frontiers.

Finally, leaving behind her the anxiety and the mourning, Carrington moves towards a reconstruction of a world in which the feminine takes charge of itself and opens up to exchanges with the outside. But Carrington's recourse to a symbolic universe in which various traditions merge leads, as with Prassinos, to the need to traverse the text in order to get to the meaning. In her, there is a refusal – or an incapacity – to represent the body *hic et nunc*, a body of flesh which does not, like her own texts, escape into the limitless world of imagination where all matter is spiritualized.

It was not until the 1970s that a feminine poetic discourse on the body, speaking directly and triumphantly about its organic, erotic and maternal reality, became acceptable – a discourse which one could no longer suspect of functioning, as Hélène Cixous would say, "within" the discourse of Man (Marks 1980, 257).

Notes

1. Whitney Chadwick finds the same general tendency among women artists associated with Surrealism to assert "their own inner reality as paramount" (Chadwick 1985, 237).

2. The pun in *gros grains de beauté* is difficult to render in English. "Gros grain" refers to "grosgrain" used by seamstresses while "grains de beauté" are beauty marks. In Prassinos's early automatic texts, the lexicon of seamstresses and milliners is constantly used, as the result of the intertwining of direct experience with imaginary transformations. In the Prassinos household, several aunts supported the family, after they arrived in France from their native Istanbul, by sewing.

3. Interestingly, we find several of the features of the bodily imagery which we have discussed in Mikhail Bakhtin's discussion of the grotesque body: the mouthlike orifices, the exaggerated outgrowths (the hump), the attention paid to the confines between the body and the world outside as well as to forms that link the human body to other nonhuman bodies (Bakhtin 1984, esp. chap. 5). We have outlined the very different basis upon which a female grotesque imagery rests, but further study is needed to construct a different model of the grotesque in women's texts.

References

Bakhtin, Mikhail. *Rabelais and His World.* Bloomington: Indiana University Press, 1984.

Bataille, Georges. *L'Erotisme.* Paris: Coll. 10/18, 1965.

Breton, André. *Anthologie de l'humour noir,* édition revue. Paris: Jean-Jacques Pauvert, 1966.

Carrington, Leonora. "L'Amoreux," in *La Dame Ovale.* Paris: G.L.M., 1939, with illustrations by Max Ernst. In English: "A Man in Love," in *The Oval Lady.* New York: E. P. Dutton, 1988.

——. "La Débutante," in *La Débutante contes et pièces.* Paris: Flammarion, 1978.

——. *En-Bas.* N.p.: Henri Parisot, 1945. Paris: Eric Losfeld, 1973. In English: *Down Below,* in *VVV* 4 (1944); reprinted in Surrealist Research and Development Monograph Series, published by *Radical America,* no. 5, 1972.

——. *The Hearing Trumpet.* New York: St. Martin's Press, 1976. In French: *Le Cornet acoustique.* Paris: Flammarion, 1976. Introduction by Jacqueline Chénieux-Gendron.

——. Interview with Germaine Rouvre. *Obliques* 14–15.

——. "The Neutral Man," in *The Neutral Man.* New York: E. P. Dutton, 1988.

——. "Pigeon vole," in *Pigeon vole: contes retrouvés.* Cognac: Le Temps qu'il fait, 1986. In English: "Pigeon, Fly!" in *The Seventh Horse and Other Tales.* New York: E. P. Dutton, 1988.

——. "Soeurs" in *La Débutante.*

——. *The Stone Door.* In French: *La Porte de pierre.* Paris: Flammarion, 1976.

Chadwick, Whitney. *Women Artists and the Surrealist Movement.* Boston: Little, Brown, 1985.

Chevalier, Jean, and Alain Gheerbrant. *Dictionnaire des symboles.* Paris: Robert Laffont/Jupiter, 1969.

Gallop, Jane. *Thinking Through the Body.* New York: Columbia University Press, 1988.

Gauthier, Xavière. *Surréalisme et sexualité.* Paris: Gallimard, 1971.

Mansour, Joyce. *Cris.* Paris: Seghers, 1954.

————. *Les Damnations.* Paris: Georges Visat, 1966.

————. *Déchirures,* in *Rapaces.* Paris: Seghers, 1960.

————. *Faire signe au machiniste.* Paris: Le Soleil Noir, 1977. (Includes, among others, *Déchirures.*)

————. "Le Cancer," in *Les Gisants satisfaits.* Paris: Jean-Jacques Pauvert, 1958. In English: "The Cancer," in J. H. Matthews, *The Custom House of Desire.* University of California Press, 1975, 189–94.

————. "L'Heure érogène," in *Carré blanc.* Paris: Le Soleil Noir, 1965.

————. *Histoires nocives (Jules César* and "Iles flottantes"). Paris: Gallimard, 1973.

Marks, Elaine, and Isabelle de Courtivron. *New French Feminisms.* Amherst: University of Massachusetts Press, 1980.

Minotaure 5, 1935.

Obliques 14–15: *La Femme surréaliste* (1977).

Prassinos, Gisèle. *Brelin le Frou.* Paris: Belfond, 1975.

————. *La Confidente.* Paris: Grasset, 1962.

————. *Le Grand repas.* Paris: Grasset, 1966.

————. *Les Mots endormis.* Paris: Flammarion, 1967. (Abbrev. *ME*)

————. *Mon Coeur les écoute.* Paris: Liasse à l'Imprimerie Quotidienne, 1982. (*MCE*)

————. *Trouver sans chercher.* Paris: Flammarion, 1976. (Includes most of the prose texts published between 1934 and 1944). (*TSC*)

————. *La Vie la voix.* Paris: Flammarion, 1971. (*VV*)

————. *La Voyageuse.* Paris: Plon, 1959.

Short, Robert. *Dada and Surrealism.* London: Calman and Cooper, 1980.

Identity Crises:
Joyce Mansour's Narratives
Judith Preckshot

Si Dieu est un cerf-volant
Qui diable est George Sand?

Who the devil is Joyce Mansour? The question is deceptively simple, for its answer depends on any number of hypothetical variables. Using the formula suggested in the final rhyming couplet of Mansour's "Incendies spontanés," if x equals a, then y equals b, we come to the conclusion that the solution to the identity puzzle is only one possible in a broad and confusing range of possibles. Indeed, Mansour is hard-put to solve that equation, and answers her own supposition, "If God is a kite (*cerf-volant*)," with the question, "Who the devil is George Sand?"[1]

Identities in literature are obscure and ambiguous by the very nature of the metaphors and masks that create them. By *cerf-volant*, did Mansour really mean a paper kite? Or did she intend the multiform god to appear as a stag beetle? Or perhaps the god was to be represented literally, just as the words state: a flying stag? In any case, "who the devil is George Sand," that French woman writing under a male pseudonym, and an English one at that! The question that Mansour raises about God and lesser creators, and their terms of comparison, invites her readers to pose the same question in her case: behind which mask(s) will we discover Joyce Mansour, English-born Egyptian but French-language poet and prose writer? As the term of comparison in George Sand implies, Mansour will not be defined other than through a writerly persona that integrates bi-national, dual-linguistic and double-gendered characteristics. By Mansour's own admission her works are autobiographical;[2] however, the life experiences at their source are clothed in fiction or metaphor so outrageous that reality is distorted beyond recognition. So, while clues to Mansour's identity may be discerned in a particular textual style, in (self-)reflecting narrative perspectives, or in the variable characters that people Mansour's short narratives, much is still left open to interpretation. After reading such tales as *Jules César*, the reader remains in a state of puzzlement: who the devil is the female protagonist, Jules César, or the wimpy Napoléon, who resembles even less another imperial namesake?

96

As it is the purpose of this essay to examine contradictions surrounding Mansour's identification with aesthetic or critical currents, as well as those emanating from her texts, we will first locate Mansour in such aesthetic and critical contexts as contribute to her authorial identity in that they reveal influences on her writing and also serve to inform readings of her work. Mansour's association with the Surrealists situates her in a particular historical moment in literature. Her ties to that movement date back to 1954, when her first volume of poetry was warmly reviewed in the surrealist periodical *Médium*. She joined the second-generation Surrealists re-grouping around André Breton in the postwar period and was a regular participant in a multitude of surrealist endeavors: most of the short narratives later published in the collection *ça* (1970) first appeared in *La Brèche* (1961–64) and *L'Archibras* (1967).[3] Another, "La Pointe," was published in the catalogue for the Eighth International Exposition of Surrealism (1959–60) dedicated to exploring the theme of the erotic; the catalogue also featured a recording on disk by Sacha Pitoeff and Dominique Farell of Mansour's playlet, *L'Ivresse religieuse des grandes villes*. Mansour embodied the communal spirit that moved Surrealism, collaborating on works with artists and writers such as Pierre Alechinsky (*Astres et désastres*, 1970), Wilfredo Lam (*Pandémonium: Orsa Maggiore*, 1976) and Ted Joans (*Flying Piranha*, 1978). And, if Mansour was surrealist in spirit and in act, her texts also bear the imprint of Surrealism.[4]

Although ensconced in the latter period of Surrealism, Mansour still played a marginal role with respect to Breton, Eluard, Aragon, and other male founders of the movement. And, ironically, it may be that her association with mainstream Surrealists, however marginal, is cause for her exclusion by feminist circles, which have evidenced a tendency to keep a hostile distance from Surrealism. Feminist readings of Mansour's work have been practically nonexistent.[5] This silence on the part of feminist critics, particularly on American shores, may stem from Mansour's adherence to aesthetic principles of male-dominated Surrealism; it may also be that her texts do not fit paradigms of women's writing currently of interest to certain feminist critics. For, unlike the novels of such women writers as Violette Leduc or Marguérite Duras, her tales tend toward the fantastic and do not stage unequivocally what might be called the "woman's experience," portrayed by some as victimization, by others as dispossession by patriarchal society, or as madness. A victim of history, Mansour arrived too late on the scene of one revolutionary moment (Surrealism) and too early for the other (Feminism) and has thus been deprived of that clear identification with aesthetic or critical tendencies which simplifies life for literary historians. We take special note of this ambivalence in the critical reception of her work, for when correlated with the ambiguous characterization of her narratives, it suggests that the very confusion of male and female roles portrayed in her texts may reflect more than a personal identity crisis; it may also be the signature of a woman writer caught between literary generations and diametrically opposed ideologies.

It is hardly surprising that a woman writer of Mansour's macabre and often shockingly frank expression would ally herself with a movement that challenged sexual mores, cultural myths and societal prohibitions, particularly the institution of marriage and the reproductive prison it represents. But as feminists of the last two decades have repeatedly pointed out, the liberation promoted by Surrealism largely excluded women and only perpetuated stereotypical images that continue to condemn them to the time-honored roles of virgin-wife-mother or whore. To be a "surrealist woman" *and* a woman writer seems a contradiction in terms. The very composition of the 1977 issue of *Obliques* dedicated to "La Femme surréaliste" reveals the fundamentally ambiguous status of the woman in Surrealism: although a goodly number of women poets and artists are represented in that volume, either by their own texts or essays on their work, a large section is also devoted to essays on the woman as she was conceived by male Surrealists, that is, as the transcendent object of their reverence as well as of their desire – the *voyante,* the *femme-enfant,* the unconscious, or the muse.[6] A feminized ideal for the Surrealists, the woman held an exalted status; a woman in reality, she existed in a position of dependence, in the shadow of better-known men: René Magritte appropriately called the surrealist woman a "pin-up girl."[7] We might ask, therefore, how the surrealist woman thus defined can be reconciled with the woman who is also a creating subject, one who writes Surrealism? Who or what is the surrealist woman writer's muse? Is her muse a feminized unconscious, mirror of the female consciousness? Or does "she" simply take the form of a male opposite?

The dedications in three of Mansour's books seem to point to a "muse" in André Breton, or at least a benefactor: Mansour had Breton to thank for early recognition of her work. But, as Renée Hubert notes, even the encouragement of the Surrealists, and of Breton in particular, was not sufficient to give women artists the visibility their work merits. It did not resolve the fundamental contradiction between male Surrealists' portrayal of the woman and the emerging group of women artists creating within the surrealist context.[8] The weakness of women's secondary position was compounded by the fact that writers such as Mansour, Leonora Carrington and Gisèle Prassinos belonged to a second generation of Surrealists publishing in the 1950s and the 1960s.[9] When viewed in the context of the movement as a whole, they are thus seen to emulate (along with their male contemporaries, we might add) the work of the movement's more inspired male originators – even though other comparisons might be equally appropriate (in Mansour's case, with the work of Henri Michaux, Jean Genet, or Georges Bataille).

One feminist approach to Surrealism suggests that the woman's creating inspiration comes from a Mother Goddess (*Magna Mater*). Gloria Orenstein stipulates that this source of creative energy is considered alienated, or mad, only when viewed from the limiting perspective of patriarchal culture. She shows further that while madness was held to be an exalted mental state and theoretical ideal upon which practicing Surrealists modeled their work, madness was a lived experience for women writers and artists associated with the Surrealists. Orenstein's subjects include Colette Thomas, Unica Zürn, Leonora Carrington, and Kay Sage, as well as the real Nadja – and not the fictional creation whose madness is documented, if misunderstood, in André Breton's book of that title.[10] She considers that all of these women are deprived of a feminine persona independent of male stereotypes and consequently "bear witness to a profound female desire to restore the original image of the centrality and awesomeness of female divinity to art and religion through reclaiming a female creation myth as a viable model for female creativity" (48). Although Orenstein maintains that their madness has cultural, rather than personal or individual roots, her emphasis on the existential nature of women's writing only further contributes (albeit unwittingly) to strengthening the gender dichotomy: men write Surrealism or madness; women are surrealist writers/painters and mad.

Orenstein's hypothesis that women surrealist artists recreate human experience in the image of a female divinity – a creative process others have termed "revisionist mythmaking"[11] – cannot fully account for narratives in which powerful matriarchal figures are not portrayed in any more positive light than male personae representing the patriarchy. Although strong female personages in Mansour's narratives sometimes usurp male positions of dominance, they do not escape the fate awaiting all characters, male or female: "emperors" or sexual amazons, patriarchs or sainted women, they all represent some degree of madness, and they are all targets for Mansour's satire. If the male myth of imperial power is undermined by Mansour's travesty of Julius Caesar in the story of that title, so also is any archetype of matriarchy: actually only a nanny to the nameless twins (who bear no resemblance to Romulus and Remus!), Jules César replaces the real mother, a "cow" of a woman incapable of caring for her children or even herself. A sexless sixty-year-old, Jules César could be played by man or woman, for her motherhood is by proxy only and her "maternal" feelings are expressed in violent and destructive ways, particularly as her charges grow up and shift their affections from the nanny, who once appeared godlike to them, to their nubile and more attractive contemporary, Lucie. Different from constructive mythologizing, Mansour's writing engages in a parody that is content to sack mythic systems preserving phallocentric power structures without proposing alternative feminist scenarios. And madness, though rampant, is rarely magical, and hardly the exclusive domain of women.

Xavière Gauthier takes the opposite point of view of the surrealist woman writer in *Surréalisme et sexualité,* a marxist-feminist account of Surrealists' representations of love and desire.[12] Rather than focus on gender difference, she frequently ignores it. Quotations from Mansour are sandwiched between male Surrealists' representation of the *femme fatale* (a praying mantis endowed with a *vagina dentata*), without any indication that Mansour's version of the male fantasy of the devouring female differs at all from those portrayed by an André Masson, Félix Labisse, or Victor Brauner. Whatever misandry that might be read in the lines from *Carré blanc,* "je dévorerai celui qui violera mes flancs / Aux pulsations / Barbares" ("I will devour the man who violates my flanks with barbaric throbbings") is attenuated by Gauthier's conclusion that woman's power is abnegated by the implicit comparison with an animal: in her view, Mansour merely reduces woman to a figure for conventionally feminized Nature (170–73). Gauthier considers that surrealist artistic production, be it by men or women, reinvests male power myths and structures of victimization with a falsely revolutionary vigor. In Mansour's case, she finds little evidence of what she calls *femellitude* (after the militant concept of *négritude*). Not to be confused with *féminité,* which for Gauthier is tainted by its opposition to everything that is traditionally associated with masculinity, *femellitude* represents "un mode de désir et d'action sur le monde qui lui appartienne en propre sans être le facile complément, le négatif affaibli de celui du mâle; un sexe différent qui ne soit pas nécessairement le 'deuxième sexe'" (275) ("a mode of desire and action on the world which belongs to woman in her own right, without being the facile complement, the weak negative of that of the male; a sex that is different but not necessarily the 'second sex'"). Gauthier opposes surrealist women writers and artists to Simone de Beauvoir, whom she portrays actively struggling against the exploitation of women but in a revolutionary framework different from, and outside of, Surrealism. Her conclusion is that while Surrealism transgressed any number of societal taboos, opening up new vistas for the human imagination, it left the institution of motherhood perhaps perverted but still intact. The continued idealization of woman as an actual or potential mother thus denies women the possibility of creating a real revolution from within the ranks of the Surrealists and breaking out of the reproductive prison it consciously and unconsciously supports.

If Surrealism refused a place to the creating woman subject, feminist re-readings of women writing Surrealism also tend to exclude Mansour. It is not through feminist writing that Mansour enjoys a certain renown in Franco-American circles but thanks to J. H. Matthews, a recognized authority on Surrealism who has championed her work for the past three decades. His earlier accounts of her work focus on its affinities with Surrealism, notably in the spirit of revolt against bourgeois society's restrictions, which finds expression in frank and shockingly erotic images reinterpreting Breton's concept of *amour fou*.[13] In a recent monograph, however, he treats Mansour on her own terms, examining in particular the traces of Mansour's Egyptian heritage in mythological references that infiltrate poetry informed by the European surrealist context.[14] He seeks to highlight the specificity of her contribution to Surrealism – not as a woman, necessarily, but as a writer whose inspiration may come also from outside Surrealism's main currents. This notion of "strangeness," or estrangement (Matthews constantly refers to Mansour as "l'étrange demoiselle"), is suggestive for the three narratives that we will examine, for they dramatize the dilemma of persons who are out of place in the spaces designated for them by fate or society. Variations on oedipal conflicts and their respective resolutions, they stage archetypical familial dramas wherein children are pitted against powerful or seductive parental figures, and women are miscast as mothers, children, and sometimes men. This sense of displacement is communicated variously by the different narrators of each story, but in all cases the search for personal moorings leads not to self-definition but to a state in between, a sort of limbo.

The narrator of "Infiniment . . . sur le gazon" speaks from the point of view of a daughter in conflict with her widowed mother, with whom she is obliged to share an apartment. The two women suffer a life of solitude and sterility, their dreariness relieved only by the noonhour visits of the daughter's boyfriend Arnaud. Arnaud, with his "porcine teeth" and dirty habits (the only place he knows to put out his cigarettes is on the rug) becomes the focus of the two women's frustrated and disturbed desires – the bone of contention, so to speak. The female narrator is known only by the term of endearment used by her lover, "femme facile"; as one might surmise, she submits to the humiliation of having sex, never with "splendor in the grass," as the title of the story hopefully suggests, but violently on the sofa or on the floor before her mother's desiring eyes. The mother accepts her pitiful role of voyeur only because her own invitations to Arnaud have been rebuffed. The daughter accepts it for reasons that become clear when the somewhat surprising dénouement of this tale is reached. The rivalry between mother and daughter for Arnaud's attentions can have but two outcomes, and both entail reducing the occasional ménage à trois to an exclusive couple. When the daughter's attempt to banish Arnaud from the household proves unsuccessful, it is the alternative scenario that is ultimately played out. So, just to get her off the younger couple's back, Arnaud finally gives the mother what she has long desired: "l'instant où la fumée de la lampe masculine noircirait son beau maquillage" (*ça*, 43) ("the moment when the smoke of the masculine lamp would blacken her beautiful make-up" [37]).

The appearance in the narrative of one of Arnaud's former mistresses sheds some light on the nature of the bond that holds the mother and daughter couple together even as it drives them apart. The woman known as Mme S . . . , who continues to support Arnaud's material needs in return for the monthly "filial" visits he makes accompanied by the narrator, is first referred to as "one of his old mistresses" and indeed is seemingly much older than he, presented as somewhat frail, "serr[ant] sa robe de chambre autour de ses maigres épaules liées entre elles par une multitude de petits os aux jointures mal ajustées" (ça, 46) ("tighten[ing] her dressing-gown around her skinny shoulders joined together by many small bones with badly adjusted articulations" [38]). Her apparent resemblance to the mother (by age) is confirmed in the commonly used epithet "la vieille" by which the daughter and Arnaud refer to the mother. This clear synonymy between mother and mistress suggests that Arnaud's forbearance of the mother's observation of his lovemaking stems less from pity than from incestuous desire. Sex with the hardly sensuous mother, with her "wrinkled pubis" and "bluish udders," is perhaps even more gratifying for him than it is with the daughter, for he can thus act out the child's fantasy of possessing his mother. In this light, a remark Arnaud made much earlier in the story, comparing the daughter to her mother, can be reinterpreted: " 'Tu lui ressembles,' me disait-il sans se déboutonner, et je devais jouir ainsi, devant elle, sur commande, et sans tendresse ni tambour" (ça, 39) (" 'You are just like her,' he said to me without unbuttoning himself, and I had to have pleasure in that way, in front of her, on command, and without tenderness or fuss" [34]). Arnaud's relationship with the daughter, then, only masks a deeper, incestuous attraction for the mother, which is also reciprocated. When the mother offers Arnaud her deceased husband's slippers and pipe, she symbolically grants him the position of father-lover and compounds the sin of one incestuous relationship (of son-mother) with another: Arnaud assumes the role, after the fact, of the daughter's father.

The story comes to a grotesque conclusion à la Lizzie Borden. The narrator's remark, "Je fis tant de bruit avec ma hache que l'on me mit au cachot" (ça, 46) ("I made so much noise with my ax that I was put in prison" [39]), hints at matricide and madness but does not entirely dispel suspicions that the murder was merely a fantasy concocted by the daughter to compensate for her continued unhappy existence and the attraction/repulsion she feels for her mother-double. The first line of the story lends credence to the latter interpretation that the murder might be only the figment of a crazed imagination. The narrator admits right from the start, "Souvent quatre, parfois trois, jamais seule: l'heure de la sieste était la meilleure de la journée" (ça, 39) ("Often four, sometimes three, never alone: the hour of the siesta was the best of the day" [34]). The mother's presence appears to be a necessary component of an erotic scenario which depends for excitement on the disequilibrium created by a third party and on the reversal of traditional roles, for it is the man who acts primarily as a catalyst, arousing passions between mother and daughter.

"Infiniment . . . sur le gazon" ostensibly sets up one conventional stereotype, which is that of the woman victimized by a male world who eventually turns her frustration on herself and her own kind. A second story, "La Pointe," plays out another oedipal drama that also seems, initially, to conform to male stereotypes. A bawdy scenario with Felliniesque overtones, "La Pointe" recounts the story of adolescent discovery of sexual identity; it is narrated by the eldest son in a family of eight boys in a bourgeois household. The ten-year-old in question is initiated into sex by the distinctly male vision of earthy femininity incarnated in the maid, "Saignée" – Saignée of the ample hips and breasts, menstrual flow, and pagan appetites. True to her stereotype, Saignée is mistress to the father, and both mistress and nurse to the young master; she is consequently a sort of surrogate mother, who entertains incestuous relations with her "son." The actual incestuous relationship between mother and son is only fully realized once the father "disappears" and the biological mother sets about seducing her son away from the maid. The father plays a marginal role in the narrative, important only insofar as his fleeting presence sketches out a primary oedipal scene for the reader. Weak and ineffectual, he is dominated by his wife; but he also receives brief mention in the text as someone who devises exquisite humiliations for his son. Whether he actually died from a fall or was pushed out the window by the mother and/or son is not clear, nor does it matter to our adolescent narrator; what is important is that his father does fade out of the picture, along with the other seven sons, and that the essential ménage à trois is reestablished, composed this time of two "mothers" and an adolescent male. In this new triangle, the gusty servant from the islands vies for the son's affections with the frustrated and unfulfilled mother. Characters may come and go, but the triangle that will come to represent the essential family structure in Mansour's narratives remains. When Saignée is also killed off by the narrator, her place is quickly taken by a mother so voracious she gives new meaning to the adjective used to describe her, "sexagénaire"; the mother's former position is occupied by the narrator's cousin-bride, a virgin who represents less of a threat to the mother's love than Saignée did because she has learned through neglect to find consolation, solo, huddled in the depths of an armoire with a pair of red, white and blue rubber gloves.

Mansour's stories generally unfold within the confines of a family unit – although that unit can be variously defined. Couples living in harmony are rare, and what is understood today as the nuclear family exists in her narratives as a perversion of accepted norms and a highly explosive potential. Mothers (and mother surrogates) are strong presences in Mansour's tales: iron-willed, sometimes violent, always creatures with insatiable sexual appetites, they either neglect their offspring, remanding them to the care of omnipresent nannies, or they are in competition with their own progeny. Fathers exist primarily through their absence, incidental only to procreation or representing a power external to the household; and if they do play a part in the story, it is as an obstacle to be removed. Children are a monstrous reflection of their parents and, more often than not, agents of their parents' destruction. In "Napoléon," the forty-year-old Julie is mother, sister and mistress to her son Napoléon; and Napoléon's father, called "le Père Armand" because he had been wearing a priest's cassock since he was twenty for purely whimsical reasons, denies his paternity symbolically just as much as the mother abdicates her strictly maternal responsibilities. The patriarch who is in appearance "strong," such as the drunken wife-beater of a father in *Jules César*, is destined for destruction: "Toute la famille détestait le père pour ses manières d'ivrogne et ses moustaches jaunies par le tabac, qui tombaient dans la soupe. Ils souhaitaient sa mort et même la chèvre mordait sa main quand il la calinait" (*Histoires*, 14) ("The whole family detested the father for his drunken ways and his mustaches yellowed by tobacco, which drooped into the soup. They wished him dead and even the goat would bite his hand whenever he fondled her" [157]). The narrator is quick to assure readers that this inverted order of cruelty and degradation is the rule rather than the exception: "C'était une famille comme toutes les familles" (*Histoires*, 15) ("It was a family like any other family" [157]).

An aphorism introducing "La Pointe" announces the topsy-turvy mores guiding behavior: "L'artichaut a des limites, l'anormal n'en a pas" (*ça*, 9) ("The artichoke has limits, the abnormal does not" [13]). The young narrator's relations with mother, wife and mistress are characterized by either physical or mental sadism. And the women clearly enjoy being neglected, beaten or otherwise debased. But the usual gender-marked positions in the sadomasochistic couple – the male sadist and female masochist – are not maintained: here all parties are equal in sexual relations constituted as "reciprocal perversions." The narrator recollects beating his mother in public for her pleasure: "Je la battais, pour sa très grande délectation, au beau milieu de la cour, sous les regards courroucés des voisins. Elle bombait la torse et me suppliait, *sotto voce*, d'arracher sa blouse, de griffer ses gros seins ou de dénuder ses fesses humides . . ." (*ça*, 21) ("I hit her, to her own very great delight, right in the middle of the courtyard, under the neighbours' incensed glances. She threw out her chest and begged me, sotto voce, to tear her blouse, to claw her big breasts or to lay bare her moist buttocks . . ." [21–22]). The mother returns the favor by insisting that her son dress as a girl – indeed, that he be married, like his bride, in a long white dress. She also ordains that he shall not attain full manhood until after her death, at which point he will "wear his sex" just as others wear black in mourning. This final rotation in the triangle, which pitted the mother against her daughter-in-law, also shifts the mother into the position usually reserved for the authoritarian father in the oedipal conflict. "Father," she courts her girlish son; emasculating mother, she tries to prevent the son from becoming a man. Once she has assumed the latter role, she must join the father in oblivion. The narrator therefore has her drown, at arm's length from rescue. He remarks cold-bloodedly on his mother's final but resolutely parental reluctance to recognize her adult child: "elle fut bien étonnée, la pauvre idiote, et ne trouva rien de mieux pour se sauver que m'accabler de sarcasmes sur ma force de volonté" (*ça,* 31) ("she was quite surprised, the old fool, and found nothing better to do to save herself than to overwhelm me with sarcastic remarks about my will power" [29]).

Mansour's language is sometimes disconcertingly frank. The text is liberally sprinkled with the words *pénis, sexe, verge,* and *pipe d'écume* (penis, sex, rod, and foamy pipe), and their female equivalents—*pubis, fourche, fente, clitoris,* and *cul* (pubis, crotch, slit, clitoris, and ass). Female characters' names and attributes in "La Pointe" (males have only the generic designation of father or son) identify them with, and as, sexual parts. This identification is confirmed in other descriptions echoing the representative terms: the fraternal Aunt Kuglov (*cul*-glov) is qualified by her "langue agile et *lux*ueuse" ("lecherous and nimble tongue"); Saignée "smelled like rotten apples" but is endowed with an "éloquence *cul*inaire"; and the virgin-bride "called" Marie was originally baptized Marie-*Culotte* [my emphases]. Were it not for the general raunchiness of Mansour's texts, the reader would be led to take these names as derogatory or disparaging to the author's own sex, even more so than the narrator's enforced transvestism. However, women are not only objects of desire but insatiably desiring subjects; in this sense, the sexes are interchangeable and sometimes confused by metaphoric substitutions which further complicate the issue of the narrator's identity. The son is described alternately as the "young man of good family," who has his way with the maid, and "mother's little girl." His sexual ambiguity appears, at first, to be no more than a whim of the mother, but this ambiguity later manifests itself through feminizing metaphors that effect a gender change through coitus and suggest, further, that orgasm has no gender. The narrator's comparison of his male member with an oyster (Saignée's "minauderies agissaient sur mon sexe comme un citron sur une huître" [*ça,* 23] ["cajoleries acted on my sex as lemon on an oyster"]) must be read through a host of associations commonly linking shellfish and female sex organs; and the metaphoric ejaculation evoked by the image of a volcano is attributed in one instance to the narrator (Saignée is described as "penchée sur mon sexe comme un nuage sur un cratère" [*ça,* 20] ["bent over my sex like a cloud over a crater"]) and in another to his mother ("mère éclata dans mes bras avec un hurlement de volcan" [*ça,* 30] ["my mother burst in my arms with a roar of a volcano"]). The "crossdressing" through metaphor is accentuated by the disparity between the narrator's possibly dormant "volcano" and the mother's orgasmic explosion. Opposite Saignée, however, the boy's maleness does persist, but takes the form of thoughts, which drop "like pollen" around Saignée's ecstasy. Or, it is hidden in *mal*, the "castrated" form of *mâle*. The narrator reflects on Saignée, "Je me faisais mal à travers toi" ("I hurt myself [became male] through you"). The play on words equates pain with maleness and penetration with the usurpation of the female body, of femaleness. In fact, the story ends with a shipwreck which only the narrator survives — through Saignée. Emerging from a submarine re-vision of memories through which he lays to rest father, mother, wife, and aunt, the narrator pays special homage to Saignée and the free and open expression of desire she symbolizes. She is not just his opposite, but an integral part of himself. Washed up on the shore of a new land, the narrator is reborn through a Saignée, half-man half-woman, "aux pensées verticales, aux orifices vibrants" ("with vertical thoughts and vibrating orifices"). The female alter ego represented in Saignée may be taken as evidence of homoerotic desire or an indication that desire cannot be so simply gender-coded as either virile or feminine.

A similar movement of transformation is also present in "Illusions de vol," with the one difference that the female narrator is originally presented as a *she* who has yet to discover that (male) side to her character which she has hidden even from herself and whose recognition would help her understand, she guesses, why she steals in stores. The mystery hinges on the unraveling of the title and the interpretation of *vol* as flight and/or theft. The double entendre is itself borrowed, if not stolen, from a general cultural storehouse of images: Apollinaire, for instance, used it before her in his depiction of Christ as the "first airplane" in "Zone" ("s'il sait voler, qu'on l'appelle voleur") ["if he knows how to fly, call him a flyer/thief"]).

The narrator's revelation comes through a piecing together of memories which ultimately link her up to childhood experiences and enable her to identify her kleptomaniac self with the visionary. The first memory involves a chess game with an old friend on Majorca who, a former scientist, had once invented a design for control sticks used in aviation. Now, it seems, the old man is touched by senility. He explains that his current "research" has taken him beyond the limits of science, and real flight, to new heights. And he proceeds to show the narrator, speechless and uncomprehending before the representations of sublimated desire the old man draws from velvet-lined cases, "des phallus de jade grandeur nature, d'autres en plastique munis de plumes gluantes" (*ça*, 72) ("life-size jade phalluses, others in plastic provided with sticky feathers" [57]). As the old man puts his penises away, disappointed by her obvious lack of appreciation, the narrator notes laconically, and without pursuing the subject further, that a certain Dorothée had emerged, all wet, from the waters of the bay.

A second recollection at a later time reconnects the narrator, by means of verbal associations, with the memory of the old man and his phallic flights of fancy. As she is preparing to board a plane one night at the Brussels airport, she is suddenly overcome by a recurrence of malarial fever and an unwonted distaste for flying (she flies often and willingly, as others take sleeping pills, she says). The sudden discomfort of real flying yields to the pleasure afforded by fantasy-flying, that is, stealing (*voler*) and desecrating or "raping," its near semantic and homophonic equivalent (*violer*). "J'aime voler dans les rues comme une femme de mauvaise vie; prendre, violer, salir l'objet futile" (*ça,* 74) ("I like to steal in the streets like a woman of ill repute, to take, to rape, to defile the futile object" [58]). Mansour allows a rare autobiographical detail to enter into the fiction at this point, mentioning that the word expressing her distaste for real flying came to her in English, her first language, rather than in French. This resurgence of early linguistic experience with the malarial fever enables her to recover, through double-language plays on words, a true sense of her identity, while still remaining under the safe cover of hallucination. "Joystick," she mutters. And a vision of the old man prompts the deduction: "Evidemment. Joyce: 'joy-stick.'"

The reader is tempted to make the obvious analogies between the author's name, a phallic instrument, and the sudden and seemingly gratuitous intrusion into the story of a female phallus (Dorothée) rising from the waters; but the story does not stop with a female identification with (or appropriation of) the male organ: its real point is how to accede to the power it represents, how to write the self, as one's (female) self. The narrator poses the question thought, if not voiced, by many a woman writer: "Comment faire pour me lever, . . . marcher, m'avancer comme un journal intime, mot après mot le long des jours, vers l'arpenteur des mirages: l'avion?" (*ça,* 74) ("How can I get up, . . . walk, move forward like a diary, word after word all through the days, towards the surveyor of mirages: the airplane?" [58]). How to fly, steal through the air? Women's writing has been variously defined as "writing the body" [15] and women writers as "thieves of language."[16] But in Joyce Mansour's case, one is tempted to elaborate on the motif: writing (or stealing) whose body, his or hers? These sorts of questions are also posed by a body of writing in which language/tongues are doubled, eroticized and questionably sexed: gender confusion goes hand in hand with linguistic confusion. Mansour's characters are often of indeterminate gender, neutralized by age (adolescence or senescence) or by physical or mental illness. Erotic images transgress gender distinctions, and all forms of sexual expression are permitted – heterosexual, homosexual, bestial, etc. This lack of differentiation occurs, however, in a context of difference; for the sex change to have its effect, it must be placed in a clear opposition of male with female.

Provocative images in Mansour's poetry recreate communication as a fundamentally sexual act; even at long distance, as is humorously implied in *Rapaces,* conversation is erotic: "Le téléphone sonne / Et ton sexe répond" ("When the telephone rings, your sex answers" [100]). All bodily orifices are endowed with the capacity for speech, for humankind is at least bi-, if not polylingual. And the relationship to language is predictably a function of sexual identification which, in turn, depends on the individual's acceptance or denial of cultural/parental structures. In "Phallus et momies," Mansour describes a linguistic past intruding on her present as a sort of menacing insemination: "Entre les cuisses de mes aïeux / Darde la langue hébraïque" ("Between my ancestors' thighs darts the Hebrew tongue"). But it is not clear that a return to a long-entombed heritage is unequivocally a good. And if the patriarchy is abnegated ("Tout casser / Briser l'image du pénis paternel" ["Break everything, shatter the image of the paternal penis"]), matriarchy is already dead, mummified: one cannot mistake the English resonance in "mummies" or the rough equivalence between daddies, mommies and death implied in the title. Mansour's conclusion, pointing to a "route parallèle à celle / Qui n'existe / Plus" ("road parallel to one which no longer exists" [Rapaces, 95–97]), rejects both paternal and maternal cultures/tongues in favor of a language analogous to one or the other of those repudiated. She prescribes, in effect, a sort of translation from dead or moribund languages to such as would give expression to a living, desiring and creating self.

In French feminist discourse of the last decade, the metaphor of bilingualism recurs with some regularity to describe both woman's natural state and the specific predicament of the woman writer attempting to insert herself into the male-dominated sphere of texts. In Les Voleuses de langue, Claudine Herrmann maintains that woman's innate bilingualism affects her general comportment for, a foreigner in her own space, she must constantly "translate" herself into a feminine other once she leaves the enclave of other women to enter mixed (i.e., male) society. The literary woman is portrayed as necessarily schizoid, inhabited by a homunculus who speaks another language, which is that of culture and knowledge; her mode of access to written language is also through "translation."[17] According to Herrmann, aggressive translation amounts to radical heresy and the ultimate antisocial – Promethean – act of challenging patriarchal rule, of stealing language. While Herrmann's rhetoric is confrontational and defines the coming to language of women as theft, Hélène Cixous approaches the same subject in "Le Rire de la Méduse" more subversively, as stealth. She engages in double-speak that shows bilingualism to be a position of neither defense nor attack, but rather one of strength that draws simultaneously on male and female "discourses": the male logos is echoed, and transformed, by the obstinate mutism of female expression, which acts on language from within. The unnamed mythic referent here is not Prometheus, but Icarus: "la femme tient de l'oiseau et du voleur comme le voleur tient de la femme et de l'oiseau: illes passent, illes filent, illes jouissent de brouiller l'ordre de l'espace, de le désorienter, de changer de place les meubles, les choses, les valeurs, de faire des casses, de vider les structures, de chambouler le propre" ("woman resembles the bird and the flyer/thief just as the flyer/thief resembles the woman and the bird: s/hes go, s/hes leave/spin, s/hes get pleasure from confusing the order of space, from disorienting it, from shifting about the furniture, things, values, from breaking into things, from emptying structures, from turning conversations upside down").[18] Whether *illes* represents graphically the male appropriation of the feminine pronoun (*elles*) or the feminization of *ils* (by adding the diminutive ending *-le*), bisexuality and the aptitude for double-tongued expression is a privilege principally reserved for women, for they can write from two perspectives, from within and without language. Cixous spells out woman's special status in the double pronoun "elle-elle" (she-she), whose phonic reproduction *elle-aile* (she-wing) is a figural reminder of woman's capacity for flight (Icarus's winged departure from his island) and for her alienation and isolation (she is also the island); *elle-aile* might be construed as the singular of *illes-îles* (s/hes/isles).

Cixous's particular attention to bilingualism could be qualified as a compensatory gesture for the profound sense of displacement that she experienced as a child, fated by history to an existence in two mutually exclusive linguistic worlds. Cixous recounts in "La Venue à l'écriture" that, born into a Jewish family displaced by the Second World War, she first learned to speak German at home and then, later, to write French at school. German was for her an "illiterate voice," the nurturing, nourishing, soulful mother tongue: "l'âmant maternel, la langue sauvage qui donne forme aux plus anciennes aux plus jeunes passions, qui fait nuit lactée dans le jour du français" (29) ("the maternal soul-lover [âm(e)ant], the primitive tongue which gives form to the most ancient, the youngest passions, which brings the milky way into the daylight of French").[19] Cixous's second language, French, was indissociable from "grammaire le loup," spelling, reason and culture. But the primacy of the written over the spoken word had the effect of reordering linguistic priorities; the first language became secondary, and Cixous's relationship to herself as a figure of speech was permanently perturbed. The child who first learned to say *Ich* cannot identify with *Je;* she comprehends the question of self ("qui suis-je?") only when it is rephrased to express the subject's unconsciousness of her selfhood ("qui, je?") or of her being in existence at all ("je suis?"). This kind of bilingualism is, of course, by no means limited to women writers. The names of Guillaume Apollinaire and Samuel Beckett come immediately to mind as notable examples of authors for whom writing in a foreign tongue is commensurate with existential or linguistic alienation. But while these two authors may put the speaking subject into question, their concerns are ontological in nature and do not ground the self as a product of language so firmly in culture and gender – at least not as explicitly as women writers and theorists tend to do.

109

The consideration of bilingualism as lived experience rather than as simple metaphor brings out a striking parallel between Cixous and Mansour. Bilingual in life, Mansour also wrote almost exclusively monolingual texts: with a few isolated exceptions, all of Mansour's published work is in French.[20] The incidence of English words in her narratives is also quite rare. That they are oftentimes detected in word-plays testifies to their oral power; French, in contrast, connotes mastery of the written. It is significant, furthermore, that the references to English in Mansour's narratives occur in the two stories that have a similar and manifestly autobiographical content. And in both these tales, "Illusions de vol" (*ça*) and "Iles flottantes" (*Histoires nocives*), the mother as character is conspicuously absent and only appears in the form of the linguistic ghost of a "mother" tongue or in the person of the Englishman, Mr. Cooper, one of the patients at the hospital which serves as a setting for "Iles flottantes." It is the father, or a paternal figure, who remains as a judgmental presence in the story and functions as a negative model for the narrator's self-definition. In "Iles flottantes," his aphorisms or other more forbidding pronouncements are interjected into the narrator's often undifferentiated accounts of real events or dreams; they reveal parental postures of disapproval against which the adult child (Mansour's autobiographical narrator) is still struggling: "'Tu parles comme une prostituée,' dit mon père" (*Histoires,* 80); "'Caca,' dit mon père toujours autoritaire" (*Histoires,* 144) ("'You talk like a prostitute,' said my father"); ("'Poop-poop,' said my father, as ever authoritarian"). Recourse to the mother tongue does not provide comforting refuge, for phallic identification (Joyce/joy-stick in "Illusions de vol") reinstitutes conflict with the patriarchal figure even as the narrator assumes his place or personality. Although the narrator of "Iles flottantes" gives the impression that she has gone to her dying father's bedside in Geneva, her confused ramblings soon let slip that it is she herself who is the patient in the Swiss sanatorium. The identification with the father, and particularly with his puritanical stance, also comes out in the narrator's relationship with Mr. Cooper, for whom she serves as interpreter. Prior to her arrival, the Englishman had been able to communicate through gestures and body language; by exhibiting his genitalia ("initiales," as they were called), Mr. C. (as he is often referred to) was able to combine pleasure with the business of getting his point across. More than the killing cancer which brought Mr. C. to the hospital in the first place, the narrator's translations precipitate the rapid decline in his health. By giving voice in French to his desires, she effectively castrates Mr. C., depriving him of a pleasurable avenue of infantile expression through the other, or "*ur*-mother" tongue. Her translations reflect the paternal agenda to rectify socially unacceptable discourse, for Mr. Cooper had been "talking" like a prostitute.

"Iles flottantes" is set in Switzerland, a country whose reputation for orderliness is in contradiction with the chaos that its polylingualism promises. It is against this backdrop that the drama of the confused narrator unfolds. The sanatorium in which she find herself is humorously represented as a modern-day Babel, where patients of diverse nationalities engage every orifice and member of the human body in vigorous conversation – properly speaking, intercourse. In one such orgy, discussion turns to the relative efficacy of national "tongues." Referring to French, German, and Russian, a Chinese patient (the English equivalent would be a Greek) responds that it is "all Hebrew" to him (87). The narration has a tendency to lapse into incoherence with the narrator, especially when she becomes lost in oneiric or hallucinatory accounts. But the paternal voice intercedes to bring the rambling narrator back to order: "Vraiment, à force de rêver tu n'entends plus que le grec ou le latin" (*Histoires,* 145) ("Really, because of your dreaming all the time, you only understand Greek or Latin" [237]). And yet, when in the position to relay these dreams or, especially, to interpret for Mr. Cooper, rendering his wishes coherent to francophone members of the hospital population, the narrator returns to the discourse of order and communication to speak (castratingly) from the position of the father. She "floats" from one role to the other, as do the islands of the title. One of the "Il(e)s/Illes flottantes" is produced by her floating between "languages" and between the gender-coded roles associated with those discourses.

In bringing this study to its close, we will bring the focus back to what is of most particular interest, namely the presence of writerly models which, invoked at the beginning of the story, underscore Mansour's relation as a woman writer not just to language, but to a literary heritage. The story opens with an abrupt "récapitulons," which hints at a summary of some past event and possibly yet another capitulation. Both suppositions prove to be true: the narrator makes a point of stating that before leaving Nice to fly to Geneva to meet her father, she had purchased Pierre Jean Jouve's *Le Monde désert* to help her pass the time en route. Jouve's book also takes place in Geneva, and thus transports the narrator to Switzerland beforehand, through the agency of another's words, and puts her in the position of retelling *his* story rather than telling her own. The narrator quite literally retraces his steps, identifying streets and places encountered in Jouve's descriptions of a walk through Geneva, as she makes her way to the hospital. She comments, "J'ai une très forte impression de vivre par procuration, respirant par les pores du livre ayant délégué mes pouvoirs à 'un autre je' situé, lui aussi, dans les neiges, dans le non-vécu de l'inactuel. Cela n'est pas désagréable" (*Histoires,* 60) ("I have a very strong impression of living by proxy, breathing through the pores of the book, having handed over my powers to another 'I' located, it too, in the snows, in the non-lived and the inactual. It is not unpleasant" [187]). Mansour's "floating isles" certainly recall Jouve's "deserted world," but the coincidence in narration does not stop at the title; the narrator's apparent inability to differentiate between the book read and the book written and her pleasurable internalization of another's discourse play out on another level the discomfort mixed with delight of the child attempting to maintain his/her difference from the parent who has engendered him/her and the society/language that has formed him/her. Although we will not presume to suggest that it is Mansour herself who is in crisis, the consciousness that is expressed in her work of mysterious influence, of being written as she writes, cannot but evoke the image of a self querying, "Who the devil am *I?*" We may well ask who Joyce Mansour is, for it is she who has first framed the question in the split personality and parallel selves of her narratives.

Notes

1.   Joyce Mansour, "Incendies spontanés," in *Faire signe au machiniste* (Paris: Le Soleil Noir, 1977), 40.

2.   Mansour is quoted in Karin Ilona Pohlmann, "Joyce Mansour's *ça* and *Histoires nocives:* Translations and Critical Interpretations," unpublished Ph.D. diss., SUNY-Binghamton, 1974, 249.

3.   Published in *La Brèche:* "Dolman le maléfique" (October 1961), "Infiniment . . . sur le gazon" (February 1963), and "Illusions de vol" (June 1964). "A la renommée de la tartine" appeared in *L'Archibras* (April 1967).

4.   In a very early essay on contemporary poets, "Three Women Poets: Renée Rivet, Joyce Mansour, Yvonne Caroutch," *Yale French Studies* 21 (Spring–Summer 1958), 40–48, Renée Hubert states that, contrary to that of younger poets who, "still half dazed by their surrealistic heritage understand only its Romantic aspects," Mansour's poetry evidences "aesthetic discoveries achieved through structure and not blindly groped for amidst lyrical storms" (48).

5.   With, to my knowledge, the sole exception of Marilyn Gaddis Rose, "Joyce Mansour's Bestiary," *Dada/Surrealism* 8 (1978), 107–14.

6.   Gloria Orenstein, "Les Femmes du surréalisme," *Obliques: La Femme surréaliste* 14–15 (1977), 61–63.

7.   Quoted in Harry Torczner, *Magritte: Ideas and Images* (New York: Abrams, 1979), 26.

8.   Renée Riese Hubert, "Surrealist Women Painters, Feminist Portraits," *Dada/Surrealism* 13 (1984), 72.

9.   Joyce Mansour's first collection of poetry, *Cris,* appeared in 1953 (Seghers), followed by *Déchirures* (Minuit, 1955) and *Carré blanc* (Le Soleil Noir, 1965). Her prose works were roughly contemporaneous: *Jules César* (Seghers, 1956), *Les Gisants satisfaits* (Pauvert, 1958) and *ça* (Editions du Soleil Noir, 1970). Quotations will be taken from the above editions, with one exception: references to *Jules César* will be to the version reprinted in *Histoires nocives* (Gallimard, 1973), which also contains "Iles flottantes." Translations for *ça* and *Histoires nocives* are taken from Pohlmann; all other translations mine.

10.   Gloria Orenstein, "Reclaiming the Great Mother: A Feminist Journey to Madness and Back in Search of a Goddess Heritage," *Symposium* 36:1 (Spring 1982), 45–70. See also Orenstein's subversive reading of *Nadja,* "*Nadja* Revisited: A Feminist Approach," *Dada/Surrealism* 8 (1978), 91–106.

11. Alicia Ostriker, "The Thieves of Language: Women Poets and Revisionist Mythmaking," in *The New Feminist Criticism: Essays on Women, Literature and Theory*, ed. Elaine Showalter (New York: Pantheon Books, 1985), 314–38; Estella Lauter, *Women as Mythmakers: Poetry and Visual Art by Twentieth-Century Women* (Bloomington: Indiana University Press, 1984), 169–70.

12. Xavière Gauthier, *Surréalisme et sexualité* (Paris: Gallimard, 1971).

13. An essay on her work figures in Matthews's *Surrealist Poetry in France* (Syracuse: Syracuse University Press, 1969), 164–77; selected poems are reprinted in his *Anthology of Surrealist Poetry,* and he contributed a review of her poetry to *Books Abroad* 40:3 (Summer 1966), 284–85. Mansour figures among the ten prose writers discussed in Matthews's *Surrealism and the Novel* (Ann Arbor: University of Michigan Press, 1966), 124–40.

14. Matthews, *Joyce Mansour* (Amsterdam: Rodopi, 1985).

15. See Ann Rosalind Jones, "Writing the Body: Toward an Understanding of *l'Ecriture féminine,"* in *The New Feminist Criticism: Essays on Women, Literature and Theory,* 361–77.

16. Claudine Herrmann, *Les Voleuses de langue* (Paris: Editions des femmes, 1976).

17. Herrmann also maintains that, historically, women have only had access to writing indirectly, through translations of others' texts and from other languages (chap. 2).

18. Hélène Cixous, "Le Rire de la Méduse," *L'Arc* 61 (1975), 49.

19. Hélène Cixous, "La Venue à l'écriture," in Hélène Cixous, Madeleine Gagnon, and Annie Leclerc, *La Venue à l'écriture* (Paris: 10/18, 1977), 29.

20. "The Sense of Smell" and "Wild Glee from Elsewhere," 67 and 107, respectively, in *Faire signe au machiniste;* with Ted Joans, *Flying Piranha* (New York: Bola Press, 1978).

Joyce Mansour and
Egyptian Mythology
Maryann De Julio

In 1953, Joyce Mansour's first collection of poetry, *Cris,* was published in Paris,[1] the city that Mansour, an Egyptian born in England, had adopted as her quasi-permanent place of residence.[2] *Médium,* the surrealist magazine that had a short run in Paris from 1952 to 1955, praised Mansour's *Cris* in particular.[3] From its inception in 1956, Mansour contributed regularly to *Le Surréalisme même,* the journal that replaced *Médium.*[4] Despite Mansour's apparent success, it is nonetheless notable that her avant-garde activity as a writer can be described as "doubly marginal" in the sense that Susan Suleiman uses the expression in her excellent article "A Double Margin: Reflections on Women Writers and the Avant-garde in France."[5] According to Suleiman, women are excluded by men from the centers of avant-garde activity, and they are perceived by critics – chiefly male – as marginal to any such literary movement which is itself, by definition, inherently marginal.[6]

Although Mansour's writing can be shown to conform generally to the broad sense of the term "Surrealism" as it was understood in the late forties, that is, as a "materio-mystical vision of the universe,"[7] her writing is of special interest for the "double center of marginality" that the work by a woman surrealist poet inevitably inscribes. My analysis of her oeuvre, especially the first collection, *Cris,* and, to some extent, the second, *Déchirures,*[8] both recollected in *Rapaces,*[9] will examine the poet's use of Egyptian mythology to put " 'woman' into discourse," as Alice Jardine describes it, and to explore the female body.[10] It can be argued that Mansour's poems particularize a longstanding tradition of eros and thanatos, and that they draw heavily upon the Egyptian cult of the dead to explore and express an inner psychic reality.[11] In short, I intend to read Mansour in the context of a universal view of culture, thereby shedding light on a surrealist aesthetic committed to the incarnation of contradictory realities which does, indeed, reinscribe the female as a speaking subject.[12]

To a great extent, the meaning of the title of Mansour's first collection, *Cris,* announces the position that she takes throughout her career as a surrealist writer. *Cris* can be understood as the expression of the pain inherent in the creative act reminiscent of birthing. Indeed, the first page of text in the collection vividly illustrates the title, recalling the tradition of the white goddess in Egypt, even though the deity Hathor, the most attractive form of this tradition,[13] symbolized by the flattened form of a female face with cow's ears, is not named explicitly:

Le clou planté dans ma joue céleste
  Les cornes qui poussent derrière mes oreilles
Mes plaies saignantes qui ne guérissent jamais
Mon sang qui devient eau qui se dissout qui embaume
Mes enfants que j'étrangle en exauçant leurs voeux
Tout ceci fait de moi votre Seigneur et votre Dieu.

(The nail planted in my celestial cheek
  The horns that grow behind my ears
My bleeding wounds that never heal
My blood that becomes water that dissolves that embalms
My children that I strangle while granting their wishes
All this made by me your Lord and your God.)

This emblematic text in *Cris* foretells Mansour's use of female body imagery to articulate a problematic attitude toward the creative act. Mansour is as ambivalent as the male Surrealists about the "whole issue of the female as the source and mechanism by which artistic creation is made possible."[14] However, Mansour's ambivalence does not exclude woman as subject in what can be read as conflicting views of her role in the creative act under the aegis of a pantheistic culture. In fact, the incantatory quality of the anaphoral structure of many of her poems seems to conjure up a female presence:

Femme debout dans un paysage nu
  La lumière crue sur son ventre bombé
Femme seule femme riche sans vice ni poitrine
Femme qui hurle son mépris dans des rêves sans repos
Le lit sera son enfer. (32)

(Woman standing in a bare landscape
  The garish light on her bulging belly
Woman alone woman rich without vice or bosom
Woman who howls her scorn in dreams without sleep
Bed will be her hell.)

The poet tends to express the anguish experienced by the individual female precisely when her creative power is most apparent. The Hathor emblem employed by Mansour in *Cris* recalls Hathor-as-fertility-goddess as well as Hathor-as-destructive-Eye sent in the form of a fierce lioness by Rê, the Great Spirit or Sun God, to devour the evil ones in the desert.[15] Mansour's use of the Hathor emblem conflates the two different Egyptian myths so that their separate outcomes are perceived in a single context, whereby the individual female is both the agent and the victim of her own creative power.

Elsewhere in *Cris,* we continue to perceive the eros/thanatos opposition on a performative level. Mansour puts eros in the service of thanatos when she uses it to represent the materiality of a preference for death:

Hier soir j'ai vu ton cadavre.
 Tu étais moite et nue dans mes bras.
J'ai vu ton crâne luisant
J'ai vu tes os poussés par la mer du matin.
Sur le sable blanc sous un soleil hésitant
Les crabes se disputaient ta chair.
Rien ne restait de tes seins potelés
Et pourtant c'est ainsi que je t'ai préférée
Ma fleur. (16)

(Yesterday evening I saw your corpse.
 You were moist and naked in my arms.
I saw your shining skull
I saw your bones thrust up by the morning sea.
On the white sand under a reluctant sun
Crabs quarreled over your flesh.
Nothing remained of your plump and dimpled breasts
And yet it is this way that I preferred you
My flower.)

The paradoxical status of the *je* in the above poem problematizes its erotic discourse: is it Mansour's poetic voice or the *je* as the other? What exactly is the subject's relation to the body in this text? Is it the poet's own reflection that she sees in a dream or is the *je* the universal subject, and the body the generic beloved? Even though the eros/thanatos opposition in the text is typical of the "materio-mystical" vision of Surrealism, our understanding of the text is enriched when we compare its 1953 literary context to an original Egyptian culture where "there was no dichotomy of spheres of activity"[16] and bisexuality was commonplace in the creation myths. From this perspective, the status of the *je* expressed by Mansour is disturbing insofar as the text must necessarily produce a split self in its contemporary inscription of a female subjectivity that reflects upon its objectification in a display of body parts.[17] The ironic stance implicit in such a position may well be characteristic of the postwar poets in France, but it is not exemplary of the surrealist project: to attain the marvelous, that point at which contradictions play themselves out.

Other examples of the eros/thanatos opposition in *Cris* recall the Egyptian cult of the dead and the two distinct beliefs about the fate of the deceased. According to one belief, "the deceased joined his ancestors who were already lodged in the cemetery on the edge of the desert and with them lived in a carefree existence on the model of that on earth – or would do so if his tomb was properly attended to. The other belief was that the soul soared up to join the stars and the sun and moon in their eternal round" (Clark 31). The mythology had to serve two purposes: to give the order whereby the universe was arranged, and to provide a series of symbols to describe the origin and development of consciousness (Clark 32–33).

The persuasive presence of the dead in Mansour's writing can be shown to serve ends similar to the original need for an Egyptian mythology even if the means by which these ends are achieved represent a deconstruction of the myth itself. For the most part, the Mansour texts collected in *Cris* do not present tombs that are properly attended to (33), nor do they present the soul on its journey heavenward. Instead, the texts alter the fate of the soul in a way that underscores the active role of the subject, *je,* in an erotic relationship with the object of its desire, *ton âme:*

Je pêcherai ton âme vide
  Dans le cercueil où moisit ton corps.
Je tiendrai ton âme vide.
J'arracherai ses ailes battantes
Ses rêves coagulés
Et je l'avalerai. (26)

(I will fish up your empty soul
  In the coffin where your body mildews.
I will hold your empty soul.
I will tear off its beating wings
Its clotted dreams
And I will devour it.)

It is known that the "Egyptians believed that the soul assumed the form of a bird in order to ascend from the darkness of the tomb to see the daylight and then returned to comfort its body" (Clark 141). By tearing off the wings of the soul ("J'arracherai ses ailes battantes"), the *je* of the above lines therefore denies the soul that ancient comfort and, furthermore, repudiates the more contemporary role of the surrealist poet as a medium who facilitates passage to the marvelous.

It can be argued that Mansour's use of Egyptian mythology strives to reclaim the power of the female subject as creator by reminding the reader of a former arrangement of the universe out of which Mansour then invents her own. In 1964, J. H. Matthews observed that "the inspiration of Mansour's poetry is not just erotic but *sadique.*"[18] And in 1958, Renée Riese Hubert stated in reference to Mansour's long prose poem *Jules César* that "God becomes a woman, but to no avail, because the rising Flood imprisons all alike."[19] I would submit that the sadism and impotence that can be found in Mansour's writing is the result of the conflict that she experiences as a woman poet in a surrealist tradition.[20] For Henri Peyre, "Surrealism rehabilitated woman and love poetry in our midst" because the Surrealists had "ceased to exile woman from poetry, as Rimbaud and his followers had attempted to do, or to worship and abuse her alternately as a vessel for all the treacheries of Satan, in Baudelairian fashion."[21] However, woman is not rehabilitated by the male surrealist poet as an autonomous subject and free agent, but rather she is rehabilitated as he dreams her to be: the agent who will liberate his imagination "from the mechanical forces which have made him a willing slave to tyranny and to war" (Peyre 33).

In a 1952 radio interview, André Breton talked about Surrealism and the "recuperation of the original powers of the spirit."[22] In Mansour's *Cris* of 1953, we find texts that attempt to "recuperate the original powers of the spirit" by "reclaiming a female creation myth as a viable model for female creativity,"[23] as Gloria Orenstein puts it with respect to the female surrealist writers and artists René (Colette Thomas), Kay Sage, Unica Zürn, Leonora Carrington, and Nadja:

Une femme créait en elle le soleil
  Et ses mains étaient belles à voir.
La terre s'ouvrait sous ses pieds fertiles
Et l'enveloppait de son haleine orangée
Fécondant ainsi la sérénité. (35)

(A woman created in her the sun
  And her hands were beautiful to see.
The earth opened under her fruitful feet
And swathed her in its orange breath
Thus fecundating serenity.)

Read in the context of Egyptian mythology, where "the rosy hue of the dawn sky, whether on the first morning or every day, is the blood emitted by Hathor or Isis – the names are interchangeable – when she bears her son" (Clark 89), the above text privileges a female brand of surrealist "materio-mysticism."

To the extent that one of the ambitions of Surrealism was to elevate the status of the dream by opening up to literature its domain (Peyre 30), Mansour's reclaiming a female creation myth as a viable model for female creativity radically questions man's dream of woman:

Femme debout épuisée épilée
  Ses jambes noires semblent en deuil de leur jeunesse
Elle appuie son dos cambré contre le mur hostile
Son dos cambré par les rêves des hommes
Et ne voit pas que l'aube est venue enfin
Tant sa nuit était longue. (13)

(Woman standing exhausted plucked
  Her black legs seem in mourning for their youth
She rests her bent back against the hostile wall
Her back bent by the dreams of men
And does not see that dawn has finally broken
So long was her night.)

It is apparent from this text that Mansour perceives man's dreams as a burden to woman ("Son dos cambré par les rêves des hommes"). Nevertheless, it is also apparent that Mansour construes woman's role as a creative one. The poet's ambivalence about woman's role in the creative act, mentioned previously, is exemplified in the above lines where woman's body is used to give birth to images whose source is not that of her own dreams.

Other surrealist ambitions and attitudes that are equally called into question by Mansour's reclaiming an Egyptian female creation myth as a viable model for her activity as a writer are the opening up of literature to the realm of insanity, the notion of the *femme-enfant,* and the definition of beauty. Mansour employs images of insanity to present the trauma of the female writer's search for originality which ends in a conflicted stance towards maternity and the materiality that wrought her own being:

Et moi je regrette ma fièvre de folle
J'ai pitié de mes parents dégénérés
Je voudrais effacer le sang de mes rêves
En abolissant la maternité. (23)

(And me I regret my madwoman's fever
I pity my degenerate parents
I would like to rub out the blood from my dreams
By abolishing maternity.)

As we have seen in the text about the birth of the sun, that is, Hathor's son, Mansour uses the point of view of the Mother Goddess to write about serenity. When Mansour writes either from the perspective of the *femme-enfant,* as in the above text where she is both autonomous subject and her parents' daughter, or when she places the *femme-enfant* into discourse as an image, i.e., the image par excellence of the surrealist woman invented by the male artist, the image loses its positive status:

Tu veux mon ventre pour te nourrir
  Tu veux mes cheveux pour te rassasier
Tu veux mes reins mes seins ma tête rasée
Tu veux que je meure lentement lentement
Que je murmure en mourant des mots d'enfant. (22)

(You want my belly to nourish you
  You want my hair to satisfy you
You want my loins my breasts my head shaved
You want me to die slowly slowly
To murmur like a child while dying.)

Although Mansour does not reject outright the image of the *femme-enfant,* the last text in *Cris* suggests that her reexamination of surrealist ambitions and attitudes causes her to reinvent surrealist images in the voice of a woman:

Les vices des hommes
  Sont mon domaine
Leurs plaies mes doux gâteaux
J'aime mâcher leurs viles pensées
Car leur laideur fait ma beauté. (38)

(The vices of men
  Are my domain
Their wounds my sweet cakes
I like to chew their vile thoughts
For their ugliness makes my beauty.)

In a sense, Mansour's text inverts the surrealist belief that woman's beauty is one of the keys to man's salvation. By making the ugliness of man's condition subject to her own discourse, Mansour's creative power assures her own beauty.

Originally, I stated that Mansour uses Egyptian mythology to put woman into discourse and to explore the female body. By means of the Hathor myth, the poet is able to present the double center of her version of Surrealism. On the one hand, her choice of Hathor – the goddess of fertility and the destructive Eye – confirms the Surrealists' ambivalent attitude toward the creative act. On the other, the Hathor myth displaces the surrealist myth of the *femme-enfant*.

Mansour continues to use Egyptian mythology and a female creation myth to reinscribe woman as subject in her second collection, *Déchirures*. In fact, we see a more fully developed metaphor in *Déchirures* for the expression of the specifically female trauma of the creative act. "Déchirures" signifies a rupture or an opening, a lacerated wound as it were, that the reader is again asked to relate to the birthing process. Although the wound connoted by Mansour's writing is female in nature, it can be seen as reminiscent of the wound in French poetry since Mallarmé, found "at the center of the text, within the I," as Mary Ann Caws puts it in her provocative study on reflection, *The Eye in the Text*, that is, the "wounded 'eye' in the mirror" that furnishes "a double vision of both passage and threshold"[24]:

Je me souviens de la matrice de ma mère
Elle était tendrement rosée
Et ses parois sentaient la peur. (120)

(I remember my mother's womb
It was delicately rosy
And its lining smelled of fear.)

Mansour thus succeeds in placing the female as speaking subject at the center of her own literary project by articulating the anxiety inherent in such a position. In "Surrealist Archives of Anxiety," Jeanine Plottel describes a similar anxiety in the "strong poet," as defined by Harold Bloom. Plottel displaces Bloom's reasoning whereby the strong poet's anxiety is a question of influence, that is, who sired his own creation, in both senses of the term. Instead, Plottel contends that the strong poet's anxiety over influence concerns whether he is a woman or a man.[25] For Plottel, the weak poet is "simply the poet who doesn't have any anxiety as to whether he is a woman or man" (123). In Mansour, it is clear that her anxiety does not arise from an uncertainty regarding her sex, but rather from the marginal status accorded her gender. Reminiscent of the surrealist game of the fifties, "L'Un dans l'autre," whose main idea was that any object can be contained in any other, Mansour gives literary expression to the history of women by means of a maternal metaphor:

Mon enfant est né dans le ventre de ma mère
Ses yeux bleus reflètent mon nom. (120)

(My child is born in the belly of my mother
Her blue eyes reflect my name.)

The image "ses yeux bleus" condenses the identities of the grandmother and the grandchild by creating a new relation between the two imagined subjects now defined by the woman writer as mother. What is most striking in the above lines is the way in which Mansour uses language to set up a reciprocity between naming and birthing, making both autonomously female activities that reclaim her past and her future.

In this way, Mansour succeeds in reinscribing herself as subject in the tradition of the great goddess, as well as modernizing Egyptian mythology, which was not a collection of texts but a language whose protagonists could be altered and whose connecting links between events in the mythical texts were generally a play on words (Clark 263–66). Mansour's adaptation of Egyptian myth to develop a new and personal mythology is thus in keeping with the surrealist exploration of myth during the immediate postwar years when the question of individual liberty emerges as a major surrealist preoccupation (Chadwick 99).

Notes

1. Joyce Mansour, *Cris* (Paris: Pierre Seghers, 1953).

2. Joyce Mansour wrote in French but she was of Egyptian origin, and born in Bowden, England, in 1928.

3. See Jean-Louis Bedouin's review of *Cris* in *Médium: communication surréaliste*, new series, 3 (May 1954), 42.

4. See J. H. Matthews, "Some Post-War Surrealist Poets," *Yale French Studies* 31 (May 1964), 152.

5. Susan R. Suleiman, "A Double Margin: Reflections on Women Writers and the Avant-garde in France," *Yale French Studies* 75 (1988), 153.

6. The case of Joyce Mansour is slightly different in that she did receive some critical attention. In 1962, in an interview with Jacqueline Peletier of *Le Monde,* André

Breton named Joyce Mansour one of the three best surrealist writers in the last 20 years. For Breton, however, Surrealism was not to be considered a movement, but rather "une méthode de connaissance, un mode de création et une éthique" (Le Monde, 13 January 1962, 9).

7. Anna Balakian, Surrealism and the Road to the Absolute (New York: E. P. Dutton, 1970), 213.

8. Joyce Mansour, Déchirures (Paris: Editions de Minuit, 1955).

9. Joyce Mansour, Rapaces (Paris: Pierre Seghers, 1960).

10. Alice Jardine, Gynesis: Configurations of Woman and Modernity (Ithaca: Cornell University Press, 1985), 33–34, cited in Susan Suleiman, "A Double Margin," 150.

11. In Joyce Mansour (Amsterdam: Rodopi, 1985), J. H. Matthews points out the direct and, more often, indirect mythological references to Egypt in Mansour's writings (28).

12. For a discussion of the "basic double center" of Surrealism, see Mary Ann Caws, The Poetry of Dada and Surrealism (Princeton: Princeton University Press, 1970), 19.

13. See R. T. Rundle Clark, Myth and Man: Myth and Symbol in Ancient Egypt (New York: Grove Press, 1960), 87–89.

14. See Whitney Chadwick, Myth in Surrealist Painting (Ann Arbor, Michigan: UMI Research Press, 1980), 26–28.

15. See Barbara Watterson, The Gods of Ancient Egypt (New York: Facts On File Publications, 1984), 124–33.

16. Clark, Myth and Man, 26.

17. See Mary Ann Caws's illuminating essay "Ladies Shot and Painted: Female Embodiment in Surrealist Art," in The Female Body in Western Culture, ed. Susan Rubin Suleiman (Cambridge: Harvard University Press, 1986), 262–87.

18. Matthews, "Some Post-War Surrealist Poets," 149.

19. Renée Riese Hubert, "Three Women Poets: Renée Rivet, Joyce Mansour, Yvonne Caroutch," Yale French Studies 21 (1958), 46.

20. For an illuminating discussion of the literary results of the repression of self-contradiction in women writers, see Barbara Johnson's perceptive essay "My Monster/My Self," in A World of Difference (Baltimore: The Johns Hopkins University Press, 1987), 144–54. Johnson focuses her remarks on Nancy Friday's My Mother/My Self, Dorothy Dinnerstein's The Mermaid and the Minotaur, and Mary Shelley's novel Frankenstein.

21. Henri Peyre, "The Significance of Surrealism," Yale French Studies 31 (May 1964), 32.

22. Cited by J. H. Matthews in "Poetic Principles of Surrealism," Chicago Review 15:4 (Summer–Autumn 1962), 42.

23. Gloria Feman Orenstein, "Reclaiming the Great Mother: A Feminist Journey to Madness and Back in Search of a Goddess Heritage," Symposium 36.1 (Spring 1982), 48.

24. See Mary Ann Caws, The Eye in the Text (Princeton: Princeton University Press, 1981), 23.

25. Jeanine Parisier Plottel, "Surrealist Archives of Anxiety," Yale French Studies 66 (1984), 122.

In the Interim: The Constructivist Surrealism of Kay Sage

Stephen Robeson Miller

In the autumn of 1938, André Breton visited the annual exhibition of the Salon des Surindépendants at the Porte de Versailles in Paris. He was accompanied by the painter Yves Tanguy and the Greek poet Nicolas Calas in the hope of discovering work that evoked what, in the *Surrealist Manifesto* of 1924, he had termed "the marvelous" – an art which, in its resolution of the seemingly contradictory states of dream and reality, conscious and unconscious, "produced a kind of absolute reality, or surreality." He was not to be disappointed. All of them quickly noticed six small paintings which showed a curious blend of flat geometric shapes and illusionistically rendered simple objects shrouded in a mood of disquiet (Fig. 1). The exhibition checklist identified the artist as "Kay Sage" and gave an address, 18 Quai d'Orleans on the Ile Saint Louis. "'Kay Sage' – man or woman? I didn't know," Yves Tanguy later recalled. "I just knew that the paintings were very strong."[1] Breton, however, felt that because of their strength, the paintings must surely have been done by a man.[2]

Although she had used her maiden name to sign her paintings since she began to paint "seriously" in 1936, Kay Sage had come to Paris in the spring of 1937 following legal separation from her Italian husband, Prince Ranieri di San Faustino.[3] Soon after her arrival in France, however, she had read Anaïs Nin's *House of Incest* and sought to meet its author. As Nin later recorded in her diary, "The Princess of San Faustino . . . an American woman . . . came to see me because she has known much anxiety and a sense of displacement. These she has recognized in the book." Nin also noted that Sage painted imaginary or symbolic "portraits of people with a few lines, an egg, a staircase, an arrow, a lightning rod, a ribbon, a serpentine, a knot, a firework, a tower, a circle"[4] – the very same paintings that had attracted Breton's attention at the Salon des Surindépendants. Both he and Nin had been quick to sense that these early surrealist paintings were imbued with an aura of purified form, geometry and silence that had an elusive identity of their own. Breton particularly responded to their atmosphere of disquieting tension, motionlessness and impending doom – emotive characteristics that Sage would continue to evoke throughout the next twenty-five years and some two hundred paintings and collages.[5] By

Fig. 1 Sage, *A Little Later*, 1938. Oil on canvas, 36 × 28 in. Denver Art Museum, gift of the Estate of Kay Sage Tanguy.

the end of 1938 and the close of the Surindépendants exhibition, Sage had become personally acquainted with the Surrealists, whose meetings were sometimes held at her Paris apartment.

The paintings that would make her work not only interesting but important to the history of Surrealism, however, were not to be executed for almost another ten years. *Interim* (Fig. 2) is one of her first mature works from the late 1940s. The distance which separates it from the compositions which Breton had admired in 1938 stems from the painting's subject. *Interim* depicts a monumental structure, vaguely reminiscent of an armature, composed of an interlocking tangle of piers, beams, wooden supports, ladders and frames, perched precariously and dramatically at the

124

edge of some steep precipice. Bits of cloth cling and furl themselves within and around the structure, while long ribbons of gauze wrap across the tower's girth. The pilings which support this skeletal construction drop off sharply at left, while creating a complex web of intricate geometry between the supports and the shadows they cast. In the distance, only the flat expanse of some desolate terrain is vaguely discernable through an immutable haze. The dramatic shadows which crawl across the scaffolding

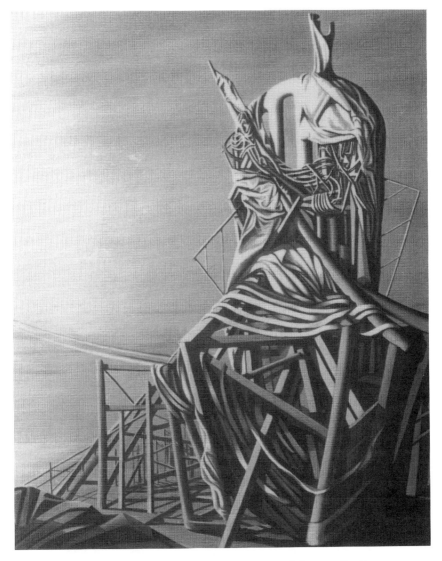

Fig. 2   Sage, *Interim,* 1949. Oil on canvas, 36 × 28 in. Private collection.

from the right are offset by the hard lines of a sulphuric light which envelopes from the left. A headlike protrusion at the top of the structure, with a smoothly cut out hole, lends a feeling of ferocity and menace to the construction. We are at a loss to explain exactly what the structure is or does or where we may be. The scene is bereft of human or biological forms and yet there is the sense that some kind of life has been here recently. A weight of doom hangs in the air and an ominous stillness prevails.

Yet while the atmospheric ambiguities and sense of enigma are found in the earlier work, it is the image which has changed. The images in the 1937–38 paintings that first caught the Surrealists' attention were identifiable, as Anaïs Nin's inventory of them proved. *Interim,* while retaining the geometric character of earlier work, now has a form which resists exact definition. This unspecified, yet authoritative, constructive subject makes Kay Sage's mature paintings unique within Surrealism. Several factors contributed to its realization. One was her ability to absorb various artistic influences to suit her needs. Another was her reliance upon the memories of past experiences which the Surrealists' interest in psychoanalysis encouraged.[6] To understand what these influences and experiences were, one must consider her childhood, her life in Italy, and the surrealist artists she came to know in Paris.

Katherine Linn Sage was born on June 25, 1898, in Albany, New York, the second daughter of a successful businessman and state senator, Henry Manning Sage, and the former Anne Wheeler Ward.[7] Although inherited wealth assured her security, Kay Sage's childhood was not to be stable by any means. When she was two years old her parents separated and her mother, an independent, high-strung and unconventional woman, began to make extended trips abroad for months at a time. Mrs. Sage always took her daughters with her. They usually traveled to London, Paris and Lucerne, and rented a villa every summer on the Italian Riviera at Rapallo. The situation caused havoc with the girls' formal education because they were constantly being taken from school to travel with their mother. As time passed, Kay and her sister, Anne, came to inhabit two completely different worlds: their mother's, which was adventurous, exotic and nomadic, and their father's, which was formal, genteel and controlled. The influence of mother and father was, however, equally strong. Kay Sage sympathized with both of them and her mature personality became an unpredictable blend of the conventional and the eccentric.

When Kay was nine years old, her mother took her for three months to Egypt, a trip which made a particularly strong impression on the little girl. They sailed up the Nile, visited Aswan, the Colossus of Memnon, the Temple of Philae, the Sphinx, the pyramids, and other ancient monuments. Here Kay felt transported. The climate and geography of the desert, punctuated by oases, the geometry of the pyramids and temples, the sharp light and sudden shadows which fell across monuments, and the

Nile itself, "brown or green, sluggish, and full of crocodiles," as she later described it,[8] is just the atmosphere evoked in the architectural forms, light and mood of her 1947 painting *Interim*.

In 1908, her parents divorced, and the split between her two worlds became emphatic. While the divorce was being settled, Mrs. Sage took her two daughters to San Francisco, where Kay had a traumatic experience that would haunt her for the rest of her life and have an impact on her art. The family arrived just after the great San Francisco earthquake, and in her unpublished autobiography, "China Eggs" (1955), she recalled:

There was never a day or night without an earthquake. The pictures would hang out from the walls and the doors would open and shut. I was in mortal terror all the time.[9]

As if this were not frightening enough, she had an experience in which she narrowly escaped being a victim. While roller-skating one day near the ruins of an old house that had been destroyed by the earthquake, she ventured down a nearby side street and found herself face to face with a horribly ugly man who proceeded to expose himself. He had

crazy green eyes and was laughing. I turned and raced down the street. When I got to the end of it, I saw that he also had turned and was going towards California Street, but he was watching me. I waited until he had gone around the corner towards my house and then I started slowly back. When I got to the corner, still undecided what to do, I saw that he had gone inside the gates of the ruined house and was peering out, waiting for me. He must have been watching me for quite a while and knew where I had come from. If I passed the gates, I know he would have pulled me in. There was no other human being in sight. I tell this only because I think that many of the fears to which I have always been subject must, in part, originate with this stay in San Francisco.[10]

Kay Sage was nearly sixty when she wrote of her experience in San Francisco, and the fact that she attributed lifelong anxieties to her sojourn there has important consequences for qualities found in her surrealist work. Through a keen interest in psychoanalysis and personal contact with Freud, André Breton encouraged his Surrealist group to turn to experiences from their individual childhoods as fuel for artistic visions. In this regard, Kay Sage was no exception. The ruins left by the earthquake that she remembered in connection with the threatening man, as well as those she saw in Egypt, are transformed in *Interim* into the incoherent architectural structure of her surrealist style. An ominous stillness prevails in *Interim* as in all of her surrealist work, much as would have been felt by the little girl on her roller skates who peered down a street knowing that, although "no other human being was in sight," a stranger lurked in the shadows ready to pull her in. There are no figures present in *Interim*, and on the rare occasions that they do occur in her surrealist work, it is usually in the guise of a threatening, shrouded phantom. The sense that a storm or even an earthquake has gouged the landscape in *Interim*, and what we see are the motionless remains, is as plausible an explanation as any for the mysterious environment the painting reveals. Clearly, in providing a record of her traumatic experiences in San Francisco, Sage left a psychological clue as to why her surrealist paintings took the form they have.

After San Francisco, Sage moved with her mother and sister to New York. In the divorce settlement it was decided that she would spend most of each year with her mother and a few months with her father on his Menands, New York, estate. Generous alimony permitted Mrs. Sage to continue her trips to Europe until the outbreak of war in 1914 intervened. Kay attended Brearley School in New York although, as usual, her education was often interrupted for traveling with her mother.

Even as a child, Sage had strong artistic inclinations and wanted "to do nothing else except draw or paint."[11] During the months of the year that she spent with her father, his house, Fernbrook, and that of his parents, Hilltop, near Albany, were the subjects of various watercolors. Even at this age Sage displayed in her watercolors a delight in depicting architecture and elements such as arches, walls and paths, which would remain an important part of her later canvases. Similarly, the residences she occupied with her mother in Italy, notably the Villa Baratta at Rapallo, would find their way into watercolors that she included with letters she wrote to her father.[12]

With the advent of World War I, Sage returned to America with her mother and settled near relatives in Middleburg, Virginia, where she attended Foxcroft School. There she illustrated the school's journal with silhouette drawings of fox hunts, and wrote her first poems. Years later, she would publish five books of verse which reflected the word games of one who had grown up speaking French, English and Italian interchangeably. It was also at Foxcroft that she became lifelong friends with Flora Whitney, whose mother, Gertrude Vanderbilt Whitney, founder of the Whitney Museum of American Art, would admire and encourage Sage's first oil paintings of the 1920s. Her formal education was completed at Foxcroft in 1916, and she spent the remaining war years with her mother in New York while working as a translator at the Censor Bureau.

After the war, in the autumn of 1919, her mother decided to return to the Riviera, but this time Sage chose to remain in the United States to study art. Her determination to study in Washington, D.C., however, had as much to do with a love affair as it did with art. She enrolled in drawing classes at the Corcoran School of Art, where she gained discipline by drawing parts of the human torso from plaster casts. When after several months the love affair ended, she coincidentally felt that she had absorbed everything the school had to offer, and chose to pursue her education in Europe.

Her art studies in Italy would be more serious. Sage settled in Rome in the fall of 1920 and began taking drawing and painting lessons privately.

Soon thereafter, she also attended the British and French academies and the Scuola Libera delle Belle Arti (Free School of Fine Arts). However, she decided that she learned more without the professors' assistance. She later wrote:

I drew from life at various academies, always staying away the day the professor came to criticize, and met an artist called Onorato Carlandi, who was to be my inspiration. He was old . . . and I was inspired not only by his painting but by his philosophy. His creed was "If you are alone, you will be completely yourself," and he used to say it endlessly. . . . He did not teach me to paint, he did not even try. But he taught me to think as I had not thought before. He was the head of a group known as the Twenty-Five of the Roman Countryside. Once a week they set out by street-car, by train (third class) or by horse-cart to some previously selected place in the campagna. There each settled down and painted. The results were judged before lunch. The winner had to pay for the lunch in the nearest Osteria. Once I paid and was very proud . . . I made no friends in Rome outside of these. I saw no one except the people I worked with. I think I was almost completely happy.[13]

And of this time in relation to her later surrealist paintings, she wrote:

I think my perspective idea of distance and going away is from my formative years in the Roman Campagna. There is always that long road and the feeling it gives that it goes a long way, and living near the Mediterranean, the sea and the boats, the feeling of the sun.[14]

In addition to the expansive vistas, many of the landscape paintings from her formative years in the Roman countryside demonstrate a compositional device which she would use frequently in her later surrealist paintings. The painting *Landscape with Poplar* (1923) (Fig. 3) is a good example. By placing large forms in the foreground or middle ground – in this case, a ruined brick building and a large poplar tree – and pushing them to the far side of the picture, as seen here at left, Sage emphasizes the expansiveness of the landscape which fills the rest of the painting. The device is used in *Interim* also, in which the large forms of the foreground are pushed to the right. The result of such staging always led to the understated dramatic effect that is a part of her mature work.

Sage settled down to paint, spending the winter months in Rome with her mother at an apartment in the Palazzo Rospigliosi on the Piazza del Quirinale, opposite what was then the Royal Palace, and her summers at the rented seventeenth-century Villa Baratta in Rapallo. At about the same time that she painted *Landscape with Poplar,* she met and fell in love with Ranieri di San Faustino, a young nobleman who was living with his mother not far away at the Palazzo Barberini. While Sage was not eager to be distracted from her painting, the prince was not like other aristocrats she had met. For one thing, he played the piano like a concert pianist and, she thought, was actually "just as mad as I was . . . could understand my fantastic imaginings and not only tolerate them but feel the same way."[15] Here, then, was a man who seemed to share her values as well as her back-

Fig. 3 Sage, *Landscape with Poplar*, 1932. Oil on canvas, 11 × 14¾ in. Mattatuck Museum, Waterbury, Connecticut, gift of the Estate of Kay Sage Tanguy.

ground. They were engaged and, two years later on March 30, 1925, married in Rome. Following a papal blessing at St. Peter's, Sage became a "Princess" – a title by which even the Surrealists would address her many years later.[16]

The first few years of the marriage were happy. Ranieri moved into the Palazzo Rospigliosi apartment and they spent their summers in Rapallo, much as she had done previously. They also had an active social life – too active, she felt – but she did not find the milieu of Roman nobility very interesting. Worst of all, her new life continually intruded on her painting activities. In time, the constant distractions which she could not avoid tired her, and she gave up trying to paint. Her husband did not have the strength of character she had originally believed. While "all his instincts were correct," he was unable to "pull up his roots and make something of his potential qualities," she later wrote. Besides giving or attending parties, "there was nothing to do in Roman Society. So Ranieri played golf and I did nothing."[17] As a result, the years she spent with Ranieri di San Faustino were her least artistically productive.

Around 1930, Sage experienced an unusual psychic event that was probably to play a role in her later surrealist imagery. One night, while sleeping in her bedroom at the Palazzo Rospigliosi, she was suddenly awakened by the sound of a roaring, crackling fire, as well as people shouting incoherently and what seemed like blocks of wood being hit together. She immediately ran to the window and opened the shutters to see where the noises came from. She knew that the façade of the Palazzo del Quirinale on the opposite side of the square was covered with wooden scaffolding for repairs, and thought that perhaps the scaffolding had caught fire. When she pulled open the shutters to check, however, there was complete silence – the scaffolding was intact and no one was in the street. She assumed that she must have been dreaming, although she was sure that she had not been. No sooner had she closed the shutters and gone back to bed, when the sound of fire, shouting and knocking wood began again. Again she opened the window only to find total silence outside. After the same thing happened twice again she ran, overcome by fright, to awaken her husband. When he checked the room, however, nothing of the sort happened. Not long thereafter, Sage learned from a priest that her experience matched exactly that of a French abbé of the sixteenth century who had described such an occurence in his memoirs. Sage was convinced that she had encountered the same supernatural forces that the abbé had.

As had been the case with her experiences in San Francisco, the fact that Kay Sage needed to record this psychic event in her memoir, "China Eggs," demonstrates the significance it had for her. The episode is interesting in relation to her surrealist work for several reasons. It places the scaffolding erected on the façade of the Palazzo del Quirinale at the center of attention. If a word could describe the forms in the painting *Interim,* it would probably be "scaffolding." Yet the scaffolding-constructive forms that were the hallmark of her mature surrealist iconography did not appear in her work until the mid-1940s, fully fifteen years after the psychic episode in which scaffolding played a central role, and ten years after she had begun painting in a surrealist mode. Perhaps the strange experience marked this particular form in Sage's mind as an enigma which would require exploration at a later time.

Toward the mid-1930s, Sage met at Rapallo the expatriate American poet Ezra Pound, who also spent his summers there. Sage and Pound spent much time together discussing poetry and art. The fact that she began painting again in 1934–35, just when she was regularly seeing Pound, is not coincidental. The paintings which she executed at this time were abstract – two-dimensional, flat, interlocking geometric shapes in muted colors – and several carried the title "Vorticist." A major departure from her earlier representational landscapes of the 1920s, these abstract paintings, by virtue of their titles, can be directly linked to her contact with Pound, for he had been a significant participant in establishing the Vorticist movement in England in the second decade of this century. Not only was he a close friend of the movement's leader, Wyndham Lewis, but he had given the aesthetic its name (from "vortex") and founded its periodical, *Blast*. It seems likely that her conversations with Pound provided the impetus which caused her, at the age of thirty-seven, to pursue her painting determinedly. From that time on she kept one of her Vorticist paintings in a prominent place in her studio, since they meant for her the beginning of her painting seriously.

Sage's resolve to follow a painting career caused her finally to bring an end to her unhappy marriage and, with it, the distractions that had thwarted her attempts to continue painting earlier. Although she had to wait until 1939 to obtain a papal annulment, she and Ranieri di San Faustino were legally separated in 1935, after which she moved to Milan. There, a year later, she exhibited her Vorticist paintings in her first solo exhibition, at the Galleria del Milione.

The abstract paintings that she did between 1934 and 1937 had important consequences for her later surrealist work. Firstly, the Vorticist paintings allowed her to consider abstraction as a viable artistic alternative to the work that she had done previously, and one which would open the way to further artistic revelations in Paris. Secondly, her abstract period allowed her to develop a sensibility for the compositional geometry of straight lines and diagonals that underlies the forms in *Interim* as well as the rest of her mature surrealist work. It could be said, therefore, that geometric abstraction predisposed her to think of composition in terms of structural components. The emphasis on structural geometry is one of the main reasons why Sage's mature surrealist work, as exemplified by *Interim,* is unique within the surrealist movement.

In 1937, following her December exhibition in Milan, Sage moved to Paris with the intention of pursuing her art career once and for all. As already noted, she took an apartment on the Ile Saint Louis and settled down to paint. On her last trip to Paris some six months earlier, she had met by chance the surrealist painter Kurt Seligmann and his wife, who were staying at the same hotel. The Seligmanns' room was next to Sage's, and when their door was open, she had walked past and seen his paintings set about the room. She introduced herself for a closer look and ended by speaking at length with him about the pictures and painting in general.[18] This was her first personal contact with a surrealist painter and probably influenced her decision to pursue painting in Paris just as soon as her Milan exhibition closed. Her first surrealist paintings, which Anaïs Nin had admired and recorded in her diary, were begun shortly after her move to the French capital.

Surrealism by 1937 was very much an established movement and, although increasingly international in scope, was French in origin. With the First International Surrealist exhibition having been held in 1936, and a large survey of the movement shown at the Museum of Modern Art in New York the same year, Surrealism was, by the time Sage settled in

Paris, a force with which to be reckoned. Breton and his group held forth at regular meetings in various cafés, and Sage quickly became aware of their dynamic presence. Ezra Pound had introduced her to the lessons of Vorticism and now she was ready to embrace the revelations that only Surrealism could provide. During almost a decade, until the mid-1940s, her work underwent its final phase of development, as she came under the influence of various Surrealists and, perhaps most especially, the proto-surrealist work of the Italian painter Giorgio de Chirico.

As the painting *Interim* makes apparent, Sage was to develop her surrealist imagery along illusionistic lines, despite the geometric character of the forms themselves. Hers would be a descriptive form of Surrealism, in which the scene is unreal, but the setting and the individual objects in it are painted with fidelity. Giorgio de Chirico provided the foundation for her work, as he had for that of Dali, Delvaux, Max Ernst, Leonor Fini, Leonora Carrington, Magritte and Tanguy, among others, in his early "metaphysical" paintings in which dissociated objects were painted literally, as if in a dream. These early works by de Chirico were held in the highest esteem by Breton, and Sage was quick to respond to their oneiric intensity. In her case, however, the influence of de Chirico would be for a time more specific: his iconography of silent squares, peopled with mannequins and mourning figures in the evening light, wrapped in shadows, bounded by far horizons, curtained doorways and ancient architecture, would find a veiled echo in many of her paintings for the next several years. Wooden planking, tilted or exaggerated perspective, shrouded figures, and eggs appear in these first surrealist paintings as direct quotations from the metaphysical de Chirico.

Yet while certain correspondences between Sage's first surrealist works and the early works of de Chirico is undeniable, they have been overstated in the past—even by the present writer. The subject matter of arches, walls and even piazzas was hardly the monopoly of de Chirico, for Sage herself had turned frequently to architectural subjects since her first adolescent works, and she had always been attracted to walls, arches, ruins and distant vistas, as her paintings done in the Roman Campagna testify. It is probably not possible, therefore, to determine for certain the extent to which many of the motifs in her first surrealist paintings actually derive from the Italian master or from her own long residence in Italy. As a result, what has formerly been ascribed solely to the influence of de Chirico in her work is, more accurately, the complex combination of this powerfully emotive imagery and her own strong attachment to Italy itself.

Sage had been in Paris nearly a year by the time the Galerie des Beaux Arts mounted its Exposition Internationale du Surréalisme in the winter of 1938. Although she was not yet personally acquainted with Breton and his group, the exhibition provided her first opportunity to see surrealist art on a large scale. This, perhaps more than any other single event, reinforced her feeling of identification with the Surrealists, and intensified her ambition to make contact with them. In March of that year, Alfred H. Barr, Jr., the director of the Museum of Modern Art in New York and organizer of the museum's 1936 survey "Fantastic Art, Dada, Surrealism," was in Paris, and Sage made it a point to contact him. Mrs. Barr wrote that Sage

would receive us and give us a drink at the end of extreme work. . . . She was immensely shy, rather awed by Alfred. She tried to suggest that she had a feeling of belonging with the Surrealists in general. I would say that . . . in 1938 she was snuggling up to the Surrealists. To us she was very kind, very nice. She spoke in vague and exalted terms about Surrealism and showed Alfred her pictures in the manner of de Chirico with their steep perspectives.[19]

It was at this time that Sage acquired her first painting, a metaphysical de Chirico titled *The Surprise* (1914) (now in the collection of the Williams College Museum of Art, Williamstown, Massachusetts), a particularly bleak work depicting a series of arches that, in their stark severity, seem close to her own taste for pared-down architectonic forms. This purchase was followed by her first surrealist acquisition, an oil painting by Yves Tanguy titled *I Am Waiting for You* (1934) – a title which would prove very prophetic indeed.

In the autumn of 1938, at the time that her six surrealist compositions were included in the Salon des Surindépendants, Sage finally made contact with Breton and his group. On the strength of her paintings, she was asked to join their circle, the meetings of which she often hosted at her apartment. When James Thrall Soby, the art historian and de Chirico scholar, and his wife accompanied the Barrs to Paris the next winter, they were to meet so many painters and writers at Sage's apartment that Soby later described it as a salon for Surrealists.[20] But Sage's acceptance as an official surrealist painter was to provide more than the camaraderie of a milieu of which she had long desired to be a part, for among the group she met and fell in love with the painter Yves Tanguy, whom she would eventually marry.

The impact that the art of Tanguy made upon her may also be felt during this period. Tanguy's paintings were among the most integral of all surrealist art, depicting biomorphic mineral forms in endless variation, casting black shadows and strewn across a submarine plain beneath a brooding sky. Sage's initial contact with Surrealism, and Tanguy's work in particular, caused her to experiment with biomorphic shapes intermittently for several years. A number of paintings (*Monolith,* 1942; *A Finger on the Drum,* 1940; *Lost Record,* 1940; *At the Appointed Time,* 1942, among others), include biomorphic forms reminiscent of shapes in Tanguy's paintings, juxtaposed among the more hard-edged architectonic forms. While Tanguy's influence in terms of form was eventually to dissipate altogether from her work, it could be said that she would come to share a state of mind with him – for Sage after the mid-1940s became as obsessed with the variety of scaffolding and hard-edged structures that inhabited her wastelands as Tanguy was with the biomorphic shapes that populated his scenes.

By the spring of 1939, Sage and Tanguy were romantically involved. They visited the art dealer Pierre Matisse at his summer house at Rambouillet,[21] near Paris, and then spent the summer at the Lac du Bourget in the Rhône valley near Switzerland. There, the painters Matta and Gordon Onslow-Ford had rented a country house, the Chateau de Chemillieu, and had invited other Surrealists to join them in painting, writing poetry and criticizing each other's work. Just as she had done in school years earlier, Sage wrote a play, but in this one all the guests at Chemillieu had a part.

With the declaration of war in September, Sage returned to Paris and began making plans with the French minister of education, Yvon Delbos, for a series of exhibitions in New York, the proceeds of which would be used to help artists involved in the crisis in France. It was decided that the artists chosen for the series would travel to America; thus, Sage made it possible for Tanguy to inaugurate the series and join her in New York in December. Her efforts resulted in the foundation of the Society for the Preservation of European Culture, which, although short-lived, came to the aid of other artists. Under its auspices, the painter Jean Hélion, incarcerated in a concentration camp in France, had an exhibition in New York; the English painter Gordon Onslow-Ford was invited by the society to deliver a series of lectures on Surrealism at the New School for Social Research (lectures which had far-reaching consequences by introducing young American painters, such as Jackson Pollock, to automatism).[22] Sage also arranged and financed the passage to New York for Matta and his wife. Later in 1941, she assisted Breton and Max Ernst, among others, to reach New York and settle in Greenwich Village. For a time, she even supported Breton and his family financially.

Having settled with Tanguy in an apartment on Washington Square in Greenwich Village, Sage began to paint once again, as Pierre Matisse planned to give her an exhibition at his gallery in the spring. In the meanwhile, her apartment became a gathering place for all the expatriate European Surrealists; the painter Matta wrote:

Kay and Yves were somehow my "Maecenas" as when she arranged for my exile to New York. I was just beginning to paint and I arrived there without work, money or knowing anyone but them. When in Waverly Place, Kay's was the meeting point of the first of us that came to New York – Buñuel, Paalen, her cousin John Goodwin, David and Susie Hare. It could be said that I personally got in touch with the young American painters through these meetings as I became through David Hare a friend of the 1054 group of 1940: Baziotes, Kamerowski, Gorky, Pollock, Motherwell and with the years each and all of them. Kay was very private about her work, almost shy, as if she was an intruder. This feeling I think came from her more "painterly" than automatistic method that was present in the surrealist group as a form of searching the infra-red side of reality that motivated us all.[23]

Fig. 4 Sage, *Danger, Construction Ahead,* 1940. Oil on canvas, 44×62 in. Yale University Art Gallery, New Haven, gift of Mr. and Mrs. Hugh J. Chisholm, Jr.

In preparing for her Matisse Gallery exhibition, Sage executed her most ambitious surrealist painting to date, *Danger, Construction Ahead* (1940) (Fig. 4). This painting illustrates the desolate wasteland that she favored and the dramatic composition, in which large forms are placed close to one side of the foreground, emphasizing distance. However, the character of the foreground forms – four spiky obelisks, and the bridgelike ramp which stretches from them across the desert plain to distant mountains at right – is probably the result of the influence of another surrealist painter whom she knew and admired, the Austrian Wolfgang Paalen. It so happened that in the spring of 1940, Paalen was passing through New York on his way to Mexico, and he had an exhibition at the Julien Levy Gallery in April. Sage acquired a small oil from the exhibition, *Study for Totem Landscape of My Childhood* (1937, Museum of Modern Art, New York, Bequest of Kay Sage Tanguy), and she entertained Paalen in Greenwich Village. One of the centerpieces of Paalen's exhibition was his monumental painting *Fata Alaska* (1938) (Fig. 5), which Sage had also seen at the 1938 International Surrealist Exhibition in Paris. Sharp obelisk forms dominate the skyline of Paalen's painting as they do in Sage's and, in addition, Paalen included a bridgelike ramp that stretches horizontally between the vertical spires much as it does in *Danger, Construction Ahead.* The parallels of these motifs, despite differences in their execution, are such that it seems likely

Sage had *Fata Alaska* in mind when she began painting *Danger, Construction Ahead,* at just the time of Paalen's exhibition. *Danger, Construction Ahead* is therefore another example of Sage's iconographic experimentation as it evolved toward the mature imagery exemplified by *Interim.*

For the next several years, Sage explored other imagery that was characteristic of more established Surrealists. She made gouaches that utilized the decalcomania technique of Dominguez and Ernst; collages that included Victorian female figures à la Delvaux; and a series of relief works with lace reminiscent of the shadow boxes associated with Joseph Cornell. Other aspects of her work – the wasteland setting, the shadows, and the titles that are unrelated to the images portrayed – belong to the surrealist

Fig. 5 Wolfgang Paalen (1905–1959), *Fata Alaska,* 1938. Oil on canvas, 48 × 36 in. Private collection, Mexico.

lexicon in general. Her concern for a wasteland setting, as in *Danger, Construction Ahead,* was shared by many Surrealists: Ernst, Magritte, Masson, Matta and Toyen had all made use of it at one time or another. Salvador Dali relied frequently upon a barren plain, and in Tanguy's work it was invariable. Similarly, the shadows which Sage often employed had long been part of the surrealist repertory, and serve to heighten the poetry and illusion of deep perspective. The wasteland setting and shadows also contribute to the sense of detachment, isolation, melancholy, loneliness and disquiet in her paintings as in those of her colleagues. Finally, her use of titles that appear unrelated to the images portrayed, and therefore contribute another dimension of poetry and mystery, was typically surrealist.[24] Considering her exploration of imagery and her embrace of characteristics particular to Surrealism, it comes as no surprise to learn that Sage gradually assembled a distinguished private collection of work by Delvaux, Ernst, Cornell, Gorky, Marcel Jean, Masson, Matta, André Breton, and Miró, among others.

While traveling in the western United States, Sage and Tanguy were married in Reno, Nevada, on August 17, 1940. Later, after visiting Alexander and Louisa Calder in Roxbury, Connecticut, and the poet Hugh Chisholm and his wife Bridgette in neighboring Woodbury, they became familiar with the rural western part of the state that still permitted easy access to Manhattan. As a result, in 1941 they left Greenwich Village and rented a house in the center of Woodbury, later buying a nineteenth-century farmhouse with barn and sixty acres on the outskirts of town. There, they transformed the house into a "surrealist museum," installed marble-topped tables and ice cream parlor chairs in the dining room, a billiard table in the living room, and entertained the exiled European Surrealists on weekends.[25] In addition to the collection of surrealist paintings and curiosities, Sage hung the bathrooms with towels on which appeared her monogram as both Princess di San Faustino and Kay Sage Tanguy.[26] All was kept under surveillance by two Siamese cats. Their neighbors from the surrounding countryside included such artists and writers as Peter Blume, André Masson, Hans Richter, David Hare, Arshile Gorky, Muriel Streeter, Malcolm Cowley, Matthew Josephson, and Julien Levy, in addition to the Calders and Chisholms. It was here that the couple lived and worked for the rest of their lives.

Sage's years in Connecticut with Tanguy were to be her happiest and most productive.[27] Ensconced in the countryside, and using the barn as a studio, she was to enter the final phase of development of her work. This full maturation of imagery occurred in the mid-1940s and, interestingly enough, at a time when Breton and many exiled Surrealists returned to Europe at the end of the war. Art historians have traditionally viewed postwar Surrealism as a movement that had lost its impetus, and which consequently did not produce any new artistic visions of consequence, but for Kay Sage nothing could be further from the truth. In 1946 she introduced into a painting called *Bounded on the West by the Land Under Water* (now in the collection of the University of Michigan Museum of Art, Ann Arbor) the scaffolding tower that marks the end of her search for a personal surrealist idiom. Scaffolding would quickly become the hallmark of her work and distinguish it from that of all other surrealist artists. However, although she had been interested in architectonic forms since her paintings done in the Roman Campagna twenty years earlier, there was no precedent for the scaffolding tower that appeared with sudden integrity in her work of 1946. It was this scaffolding and its attendant architectural forms that she would explore obsessively in many guises for the rest of her life. As has been seen, the scaffolding assumed a particularly monumental and refined character in her painting *Interim*.

Questions remain: Why, in the forties, did the structural iconography of a painting such as *Interim* suddenly take form? And why did Sage become so obsessed with it? The answers are probably best understood as a combination of reasons. As much as the scaffolding imagery can be identified as particular to Kay Sage, so must she have identified with it. Considered in this way, the idea of the scaffolding can be seen in relation to the troubling personal experiences of her life. It must be remembered that she had known an unsettling and lonely childhood, marked by many problems: her parents' separation and subsequent divorce; the peripatetic existence that followed as she was shuttled between Europe and America; her frightening experiences at an impressionable age in San Francisco; her mother's addiction to morphine and her sister's early death from tuberculosis; an unhappy first marriage; the devastation of two world wars on a continent she knew even better than her native country. When viewed as a structure that is fragile yet unyielding, protective yet vulnerable, the scaffolding may be seen for what it must have meant to her – a metaphor for the self and the painful experiences she had known and was able to surmount. Her *identification* with the scaffolding imagery that informs *Interim* therefore accounts for her obsession with it.

It must also be remembered that in Italy some fifteen years earlier, she had had a psychic experience in which the scaffolding that she could see from her bedroom window played an important part. The fact that she not only wrote of this episode many years later in her memoir, but spoke of it to Naum Gabo and his wife in Connecticut, may be an indication that she considered it a factor in the realization of imagery in a painting such as *Interim*. Gabo himself could have played a role in its development. In 1946, the same year that Sage introduced the scaffolding into her painting, Gabo moved to America and settled in Woodbury, Connecticut. Although Sage did not meet him until 1947,[28] after completing the painting in which the scaffolding first appears, the presence of the Russian Constructivist sculptor and their subsequent close friendship could only help to reinforce and encourage the *constructed* character of the scaffolding as it appears in *Interim* and later paintings. It is interesting to note, too, that Sage owned a work by Mondrian (which she later sold to the painter Leon Kelly),[29] and his purist aesthetic of lines intersecting at right angles could have reinforced this aspect in *Interim* and other paintings.

With regard to possible specific influences of surrealist imagery, several correspondences are worth noting. In 1931, Alberto Giacometti made a wooden construction called *Cage* that could be the sculptural equivalent of the structure in *Interim,* and which Sage may have remembered. Or, through her admiration for the early paintings of de Chirico, she may have been intrigued by the studio carpentry that occasionally crowded his pictures from 1916 to 1918. Even the wirelike mesh in Oscar Dominguez's *Nostalgia for Space,* then in the collection of Peggy Guggenheim's Art of This Century Gallery in New York, could have affected her. To some degree, all these examples may be relevant. A combination of artistic and psychological factors contributed therefore to the creation of an imagery with its own identity.

With the distinctive individuality of her work after 1946 came its inclusion in an increasing number of group and national exhibitions. Sage participated in the 1947 Paris and Prague international surrealist exhibitions, as well as the 1955 Tokyo exhibition. She was also represented in over fifty national shows during her lifetime, including exhibitions at Art of This Century, the Whitney Museum of American Art, the Carnegie Institute, the San Francisco Museum of Art, the Art Institute of Chicago, and the Museum of Modern Art. She had solo exhibitions at the Pierre Matisse Gallery in 1940 and the Julien Levy Gallery in 1940 and 1947; in 1950 the Catherine Viviano Gallery of New York became her dealer. By the time of her death in 1963, Sage's work was in the collections of the Metropolitan Museum of Art, the Art Institute of Chicago, the Museum of Modern Art, and the Whitney Museum of American Art, among others.

Sage's mature painting years were not to last as long as they might have, had circumstances been different for her. Early in 1955, Yves Tanguy died suddenly from a cerebral hemorrhage, and the emotional loss for Sage was one from which she never recovered.[30] After his death, she withdrew and wrote her memoir, "China Eggs," although she did not write about her life with Tanguy because it was too close to her. When she finally began to paint again, later in the year, her pictures were particularly dark and brooding, reflecting her state of mind. Then in 1956 Sage began to have symptoms of double cataracts, and as her eyesight deteriorated over the next several years, her anxiety increased. It was hard enough for her to live without Tanguy, but the gradual loss of her eyesight – which would eventually force her to stop painting entirely – was unimaginable.[31] In her private notebooks she began to contemplate suicide.

Alone and with health problems, Sage began to put as much energy into writing poetry as into painting. She had written poetry occasionally since her school days in Virginia and in Milan in 1937 published a small book of children's verse in Italian called *Piove in giardino* (It's Raining in the Garden). Now, in the late 1950s, she published three more books of poetry: *Demain, Monsieur Silber* (Paris: Seghers, 1957); *The More I Wonder* (New York: Bookman Associates, 1957); and *Faut dire ce qui est* (Paris: Debresse-Poésie, 1959). The verse in all these books betrays, in typical surrealist fashion, a delight in double-entendre word games but with an edge particular to their trilingual author:

English, French and Italian
I can read and write in all of these;
But actually they are translations
I think in Chinese.

With regard to her two creative outlets, she was to comment in "Occupations":

When I'm tight
I write.
To paint
I must be sober.
There might be something in this
that I should think over.

Allusions to her painted images, the titles of her paintings or her despairing state of mind also appear in the verse:

I have built a tower on despair
you hear nothing in it, there is nothing to see;
There is no answer when, black on black,
I scream, I scream, in my ivory tower.

Jean Dubuffet, who contributed the illustrations to her last book of verse, *Mordicus* (Alès: P. A. Benoit, 1962), wrote:

These poems impressed me deeply with their startling elliptical brevity, their tacit violence and, above all, their radically anti-intellectual, anti-intelligent stand. They seemed very exceptional to me, unlike any other poems that I knew, and curiously in accord with my own humor and positions. My attachment to these poems never diminished and I feel about them today as strongly as when I first read them.[32]

By 1958, her eyesight had deteriorated to the point where she found it difficult to continue working in oil, and decided to turn to collages instead. The collages depict various arrangements of rocks; some are strewn across what may be the sandy bottom of a river bed, while others are piled high to form monoliths. Occasionally, they include pieces of drapery or floating white cloths that contrast with the dark solidity of the stones (Fig. 6), just as she used drapery in the oil paintings to contrast with the scaffolding's angular lines. The rock collages with their inky black shadows bear a re-

Fig. 6 Sage, *The World of Why*, 1958. Collage, ink, wash, and watercolor on paper, 16¾ × 12¾ in. Private collection, Connecticut.

semblance to Tanguy's paintings, but unlike his, the forms are clearly identifiable. According to an eyewitness, the photographer Alexandra Darrow, Sage executed collages by taking a sheet of paper and brushing it at random with diluted bluish gouache, then cutting shapes from the sheet and darkening one side with ink to create volume. The shapes were then attached to a second sheet of washed gouache.[33] As always with Sage, an economy of means and form produced a dramatic and monumental effect.

Sage finally underwent an operation for her double cataracts in 1959 in Boston, but the results were only partially successful. She had to resign herself to the fact that she would never see normally again, but this was difficult for her to accept. In desperation, she attempted to take her life using barbiturates. As a result, her friends rallied and her dealer Catherine Viviano mounted a retrospective exhibition of her work in 1960. Pierre Matisse urged her to continue the compilation of a catalogue raisonné of Tanguy's work, and there was the project with Dubuffet of the poem book, *Mordicus*. "The only time I ever saw her happy in her later years – as happy as she had been when Tanguy was alive – was when she was working on that book with Dubuffet," Hans Richter commented.[34]

Friends remember that one day while visiting at Town Farm, Sage suddenly interrupted the conversation and reached for a wicker basket that lay nearby. She began to pull pieces of wicker from the basket – and that action was the beginning of a group of about twenty mixed-media collage reliefs.[35] She had not painted or made collages for three years and now, with a final burst of energy, she poured herself into making relief works that were a visually less demanding outlet for her creativity. Using tinfoil, marbles, glass, wire, hypodermic needle covers, empty bullet cartridges, small stones and plywood, as well as wicker, the collage reliefs preserve the imagery of earlier work. *Contraband* (Fig. 7) is a complex arrangement of rocks and strips of wood that, as a result of its relief, introduces actual shadows as an integral part of the composition. Through the use of mixed media, Sage was able to create works that still preserved the imagery of *Interim* and other paintings. The relief collages were the basis for her last exhibition, at the Catherine Viviano Gallery, in 1961. She even wrote a poem about these works for the catalogue of the exhibition:

These are games without issue
some have been played
and are therefore static.
Others will be
and can still be played.
There are no rules;
no one can win or lose.
They are arbitrary,
and irrelevant,
but there is no reason why
anything should mean more
than its own statement.

Two and two
do not necessarily make four . . .

If that is a scientist at my door,
please tell him
to go away.

Fig. 7 Sage, *Contraband*, 1961. Stones and playwood on cardboard, 20×15 in. Mattatuck Museum, Waterbury, Connecticut, gift of the Estate of Kay Sage Tanguy.

In December 1962, in an effort to bring her out of her depression, the art dealer Julien Levy bought her a tape recorder and encouraged her to become interested in music. "It's no use, Julien," she replied, "I am only interested in Surrealism."[36] A few days later, on a dreary January afternoon, she shot herself in the heart.

Kay Sage's surrealist work succeeds on several levels. It captures "the marvelous" – the beauty which Breton championed for its provocation of contradictory states simultaneously: the real and the unreal, the factual yet secretive. At the same time, a painting such as *Interim* impresses us in aesthetic terms: the dramatic composition and technical control in the execution of form, light and shadow. Finally, on the level of iconography, Sage developed in the scaffolding an imagery that was identifiably hers, and which became a personal symbol expressing the self – herself – struggling to stand in the void. For these reasons, Kay Sage's Surrealism evokes *a sense of revelation* that enriches our experience of the world.

Fig. 8   Kay Sage in her studio, Town Farm, Woodbury, Connecticut, 1957, standing before her easel and her painting *Suspension Bridge for the Swallows* (1957, oil on canvas, 36 × 28 in. Currier Gallery of Art, Manchester, New Hampshire).

Notes

1. Quoted in Ralph Minard, "Dream-World Artists Use Woodbury Barn," *Hartford Times,* Hartford, Connecticut, August 14, 1954.

2. Nicolas Calas in conversation with the author, New York City, August 28, 1974.

3. Donna Topazia Alliata in conversation with the author, Rome, March 23, 1977.

4. Gunther Stuhlmann, ed., *The Diary of Anaïs Nin, 1934–1939* (New York: Harcourt, Brace and World, 1967), 243, 290.

5. Catalogue Raisonné of the Surrealist Work of Kay Sage, Archives of American Art, Smithsonian Institution, Washington, D.C., microfilm rolls 2886–88, compiled by the author.

6. Lisa Vihos, graduate student at the University of Michigan Art History Department, has given me the benefit of her insights concerning Sage's artistic and psychological influences in San Francisco and Rome.

7. Much of the biographical information throughout the essay appears also in my article "The Surrealist Imagery of Kay Sage," *Art International* 26:4 (September–October 1983).

8. Kay Sage, "China Eggs," unpublished memoir, 1898–1935 (1955); Archives of American Art, Smithsonian Institution, Washington, D.C., microfilm roll 685, 15.

9. Ibid., 18.

10. Ibid., 18–19.

11. Julien Levy, "Tanguy, Connecticut Sage," *Art News* 53:5 (September 1954), 27. Hereafter cited as *Art News.*

12. The letters are also on microfilm at the Archives of American Art, rolls 2886–88. Their preservation is due to the efforts of Kay Sage's nieces, Leslie Mackin Rand and Susanne Sage Walcott.

13. "China Eggs," 51.

14. *Art News,* 27.

15. Letter to Flora Whitney Tower, May 5, 1924; courtesy of Mrs. G. Macculloch Miller.

16. Meret Oppenheim in conversation with the author, New York City, May 23, 1978.

17. "China Eggs," 100.

18. Arlette Paraf Seligmann in conversation with the author, New York, March 20, 1976.

19. Mrs. Alfred H. Barr, Jr., in a letter to the author, March 30, 1977.

20. James Thrall Soby in conversation with the author, New Canaan, Connecticut, August 16, 1978.

21. Mrs. Eleanor Howland Bunce in conversation with the author, Hartford, Connecticut, April 30, 1978.

22. Onslow-Ford considered Kay Sage responsible for saving his life, as the boat on which he would have been stationed was destroyed without survivors in the first month of the war. (Gordon Onslow-Ford in conversation with the author, Inverness, California, September 22, 1984.)

23. Matta in a letter to the author, March 11, 1977; the full text of the letter appears in the catalogue of the Matta exhibition, Centre Georges Pompidou, Paris, 1985.

24. The source for the titles of several of her paintings can be traced. *Page 49* (1950) (Williams College Museum of Art, Williamstown, Massachusetts) derives from the fact that in 1950 an article about her called "Serene Surrealist" appeared on p. 49 of the March 13 issue of *Time* magazine.

25. Wilfredo Lam in conversation with the author, Paris, March 14, 1977.

26. Sir Roland Penrose in conversation with the author, London, July 2, 1977.

27. William N. Copley in conversation with the author, New York, December 22, 1973.

28. Mrs. Miriam Gabo in conversation with the author, London, October 1984.

29. Leon Kelly in a letter to the author, July 1976.

30. Patrick Waldberg in conversation with the author, Paris, May 31, 1977.

31. Polly Clapp in conversation with the author, Roxbury, Connecticut, February 1972.

32. Jean Dubuffet in a letter to the author, December 29, 1974.

33. Alexandra I. Darrow in conversation with the author, Woodbury, Connecticut, March 1976.

34. Hans Richter in conversation with the author, Southbury, Connecticut, October 10, 1973.

35. Elizabeth Wade White and Evelyn V. Holahan in conversation with the author, Middlebury, Connecticut, April 1975.

36. Julien Levy in conversation with the author, Bridgewater, Connecticut, December 16, 1972.

I would like to express my gratitude to Mr. and Mrs. F. R. Miller, Susan W. Nessen, H. Wade White, Mrs. Sarah Barrett Matisse, Marie-Pierre Driot, John S. Monagan, Dominique Miller, Marc Chabot, Enrico Donati, Cleve Gray, Maurice Lefebvre-Foinet, Marcel Duhamel, Whitney Chadwick, and Frieda Gauthier. The essay is dedicated to Darrel P. Sweet.

The Flight from Passion in Leonora Carrington's Literary Work

Peter G. Christensen

Relationships between men and women have been one of the central concerns of Leonora Carrington's literary work. Unfortunately, the publishing history of her texts has concealed the course of her development in thinking about this issue. In order to understand Carrington better, we need to pay closer attention to a diminishing interest in romantic love in her writings. Although a general movement in her work away from Surrealism toward hermeticism has often been noted, a progress from heterosexual passion to androgynous union to the autonomy of women's communities will be presented here for the first time.

Most of Carrington's fame as a feminist rests with her most accessible and enjoyable literary work, the novel *The Hearing Trumpet,* published in the 1970s but written c. 1952, when she was about thirty-five. However, the recent appearance of two retrospective collections shows that her position here was not one that she held in her early twenties. *La Débutante, contes et pièces* (1978) and *Pigeon vole: Contes retrouvés* (1986) include texts (stories and plays) written between 1937 and 1941 which focus on surrealist *amour fou* and other passionate feelings of women toward men. This essay will examine some of these neglected works from her early period (1937–40), offer a revised reading of androgyny in the middle period (1941–46), and recontextualize feminism in her latest period (1946–present). I will omit discussions of her very brief stories, as they are less rewarding than her longer works. My analysis will briefly examine nine texts: (1) "Quand ils passaient," (2) "Histoire du petit Francis," (3) *La Fête de l'agneau,* (4) *Pénélope,* (5) *En-Bas,* (6) "Une Chemise de nuit de flanelle," (7) *The Stone Door,* (8) *The Hearing Trumpet,* and (9) *Opus Sinistrum.* This approach will show Carrington to be constantly rethinking and modifying her ideas.

Carrington's oeuvre has already been studied from feminist perspectives and with reference to Surrealism and hermeticism. Since 1969 her writings and paintings have been sympathetically discussed by Gloria Orenstein, Ida Rodriguez Prampolini, Bettina Knapp, Whitney Chadwick, Jacqueline Chénieux-Gendron, and Nancy Mandlove. All locate her with reference to a surrealist tradition, although Rodriguez Prampolini writes that her paintings participate in "expressionistic-fantastic" art rather than in French Surrealism (73).

Despite the many debates within the women's movement, Carrington has not provoked critical controversy. She has treated such contested topics as androgyny, matriarchy, and revolution, but these have not been taken up by feminist critics unsympathetic with her project. Analyses of Carrington's works have been what Peter J. Rabinowitz calls "authorial readings," accepting the author at her word and following her as she would like to be read.

Orenstein's approach stresses the Goddess as a source of inspiration and a reference point for female creativity. She gives value to androgyny as a concept, with reference to the alchemical and Jungian systems (1985, 565) which have influenced Carrington. Bettina Knapp, Whitney Chadwick, and Jacqueline Chénieux-Gendron also explicate the difficult hermetic and esoteric references in her work. In contrast, Nancy Mandlove mostly bypasses these traditions. She stresses the feminist revolution without violence and sacrifice in *The Hearing Trumpet,* but she does not investigate earlier works in which violence and sacrifice are present. As Carrington becomes more and more popular, the need to offer yet another short explication of her esoteric system diminishes. We can resist concentration on her hermetic symbolism in order to view the interaction between women and men in a feminist context.

Feminists less oriented toward myth may have three reservations about Carrington's writings. First, her allegiance to the hermetic tradition opens up the possible objection that her work is inherently ahistorical and that it lacks a sense of the role that women have played in society. Carrington does not depict the relationships of women and men as products of complex social and economic forces. Even *The Hearing Trumpet,* which has a historical dimension lacking in her other writings, departs from realistic probability to create a historical fantasy around Doña Rosalinda. Reverence for the Goddess may also keep readers distanced from the realities of women's existence in the twentieth century. Carol P. Christ and Judith Plaskow in their introduction to *Womanspirit Rising* point out the paradox that those feminists who try to develop a new spiritual vision based on the prebiblical past run the double risk of both not breaking sufficiently with the past and "distorting the past through romanticizing it" (11). Finally, Carrington's Jungian sympathies lead her to valorize the feminine and the masculine as timeless concepts, although they are not coded traits possessed by women and men, respectively. Some feminists, such as Naomi Goldenberg, wish to disassociate themselves from the Jungian categories. Carrington's use of both a timeless, antisocial, passionate love (sometimes symbolized by bestiality) and her alchemical framework for the union of lovers have their roots in Surrealism, but her eventual turn to the community of women and the Goddess represents a departure in a new direction.

Even at the start of her career Carrington wrote well. "Quand ils passaient," one of the best of the stories first published in *Pigeon vole*, depicts the vengeance of Virginia Fur, a forest dweller, on the religious community of Saint Alexandre, which was responsible for the death of her lover, Igname, a wild boar. Saint Alexandre, a pretentious local preacher, has led huntsmen to the animal. After her lover is killed, Virginia gives birth to their seven little boars. She keeps one, and she and her cats eat the others at the funeral meal. In the forest where she travels about on a wheel she gains the help of horses who vow death to Alexandre. Then in disguise she accompanies a dying woman to the convent where he preaches. When the body of her lover is brought in for a banquet, a thousand horses storm the building, and Virginia is visible amid all the destruction, seated on her wheel. She cries "death" to Alexandre and his bevy of nuns.

This story sympathetically treats a marginal woman who initiates a great slaughter when she loses her lover. The community of women at the convent is subservient to the "saint." The possibility of healthful relations among women is nil. On the way to the convent, for example, Virginia, in her disguise as Engadine, does not have any desire to accept her companion's request for an embrace. Virginia sees her revenge as "duty," and she does not depart from it. She and her lover needed nothing from society. They made love beneath a pile of cats and had no wishes for integration in the human community.

The longest story from the 1937–40 period, "Histoire du petit Francis," a novella of eighty-six pages, is another study of a female's revenge, but this time the avenger is the villain. The selfish girl Amélie is left home in Paris while her father, Umbriaco, and his nephew Francis go off on a tour of southern France. They have many enjoyable times together, but Amélie's long-distance nagging exasperates them. They split up, and Amélie, in a passionate rage at Francis for presumably alienating her father's affection for her, hits him on the head with a hammer "until a great hole appeared in his skull" (1986, 146). Francis's mother has a white coffin prepared for him, but Umbriaco sneaks in at night to paint it in black and yellow wasplike stripes, which his nephew would have preferred.

In her preface to *Pigeon vole* Jacqueline Chénieux proposes to read this story as a *roman à clef* in which Carrington is Francis; Max Ernst, Umbriaco; and Ernst's wife, Amélie. It refers to their emotional lives in early 1940 before the war brought imprisonment for Ernst and forced Carrington to try to escape to freedom through Spain. Such a reading refuses the gender distributions in the story. The ideal life is led by the two men, and a crazy girl with what appears to be an Electra complex is incapable of accepting it. Never again will Carrington deal with the friendship of men put in jeopardy by an unreasonable female. Both "Histoire du petit Francis" with its male bonding and "Quand ils passaient" with its heterosexual passion and vengeance show Carrington at a stage of writing before androgyny becomes important.

From around the same time period come two plays which treat the transcendent love of women for nonmortal men. In Carrington's longest play, *La Fête de l'agneau*, the heroine, Théodora, an eighteen-year-old, is in love with a phantom, Jérémie Carnis, who is her husband's dead brother. He kills sheep and shepherds and decapitates them as well. Jérémie and Théodora drink the blood of Joe Green the shepherd together, served up by a vampire bat. However, despite the ecstasy occasioned by their reunion, the end is near. Jérémie has a terrible fear that Théodora will grow old and lose her beauty. If she does, he will stop loving her. While Théodora fantasizes about the great future they will have together, rolling in the snow while he bites her, he tells her that he must leave now and that they can look forward to being together in hell. She must not come with him, as he does not think she can bear the cold. Although she declares that her life means nothing without him, he goes off. She is left alone on stage crying.

In this play the mad love of the protagonists is the only value, but even this relationship is an extremely compromised one. Jérémie's attitude toward women is blatantly sexist. Although there is no one in the play to tell Théodora that she is being used, the sudden unhappy ending makes it clear that Jérémie is responsible for most of Théodora's misery.

Pénélope, another full-length play, published in 1946 but based on the same material found in the early short story "La Dame ovale" (1938), serves as a companion piece to *La Fête de l'agneau.* Both plays have a level of everyday reality which is mixed with fantasy. This play, however, provides a happy ending for the passionate lover, Pénélope, a girl, and her rocking horse, Tartar. In the last scene Pénélope and Tartar emerge in a white light, and Pénélope is transformed (for a second time) into a horse. They appear as a couple of white colts holding hands. Meanwhile the patriarchal father throws himself out of the window along with all the other "blocking characters" in the drama. Although the ending here has been said to represent "the hope of salvation through androgynous union" (Orenstein 1975, 136), it might make more sense to see the ending as confirming the value of heterosexual passion. Although a cow has previously told Pénélope that men belong to a feeble and bad race (1978, 134), the united couple suggests that a woman can still find salvation by choosing a male who is an exception to the general rule. In later works androgyny will be divorced from romantic passion. If we place *Pénélope* in the early period because of the conception of the story in the 1930s, we see with *En-Bas* (published in 1944) a shift to a stronger feminism and a greater reliance on the idea of androgyny.

In the harrowing autobiographical experiences of 1940 recounted in *En-Bas,* Carrington moves toward a feminist revision of Christian traditions that is surprising, as the early stories reject Christianity outright. Carrington is given Cardiazol, a powerful drug, by her cruel Spanish captors, and she has visions which straddle the boundary between revelation and madness. At one point she declares that she is the lunar element (the opposite of the sun), and that she is going to take the dead Christ's place, for the Trinity has been deprived of a female figure (1973, 48). She is the Christ on earth in the person of the Holy Spirit. At another time she finds the description of Pentecost in the Bible and again identifies herself with the Holy Spirit (61), which according to some traditions is portrayed as feminine (Ruether 24). In believing herself the Holy Spirit, Carrington announces herself as one part of a larger whole, a type of incomplete cosmic entity. Whereas the narrative represents a move to feminist consciousness, it also opens Carrington up to the limits inherent in some concepts of androgyny.

The problems in the conceptualization of androgyny (bisexuality) have been expressed succinctly by Hélène Cixous in her discussion of this concept in "Sorties," her part of *The Newly Born Woman*. For her there are good and bad versions of androgyny. Of the first she writes:

Bisexuality as a fantasy of complete being, which replaces the fear of castration and veils sexual difference insofar as this is perceived as the mark of a mythical separation – the trace, therefore, of a dangerous and painful ability to be cut. (84)

To this false ideal, Cixous sets up a bisexuality which involves an erotic universe, "the multiplication of the effects of desire's inscription on every part of the body and the other body" (85). *En-Bas* does escape from the false ideal, but in the following two works there is an abstraction in the treatment of it which is partly desexualized.

"Une Chemise de nuit de flanelle" ("A Flannel Nightgown") and *The Stone Door*, both written around 1945, are the two works most indebted to the hermetic tradition. "Une Chemise," the most successful of her four plays and an excellent example of a text as a ritual center of pilgrimage (see Caws 15), is concerned with a form of ritual violence in which a patriarchal figure is killed in order to make way for a new Goddess-oriented order. When the beleaguered serving woman Prisni drinks the blood of the dead man, we have not only the symbol of the union of male and female, but a suggestion that matriarchy will be sustaining itself on the ruins of patriarchy. The issue of ritual sacrifice is a troubling one on two counts. First of all, the peaceful revolution in *The Hearing Trumpet* is preferable. Second, in the light of René Girard's *Violence and the Sacred*, we are allowed to discountenance the close connection of violence and the sacred in any example of mythmaking.

The Stone Door successfully uses ritual without violence and, although it requires some hermetic knowledge, is one of Carrington's most attractive narratives. Here the alchemical union of masculine and feminine is worked out in the union of Zacharias, the poor Hungarian Jew, and the nameless heroine. A giant tells Zacharias that man is mistaken in thinking that he is one, for he has another part of himself (112). He says that the Ram must become woman, and Air must become man. Zacharias, as Air and the Scales, soon after meets the woman, incarnate as Fire and the Ram. They make it through the Stone Door together into life. The androgynous ideal here is not undercut by violence, as in "Une Chemise" or by threats of madness as in *En-Bas.*

In *The Hearing Trumpet* women's community becomes a value for the first time. The ninety-two-year-old heroine, Marion Leatherby, her longtime friend Carmella, and their friends at the old age home Lightsome Hall recover the Holy Grail, which is really the Cup of the Goddess, and return it to her. Nancy Mandlove writes that this event constitutes a restoration of "matriarchy" (121), but the closing pages of the novel do not clearly establish that the new society will be constituted by women in power. Instead of a condemnation of men for wrecking the world, we find hope that animals will do better where humans have failed. Marion writes:

After I die Anubeth's werecubs will continue to document, till the planet is peopled with cats, werewolves, bees, and goats. We all fervently hope that this will be an improvement on humanity, which deliberately renounced the Pneuma of the Goddess. (158)

It is to Carrington's credit that she shows the restoration of Goddess worship, rather than a "return to matriarchy," as the existence of matriarchy in the West has been doubted. In her investigation of the Middle East in *The Creation of Patriarchy,* Gerda Lerner proposes that the dethroning of the powerful goddesses and their replacement by a dominant male god was not the equivalent of the overthrowing of a matriarchal order. She finds no evidence of an early matriarchal period even though there was widespread Goddess worship, and she reminds us that matrilinear societies are not the same as matriarchies.

Although Marion can be considered a counterpart of Sir Perceval in this quest romance, as Gloria Orenstein points out (1977, 231), we should note that Carrington stresses group achievement as much as the heroism of one woman with visionary powers. Marion is aided not only by Carmella, a very close friend, but by a half-dozen fellow residents at the retirement community. She and these residents initiate a hunger strike to protest the behavior of the Gambits after Maude (i.e., Arthur) Somers dies from eating poisoned fudge. These nonviolent women are able to regain the Cup of the Goddess with the help of bees and wolves who do not even attack the men who guard it. They then worship the Goddess in her triple aspect. She is not divided into asexual Sky Goddess and sexual Earth Mother as in the systems of Jung and Neumann. (See Ostriker 246.)

Men are still welcome in the new world of the Ice Age, but they are not allowed to participate in the ritual of Goddess worship. Marriage is accepted, but it is associated with companionship, not passion. Four heterosexual couples are shown in the novel, two good and two bad. Both Dr. and Mrs. Gambit and Marion's son Galahad and his wife Muriel are satirized. Galahad is presented as a weak man and prey to his nasty wife. Arthur Somers apparently had a happy life with his wife, Veronica Adams, and they fled together to Lightsome Hall when he was in trouble with the law. The sister of Marion's friend Marlborough, Anubeth, is a wolf-headed woman who has a happy marriage with King Pontefact of the wolves. They have a litter of six werewolf cubs of which they are very proud. Thus we see that marriages may be good or bad, but women can live rewarding lives entirely separate from men. Marriage does not offer something essential to life.

Although the principle of androgyny is still endorsed by one of the alchemical documents discovered by Doña Rosalinda's biographer (94), this alchemical androgyny is never brought to bear on the lives of the characters. The document reads in part:

At the beginning the two spirits which are known as Twins are the one Female and the Other Male. They established at the beginning Life, the Pneuma, and the Holy Cup to hold the Pneuma.

And when these two Spirits met such was the manner of the birth of the Winged One [or the Feathered Hermaphrodite, Sephirá]. (94)

Despite this formulation, the aphrodisiac Musc Madelaine that enables Doña Rosalinda to levitate and presumably copulate in midair is not viewed as a potion for this type of alchemical union. The Musc is valued for enhancing sexuality in a repressed cloister.

Marion notices the portrait of Doña Rosalinda winking at her, and a connection is set up between women's communities across the ages. Although neither the nuns nor the old women are presented as lesbians, the existence of such women is acknowledged by the novel. Marlborough says that Anubeth had tried to organize at the Vatican a fancy-dress ball for "destitute lesbians," but her plan was not successful, for the Pope was not impressed (150).

Male homosexuality exists peripherally in the novel through the mention of the Knights Templar, around whom various stories of homosexual practices accrued. In addition, one specific example of homosexual behavior is presented in the person of Fernand, Bishop of Trève les Frêles, who is interested in choirboys. He writes to his associate, Doña Rosalinda:

Finally I felt strong enough to negotiate a few leagues, as far as Avignon, in order to refresh my soul with artistic enjoyment in the form of elevated music. As you know, song is the food of the soul, and I was impatient to get to the cathedral to hear the Nordic choirboys sing Mass.

I will not enter into a lengthy ecstatic description of those gentle singers. Let me say simply that if they indeed resemble angels then let me enter paradise and frolic amongst the cherubim. Such delicate fair skins and innocent blue eyes! Their pure trilling song transformed the mass into an experience of pure delight. This, My Dear Rosalinda, is something I feel sure you have never experienced. (89)

Eventually the bishop gives spiritual instruction to one of the boys who has had to leave the choir because his voice has changed. In the context of the novel the bishop is not being satirized. Instead Carrington writes with a gentle humor which acknowledges that homosexual behavior cannot readily be explained with recourse to theories of androgyny.

Through the depiction of religious communities from the Spanish past *The Hearing Trumpet* takes up the same question about history that has recently been confronted by Christa Wolf in *Cassandra*. Rather than reproduce the absence of women from history, Wolf revises history from a feminist standpoint. As Ruth Hoberman indicates, Wolf asks us to see what would happen if the great male heroes of the past were replaced by women. Thus she creates a novel that "flies in the face of probability, plot, the distance of past eras from our own" (3). Doña Rosalinda is a figure similar to Cassandra, for she takes actions that exceed her station. Not content to be another male-identified Saint Teresa in Ecstasy at best, she seeks out the Cup of the Great Goddess.

The Hearing Trumpet continually makes fun of Christianity, which is seen as entirely patriarchal. Recent scholarship has shown a larger place for women in the early history of Christianity than would have been suspected in 1952 (Fiorenza 1988). The triumph of the antifeminist Augustinian idea of sexuality over less sexist views in the early Christian church has been investigated by Elaine Pagels in *Adam, Eve, and the Serpent.* Greater knowledge of women's culture in ancient history is bound to affect our individual responses toward the rewritings of history offered by authors such as Carrington.

Opus Sinistrum, Carrington's fourth and last play, dated seventeen years after *The Hearing Trumpet,* moves back away from history. Although Carrington has not written the kind of matriarchal magic play called for by Heide Goettner-Abendroth in "Nine Principles of a Matriarchal Aesthetic," she does show us the overthrow of male domination in its three and one-half scenes. The second scene opens with a male ritual taking place in an African jungle. Cannibals representing the twelve houses of the zodiac are presiding over a cauldron which symbolizes the planet Earth, but the men are not good guardians of it. The cauldron, as Orenstein points out, is also connected with the Grail (1975, 44). Male society is lampooned for its obliviousness to its responsibilities to our planet. The tone is much more acerbic than in *The Hearing Trumpet.* At this point men and women seem radically separate from each other.

At the end of the play a huge eighty-year-old woman, Mina Mina, destroys the computer of the male Bogeyman. He childishly calls for his mother and disappears into the earth. There is some danger in such symbolic actions. Freed from the constraints of realism, one risks falling into the false dichotomy of Cartesian Man versus Witch Woman. Mina Mina, the victor, is left onstage eating an apple. She triumphs where Eve failed, but there is no community of women around her at the end of the play. Since 1969 we have no extended published text by Carrington, and we must leave our survey at the tensest point for men and women in her literary career.

Elaine Showalter has described four models of women's writing: biological, linguistic, psychoanalytical, and cultural (249). Of these, the cultural has been most engaged with history, and from this standpoint *The Hearing Trumpet* must be considered Carrington's richest work, particularly for its valorization of communities of women in a framework in which heterosexual unions are made secondary.

Currently almost all of the writing published by Leonora Carrington in French is in print in five separate volumes. In English the situation is not as good, as *Pigeon vole* and some of the selections in *La Débutante, contes et pièces* have not been translated. Thus this necessarily brief overview has been geared especially for the English-language reader. As Carrington has written in both English and French, translations of her work have operated in two directions. Let us hope that more translations into English are forthcoming.

Carrington's plays all require a certain ingenuity in staging in order to have their effect. *Pénélope* was produced in 1957 in Mexico by Alexandre Jodorowsky. If there have been other stagings of her plays, they have not been mentioned in the previous literature on her. Certainly an innovative production of "Une Chemise de nuit de flanelle" would bring this fine one-act play to public attention.

Since 1952 Carrington has assured her reputation as one of the greatest living painters with a prolific volume of work. Her plays, stories and novels, which make up her important literary expression, need to be analyzed now in relation to her visual work.

References

Carrington, Leonora. *La Débutante, contes et pièces*. Trans. Yves Bonnefoy, Jacqueline Chénieux, and Henri Parisot. Paris: Flammarion, 1978.

———. *En-Bas précédé d'une lettre à Henri Parisot*. Paris: Le Terrain Vague, 1973.

———. *The Hearing Trumpet*. New York: St. Martin's Press, 1977.

———. *The Oval Lady*. Trans. Rochelle Holt. Santa Barbara: Capra Press, 1975.

———. *Pigeon vole: Contes retrouvés*. Trans. Jacqueline Chénieux and Didier Vidal. Cognac: Le Temps qu'il fait, 1986.

―――. *The Stone Door*. New York: St. Martin's Press, 1977.

Caws, Mary Ann. *A Metapoetics of the Passage: Architextures in Surrealism and After*. Hanover: University Press of New England, 1981.

Chadwick, Whitney. *Women Artists of the Surrealist Movement*. London: Thames and Hudson, 1985.

Chénieux-Gendron, Jacqueline. "Hermetisme et Surrealisme dans les oeuvres de Leonora Carrington." *Proceedings of the 10th Congress of the International Comparative Literature Association, New York, 1982*, vol. 2. Ed. Anna Balakian. New York: Garland, 1985, 512–18.

Christ, Carol P., and Judith Plaskow, eds. *Womanspirit Rising: A Feminist Reader in Religion*. New York: Harper and Row, 1979.

Cixous, Hélène, and Catherine Clément. *The Newly Born Woman*. Trans. Betsy Wing. Minneapolis: University of Minnesota Press, 1986.

Fiorenza, Elisabeth S. *In Memory of Her: A Feminist Theological Reconstruction of Christian Origins*. New York: Crossroad, 1983.

Girard, René. *Violence and the Sacred*. Trans. Patrick Gregory. Baltimore: Johns Hopkins University Press, 1977.

Goettner-Abendroth, Heide. "Nine Principles of a Matriarchal Aesthetic." In *Feminist Aesthetics*. Ed. Gisela Ecker. London: Women's Press, 1985, 81–94.

Goldenberg, Naomi R. "Dreams and Fantasies as Sources of Revelation: Feminist Appropriation of Jung." In *Womanspirit Rising: A Feminist Reader in Religion*. Ed. Carol P. Christ and Judith Plaskow. New York: Harper and Row, 1979, 219–27.

Hoberman, Ruth. "Feminist Historical Fiction in the Twentieth Century." Paper presented at the NEH Summer Seminar on the British Novel in the Early Twentieth Century, Cornell University, August 28, 1988.

Knapp, Bettina. "Leonora Carrington's Whimsical Dreamworld: Animals Talk, Children Are Gods, a Black Swan Lays an Orphic Egg." *World Literature Today* 51:4 (Autumn 1977), 525–30.

Lerner, Gerda. *The Creation of Patriarchy*. New York: Oxford University Press, 1986.

Mandlove, Nancy B. "Humor at the Service of the Revolution: Leonora Carrington's Feminist Perspective on Surrealism." *Perspectives on Contemporary Literature* 7 (1981), 117–22.

Orenstein, Gloria Feman. "Hermeticism and Surrealism in the Visual Works of Leonora Carrington as a Model for Latin American Symbology." *Proceedings of the 10th Congress of the International Comparative Literature Association, New York, 1982*, vol. 2. Ed. Anna Balakian. New York: Garland, 1985, 565–75.

―――. "Leonora Carrington's Visionary Art for the New Age." *Chrysalis* 3 (1978), 65–77.

―――. "Manifestations of the Occult in the Art and Literature of Leonora Carrington." In *Literature and the Occult: Essays in Comparative Literature*. Ed. Frank Luanne. Arlington: University of Texas Press, 1977, 216–33.

―――. "Reclaiming the Great Mother: A Feminist Journey to Madness and Back in Search of a Goddess Heritage." *Symposium* 36:1 (Spring 1982), 45–70.

―――. *The Theater of the Marvelous: Surrealism and the Contemporary Stage*. New York: New York University Press, 1975, 122–47.

―――. "Towards a Bifocal Vision in Surrealist Aesthetics." *Trivia* 3 (Fall 1983), 70–87.

157

————. "Women of Surrealism." *The Feminist Art Journal* 2:2 (Spring 1973), 1, 15–21.

Ostriker, Alicia. "The Thieves of Language: Women Poets and Revisionist Myth-making." In *The New Feminist Criticism: Essays on Women, Literature, and Theory.* Ed. Elaine Showalter. New York: Pantheon, 1985, 314–39.

Pagels, Elaine. *Adam, Eve, and the Serpent.* New York: Random House, 1988.

Rabinowitz, Peter J. *Before Reading: Narrative Conventions and the Politics of Interpretation.* Ithaca: Cornell University Press, 1987.

Rodriguez Prampolini, Ida. *El Surrealismo y el Arte Fantástico de México.* Mexico City: Universidad Nacional Autónomo de México, 1969.

Ruether, Rosemary Radford, ed. *Womanguides: Readings toward a Feminist Theology.* Boston: Beacon Press, 1985.

Showalter, Elaine. "Towards a Feminist Poetics." In *The New Feminist Criticism: Essays on Women, Literature, and Theory.* Ed. Elaine Showalter. New York: Pantheon, 1985, 125–43.

"Variations on Common Themes." Trans. Yvonne Rochette-Ozzello. In *New French Feminisms.* Ed. Elaine Marks and Isabelle De Courtivron. New York: Schocken Books, 1981, 212–30.

Beauty and/Is the Beast:
Animal Symbology in the Work of
Leonora Carrington, Remedios Varo
and Leonor Fini

Georgiana M. M. Colvile

> The House of Beasts drew nearer each moment.
> Leonora Carrington, "The Royal Command"

Iconographic representations of both familiar animals and fabulous beasts are as old as human history. The basic belief in a "woman and nature" association can be traced back almost as far. Some feminists have objected to this cliché (Marks and Courtivron 220–22); others, like the painters I am about to discuss, have turned it to their advantage.

Carroll's Alice, who has fascinated Surrealists and feminists over the years, is led on her two oneiric journeys by animal guides: the White Rabbit takes her Underground (until recently the only place for women's creative expression) to Wonderland; the dream metamorphosis of a black kitten helps her both into and out of the Looking Glass. In these strange places, humans, ordinary animals and fantastic creatures interrelate quite naturally.

Todorov bases his definition of the fantastic on the hesitation and ambiguity which occur between reality and the inexplicable (28–45), much like the gap the Surrealists sought to bridge between everyday contingencies and secondary states, such as dream, fantasy, illusion, madness, death, etc. To Todorov, any phenomenon which can eventually be rationalized is merely strange, like Freud's "uncanny" and the mechanisms of dream-work, whereas the utterly undefinable in terms of "real world logic" belongs to the category of the "marvelous" (46–62). To André Breton, "the marvelous is always beautiful, anything marvelous is beautiful, in fact only the marvelous is beautiful" (Lippard 15). Breton and his friends included women in this pattern, conveniently putting them on a distant pedestal and maintaining them as inexplicable creatures like the Sphinx and the Chimaera. Xavière Gauthier, in *Surréalisme et sexualité,* was one of the first to expose the Surrealists' inconsistency toward sexuality and their own ideology. She catalogs the ironic metamorphoses to which they sub-

jected the female "objects" of their desire: reconstitution of the lost androgyne, woman as nature, earth, flower, fruit, star, witch, voyante, threatening beast, etc. . . . .

Except for the indomitable Leonor Fini, most women artists first became connected with the surrealist movement as wives or companions of
members of Breton's circle or of other internationally recognized avant-
garde artists. However quiet and subdued they may have appeared within
the group (Kaplan 55–56), they continued to weave their own independence as artists, using all the material and freedom the surrealist framework could provide them with. As Whitney Chadwick has pointed out:

> In recognizing her intuitive connection with the magic realm of existence that gov-
> erned creation, Surrealism offered the woman artist a self-image that united her
> roles as woman and creator in a way that neither the concept of the femme-enfant
> nor that of the erotic muse could. (182)

Just as Judy Chicago chose "women's work" like embroidery and china
painting to make a feminist statement in her 1979 exhibit *The Dinner Party*,
women Surrealists made extensive use of their own beauty in self-
portraits and explored the worlds of childhood and madness, where men
tried to confine them, as passages to their true identity (Chadwick 35–38).

Most of these women's animal imagery comes from dreams or from various myths they chose to refer to. Animals appear frequently in dreams.
Freud identifies small animals as genital symbols (the snake being specifically phallic), wild beasts as representing passionate impulses, and beasts
of prey or wild horses as substitutes for a dreaded father figure. Jung relates animals to various unconscious manifestations of the "animus" and
"anima" and man's basic instinctive drives.

In Genesis, though the animals were created before Adam, the latter
appropriates and dominates them by naming them, prefiguring his subsequent treatment of Eve. The alliance between Eve and the snake is a deformed version of the older matriarchal Celtic myth from the time when
"all totem societies in Ancient Europe were under the dominion of the
Great Goddess, the Lady of the Wild Things" (Graves 422). According to
Graves, the Goddess could undergo any number of animal metamorphoses—into a mare, she-bear, sow or hind, for example. She mated
yearly with her snake-son, killed him and burned the egg she had laid: he
would be reborn each year from the ashes (387–88). Graves has traced the
gradual shift in Western civilization from Goddess cult to God worship.
Vestiges of the former often appear in animal form, like the Old Testa-
ment golden calf and the male preference for female or animal masks at
carnivals.

Links between women, children, animals, and various forms of magic
are a constant in western art. Borges comments on children's fearlessness
in front of fierce animals in zoos, and on the legend that only virgins could

approach and catch unicorns (9, 183). Fabulous beasts, like sphinxes, chimaera, and gorgons, tend either to be female or to symbolize male fear of female sexuality. In his study of monsters in western art, Gilbert Lascault associates the artist's creative anguish with the death drive and a terror of procreation, all of which find an outlet in vampiric representation. He looks to women to break that pattern: "It is only by retrieving the naïve power within themselves, that women can avoid the sterile, perverse pitfall of male sexuality, which is rooted in violence" (424, my translation).

In order to find herself, the surrealist woman artist was not appropriating nature as divorced from culture, but retracing her steps back to matriarchy and Goddess cult, to the prehuman world of animals, to "the original confusion between man and animal species" (Chénieux-Gendron, *Surréalisme* 254), to her own prelinguistic infancy and intimacy with the mother, to the nursery world of toys, pets, and animal fairy tales in which the father becomes the monster.

Baudrillard insists on the perfectly ritual fascination emanated by animals, and equates it with female charm (122–25). He maintains that the attraction of animals lies not in their wildness but in "the feline, theatrical nostalgia for parade and ornament they arouse in us." Leonor Fini's elaborate costumes and catlike attitudes come to mind. Despite his masculine focalization, Baudrillard's definition of the "paradoxical space, where the distinction between nature and culture is abolished . . . in the concept of ornament and parade in which woman and animal alike are reflected" (122), points to a place from which woman can create.

Each of the women artists I have chosen favors one specific animal, although others will appear in her work. Like the Mayan "Naguals" (Nicholson 41–42), these animals can be seen as personal totems, symbols of another world, alter egos, and mirror images, or as a metamorphosis of the loved one. Hence Beauty and/is the Beast.

Beauty in the fairy tale is a model daughter, who asks her father for no more than a rose (respect for her virginity). He steals the rose from the Beast's garden. Beauty goes willingly to the Beast's kingdom, first to save her father, then to save the Beast, who is dying without her. When she discovers she loves him and agrees to marry him, he turns into a handsome prince. According to Bettelheim, Beauty has normally crossed the oedipal bridge from father to husband (401–12). She is able to love the Beast when sex (his bestial form) has ceased to threaten either her or her father. Jung sees the tale as illustrating a "process of awakening" which instructs women on how to recognize their "true function of relatedness" and the required feminine submissive response to the "animal man" (Jung 137–40). Another reading: Beauty's father is poor, foolish, and steals other people's flowers. His absence and mistakes lead her to discover a new enchanted realm, the Beast's palace, where all her wishes come true and a magic mirror abolishes time and space. She returns to the imaginary world of childhood, where her companion resembles the fuzzy toys and furry pets she once cherished. She falls in love with the Beast, not the prince. The prince is her father's fantasy, a mirror image of his younger self, who will enable him to possess her vicariously. This leads us to Leonora Carrington, who rewrote "Beauty and the Beast" at least twice.

The Bride of the Wind Whinnies Unbridled: Leonora Carrington

At the beginning of her career as an artist and writer, Leonora Carrington obviously chose the horse as her personal totem. In two early texts, the short story "The Oval Lady" and the play *Pénélope,* Carrington's adolescent Beauty (Lucrecia/Penelope) is in love with her hobby-horse (all at once toy, animal and fantastic Beast) Tartarus (Tartar in the original French versions). Tartar returns the girl's love. Her father threatens to burn the hobby horse to stop her from "playing" with him/it. Penelope escapes by turning into a horse herself and flying off like Pegasus with her uncanny lover. As Gloria Orenstein has explained:

Tartar, derived from Tartarus, the Greek underworld, links another Celtic white horse divinity, Epona, to the realm of the otherworld. Shortened to Tartar, a double anagram of ART, it indicates that through ART we can attain divine and occult knowledge. (*Theater* 132–33)

ART is also the archaic "thou" form of the verb "to be" and the girl could thus address her inanimate horse-lover as he comes alive, and/or her newly found identity: "ART! ART!" In addition, Leonora Carrington has practiced mirror-writing since childhood, and "TARTAR" in the mirror would read "RAT RAT"! An appropriate insult for the murderous father, the epithet probably refers back to Apollo's other name, Smintherus, meaning "rat."[1] For the Greeks and Romans, the rat was a noxious chthonian beast, propagator of the plague. Such animals hardly appear in the matriarchal Celtic mythology Carrington has always adopted, and she seems to have banished them, like the father, from her work. In dream symbology, rats represent gnawing sexual desires: the father's problem, as in "Beauty and the Beast."

Like her symbolic animal carrier, Leonora Carrington was almost constantly on the move from 1926 to 1942, when she finally settled in Mexico. Her bestiary increased as she went through the various "passages" of her life, from her Celtic ancestry to the land of the Mayas. Her later paintings and writing are marked by the multiplicity of her experience, including the hybrid creatures of her imagination, part human, part beast, anchored in Todorov's uncertain space of the fantastic.

In Carrington's early work, the horse remains the dominant animal. From the beginning, she has sought to abolish the difference between humans and other animals even in love, as she told Germaine Rouvre: "In l'amour-passion, it is the loved one the other who gives the key. Now the question is: who can the loved one be? It can be a man or a horse or another woman" (Interview. Chadwick 105). She then admitted her own preference for men but insisted that she had absolutely no prejudices concerning other people's tastes (*Obliques* 91–92). The connection with the Earth Goddess, who was able to take almost any animal form, seems obvious.

Man, bird and horse, Max Ernst provided Carrington with the first crucial key. The already white-haired Ernst was the White Horse who helped her escape from her stuffy upper-class British environment, and the White Rabbit who led her to the Underground of the surrealist group in Paris. Ernst had already created his own totem and legend: Loplop, the Bird Superior, reborn after "the death of Max Ernst in 1914" (*View* 2: 30). For Carrington, he was also a horse. They both appear in equine form in her twin portraits *Self-Portrait* (1937) (Fig. 1) and *Portrait of Max Ernst* (1940).[2] The former gives animal and mythical expression to newly found love and freedom.

This first important picture contains the basics of the magical code Carrington was to develop in her later work. As Whitney Chadwick and Jacqueline Chénieux-Gendron have already demonstrated, the horses are intertextually related to the written works *Pénélope* and "The Oval Lady," and the hyena reappears in "The Débutante" (Chadwick 78–79; Chénieux-Gendron, *Surréalisme* 254–55). In *Self-Portrait* the seated woman's mane-like hair finds an echo in the horse's mane and the hyena's color.[3] The black female hyena coming toward the seated Leonora from the left (*sinistra*, evil) has its feet on the earth-brown floor and matches the woman's black shoes. The white rocking horse (Tartar), on the right, is positioned in the air, above her, his rocker touching her mane, his white color matching her riding breeches, apparently galloping toward the window in the background. The color of the window wall and of the sky seen through it is blue, the color of imagination and the other side of the mirror: time and space have been abolished outside the room, where the hobby horse has become a real steed speeding into the trees. The natural green landscape reflects the color of the woman's jacket; she is also both outside and in. Green is the color of the plant world, of regeneration, life's awakening, strength and hope; also of acidity and of Persephone's pomegranate seeds, Hades' gift of male temptation. Green is the color of Carrington's mother's native Ireland, her earliest source for the Celtic mythology so essential to her work. The yellow-gold curtains are a sign of renewal and of the earth's fertility, as well as of the knowledge of celestial light conveyed by the alchemists' precious metal. The red and blue chair Carrington is sitting on represents an alliance between the male and female principles and at the same time the competitive struggle between heaven and earth. The three colors of the alchemists and of the Moon Goddess are already manifested here: Abraham Juif represents three riders on three lions, black for gold in maceration, red for its inner ferment, white for the conquest of death

Fig. 1 Leonora Carrington, *Self-Portrait,* 1937. Oil on canvas. Reproduced courtesy of the Pierre Matisse Gallery, New York.

(Grillot de Givry, 362–63). The New Moon is the White Goddess of birth and growth, the Full Moon the Red Goddess of love and battle, and the Old Moon the Black Goddess of Death (Graves 70). The two animals, the white horse and the black hyena, represent the goddess's duality – positive versus negative, life versus death, Earth Mother versus devouring monster (this last aspect becomes even more apparent in the Aztec divinity Coatlicue [Nicholson 84; Andrade 85–89]) – so inherent to human nature and to man's fear of woman. *Self-Portrait* contains all the components of a young woman's initiation to the world.

The hyena never reappears in Carrington's later work. It is no doubt connected to a childhood fantasy and seems to come straight out of Lewis Carroll's *Through the Looking Glass:* "Nurse! Do let's pretend that I'm a hungry hyena and you're a bone!" (112). The animal's presence, like its devouring role in "The Débutante," adds an element of malicious humor to the picture: the little girl has grown up and the nursery is undergoing a perverse transformation! A definitely antiestablishment animal, the hyena was already despised as "a dirty brute" for its apparent androgyny in an early medieval bestiary (Freeman 80).

The *Portrait of Max Ernst* is situated on the other side of the window. Max, with a pinched stubborn expression, appears as a hybrid creature: his own human head, hand and foot (the yellow-and-black striped sock evoking a stinging insect) emerge from an aggressively male red fur garment in the shape of a seahorse. He is standing in a desolate blue-and-white Arctic landscape, with a symmetrical horse made of snow and icicles behind him (probably Carrington, the abandoned or about-to-be abandoned mate). He is nonchalantly carrying at arm's length an oval green lamp, an alchemical egg, with the moon's face on it, which also represents a prancing horse (Chadwick 80–81). He is walking forward, probably to dump it (her) into the icy water. He seems to be leaving her, just as Uncle Ubriaco abandons Little Francis in Carrington's tragicomic story "Histoire du petit Francis," which Jacqueline Chénieux-Gendron reads as a barely disguised account of the couple's years in St. Martin d'Ardèche, where they had moved from Paris in 1937; the war brutally dislodged and separated them in 1940 (Chénieux-Gendron, Preface 7–9).

Whitney Chadwick's description of their extraordinary dwelling place posits it as the obvious model for Carrington's first published story, "The House of Fear" (1938),[4] illustrated by Max Ernst:

Carrington's life with Ernst strengthened both their associations with nature. At St. Martin d'Ardèche . . . they renovated a group of ruined buildings, covering the walls with cement casts of birds and mythical animals. Carrington's paintings of the period reveal a growing vocabulary of magical animals, at the center of which lies the image of the white horse. (75)

In 1940, Ernst painted *Leonora in the Morning Light* (*View* 2: 9), in which Carrington's head and shoulders, framed by her dark mane, are seen emerging from a frottage jungle of fantastic flora and fauna, from which she remains inextricable, a vision of the Earth Goddess. The horse Ernst is again the helpful animal guide in "The House of Fear." He wrote a little introductory story, "Loplop Presents the Bride of the Wind," in which she reads her tale to a group of fascinated animals (*Obliques* 81). (Carrington refers to her orphic power over animals at the end of *En-Bas,* her lucid account of her nervous breakdown in 1940, following Ernst's internment in a concentration camp [65]. Her sensitized state gave her a strange insight, still manifest in her painting.[5]) Carrington replied in 1942 with the text "The Bird Superior, Max Ernst," illustrated with her portrait of him (*View* 2:13). Chadwick has described these mutual tributes written in their magical animal code extensively, so I will linger only on the appellation "The Bride of the Wind." According to Graves, the White Goddess was in charge of the winds, one of which was the answer to a riddle, just as man was the answer Oedipus correctly gave the Sphinx: "Furthermore only pigs and goats (sacred to the Goddess) could see the wind and mares could conceive merely by turning their hindquarters to the wind" (435). This equine myth was transmitted to the Greeks, who personified the North Wind as Boreas, the sire of twelve wondrous colts. These legends posit the wind as a prepatriarchal male, giving his Bride an original matriarchal context.

In another early picture, *Horses* (1941) (Fig. 2), Carrington uses the same colors as in *Self-Portrait,* but here the noble animals have the world to themselves; no Yahoos or other creatures are to be seen in the reddish brown landscape, resembling the decor of a Western. The foreground shows a closeup of a black-and-white stallion and a golden mare happily

Fig. 2   Leonora Carrington, *Horses,* 1941. Oil on canvas. Gallery 1900-2000, Paris.

copulating, an energizing green blanket loosely wrapped about her neck. Other horses of various hues are scattered in the background, some inside of or atop a building. In the distance a miragelike blue lake hints at the unreality of this prehuman paradise.

Carrington's later painting, after her arrival in Mexico in 1942, becomes increasingly rich and hermetic. She has evolved from more personal themes to what Gloria Orenstein calls a "pictoral cosmology," the key to which is her "underlying feminism" (*Chrysalis* 66-77). Her paintings are invitations to an alternative world of harmony, where humans, animals, plants and inanimate objects are on an equal footing, just as they all speak the same language in her stories and plays. Fabulous hybrid creatures abound, such as the Chimaera of *Who Art Thou, White Face?* (1959) and the butterfly-people of *Lepidoptera* (1969) (Orenstein, *Theater* 122-32).

In her quest for woman's freedom and wholeness, Carrington uses her own experience, her accumulated knowledge of Celtic and Mayan myths (she studied with the Chiapas Indians before completing her 1963 mural *El mundo mágico de las Mayas*), alchemy, the Tarot, the teachings of Gurdjieff, Carlos Castaneda et al. . . . Her symbology and color wheel have no doubt been influenced by the Irish Book of Ballymote, which divides the year into a system of letters, numbers and colors (Graves 296-300), and by the even more complex Aztec calendar (Nicholson 43-53). In the latter, days were regarded as animate beings and individually represented by deities corresponding to numbers, animals, plants, elements, planets, death, etc. – in fact all the essential components of the life cycle.

Both sides of the paradoxical eating theme as related to the Goddess – provider of good crops and natural foods, on the one hand, and devourer of her own young (an attribute of two of her animal forms – the sow and the cat [Markale 93–103]) on the other – are amply represented in Carrington's fiction. People enjoy good meals in *The Hearing Trumpet* and in "Jemima et le loup," for example, but violence and cannibalism color "The White Rabbits," "The Débutante," and "The Sisters." Yet in Carrington's paintings meals seem to consist uniquely of fruit, herbs and vegetables, the Goddess's peaceful gifts. In *Edwardian Hunt Breakfast* (1959),[6] a table has been set in a forest clearing, surrounded at a distance by live game, deer, and wild boar (two of the goddess's main forms), while the meal, like the *Lepidoptera*'s, is composed only of fruit. Two "huntsmen" are arriving with a gift of live birds. The hostess has a butterfly's head, perhaps in reference to the Mexican Zapotec butterfly god symbolizing rebirth (Nicholson 13, 43). The message is clear: the butterfly goddess has transformed the hunting ritual into peace and harmony between men and animals.

There is little left to say about Carrington's use of alchemy and the magic arts after Gloria Orenstein's thorough and stimulating analyses. Alchemy has been defined by Arturo Schwarz as an all-male, misogynous, celibate activity, reducing the still and the reconstituted androgyne to the alchemist's onanistic fantasy (156–71). Carrington, Varo, and Fini invented their own alchemy, seeking to create the gold of a fulfilling woman's world. In their work, the recurring egg is a fertility symbol. Carrington's fantastic creatures resemble both the winged dragons and bird-serpents of alchemists like Abraham Juif and Nicolas Valois (Grillot de Givry 354–63), and the Mayan plumed serpent Wind and Corn God Quetzalcoatl. She pointedly titled one of her medieval-looking paintings *The Chrysopeia of Mary the Jewess* (1964) (*La Femme et le Surréalisme* 160), combining Mary the Christian goddess figure with a feminized (Abraham) le Juif. The White Goddess of the Celts and the Aztec Coatlicue are both Earth and Moon Goddess. Carrington portrayed her in these two functions in two separate pictures, one titled *The Ancestor* and the other *The Godmother*. The first (Fig. 3)[7] seems to represent the nocturnal Moon Goddess. Cloaked and hooded in white, against a misty Irish green background, she has the appearance of a ghost. The white of passage and the green of regeneration and hope situate her between both worlds. Green was also the color of the north and of royalty to the Mayas. Moreover, she is standing at the crossroads of the four cardinal points, each of which is guarded by a little lemur, symbol of the lost continent of Lemuria. They are white like her, and her jet black left eye matches theirs. Her other eye (a red rose) and the green cabbage she is holding in her hands point to life. She is human, animal, and vegetable. The celestial vault behind her and the fading moon in the upper right-hand corner suggest that dawn is near, but the picture remains obscure and mysterious, like the strange appari-

Fig. 3   Leonora Carrington, *The Ancestor*, 1968. Oil on canvas. Private collection, Mexico.

tion of the mother's ghost in *Pénélope. The Godmother* (1970) (Fig. 4) is bursting with animal vitality. Her colors – black, gold, and red – symbolize west, south, and east in Mayan mythology. This fat fertility figure, whose black head and shoulders could belong to either an owl or a she-bear, is holding out her arms as perches to two birds: the dove of peace and the wise owl. Her large body is made up of the golden-haired heads of countless women, with a round celestial fire in her center. Her top is haloed with red, matching her red feet. The background creates a bluish white diaphanous light. Her shape is that of the Grail or the half-egg of the alchemical still. The dark matter of her top is being turned into gold and light. Her vase-body is upside down, like the values put forward by Carrington: the Goddess has devoured the women to unite them and their strength; the gold color of alchemy, the sun, and corn have been feminized.

Carrington never discards the male principle, and between *The Ancestor* and *The Godmother* she painted *Forbidden Fruit* (1969) (Fig. 5). A small, disproportionate woman is doing a headstand and rubbing noses with a long snake, twice curled around her in egg-shaped coils. They are sharing fruit, more like pomegranates than apples, and are guarded by sacred animals, two oxen and a lemur. The title seems ironical, as the goddess's pleasurable mating rite eclipses the guilt-ridden Eve story. The picture is prob-

Fig. 4 Leonora Carrington, *The Godmother*, 1970.

Fig. 5 Leonora Carrington, *Forbidden Fruit*, 1969. Oil on canvas. Private collection, Paris.

ably a humorous reference to Graves's description of Osiris's "fifty-yard-long phallus . . . looped around the world like a serpent" (380).

Carrington's animals are often the guardians of the goddess or a substitute female figure. In *The Return of Boadicea* (1969) (*A Retrospective Exhibition*), the Celtic warrior queen is represented with a double bird and horse head. Her fiery chariot is being drawn and protectively surrounded by a team of fierce and sturdy half-horse, half-ox hybrids. The sheep and goats of *Round Dance* (*A Retrospective Exhibition*) form a ring around a compact circle of women dancers. Here the central female principle unites Christian sheep and pre-Christian goats (Graves 425).

With the secret magic of her art, Carrington is forever trying to create a wondrous creature in whom feminine, childlike, animal, and plant qualities would harmoniously merge. She/it appears at the beginning of her story "Quand ils passaient":

> It was quite a sight: fifty black cats, fifty yellow cats and her. Whether or not she was really human, was impossible to determine. Her very smell made it seem doubtful. She exuded a blend of spices, wild game, stables and fur-like herbs. (*Pigeon vole* 33)

The Owl and the Pussycat: Remedios Varo

Varo's exquisite draftsmanship and scientific precision place her technique somewhere between Leonardo and Magritte. Like Carrington, Varo projected another world and was fascinated by the magic arts. Her transformational process through painting is, however, a different one: whereas Carrington used her art to create a potential metamorphosis of the world according to the female and animal principle of the Goddess, Varo's alchemy consisted in transforming her own inner world of nightmarish visions and closing-in contingencies into art. The close friendship between the two women, who shared each other's dreams, studied the hermetic arts and belonged to a Gurdjieff group together, has been described by several critics (Chadwick 191–95).[8]

Varo's wild, wandering youth resembles Carrington's: she escaped from a stifling family life in Madrid to the avant-garde circles of Barcelona. There she met French surrealist poet Benjamin Péret, followed him to Paris, and frequented Breton's group. The war took the couple to Mexico, where Varo settled for the rest of her life. She produced the main body of her work there from the early 1950s to her premature death in 1963.

In his novel *The Crying of Lot 49*, Thomas Pynchon's heroine Oedipa Maas gazes at Remedios Varo's painting *Embroidering the Earth's Mantle* (1961, the center panel of a triptych), recognizes her own Rapunzel pattern, and weeps (10–11).[9] On the one hand, Varo's picture of maidens emprisoned in a tower, weaving a world they cannot reach or see with threads emerging from an alchemist's still, reflects the predicament of Pynchon's Everywoman heroine; on the other, the latter's first name, Oedipa, perfectly suits Varo's omnipresent specular woman protagonist, described as follows by Janet Kaplan:

Most of Varo's personages bear the delicate heart-shaped face with large almond eyes, long sharp nose and thick mane of lively hair that marked the artist's own appearance. The personae she created serve as self-portraits, transmuted through fantasy. (9)

Oedipa's sphinx remains invisible, the riddle purloined, and the only answer is to go on painting.

There is less marvelous in Varo's universe than in Carrington's, but an eerie viewpoint pervades it, similar to the one Todorov attributes to Sartre, Blanchot and Kafka (181–82). The only fantastic object is (wo)man him/herself; the fantastic becomes the norm. To Varo, dreams, real and metaphorical voyages or quests, and the magic arts are interwoven with everyday "reality." Her canvas reflects the deforming mirror of the mind.[10]

Varo's animal imagery is more limited and more intimate than Carrington's. She often uses birds as symbols of escape or simply as decorative motifs, which is the case in *Troubadour* (1959).[11] Were it not for Varo's characteristically uncanny way of making animate and inanimate matter merge and overlap, the wandering orphic minstrel in his little boat, surrounded by attentive birds, might well be part of a sixteenth-century *fine fleur* tapestry. Varo's birds, which often accompany human figures, can also be "Jungian symbols of transcendence" (Kaplan 163).

Two compatible nocturnal beasts stand out in Varo's work: the owl and the cat. She must surely have known Edward Lear's famous nursery rhyme "The Owl and the Pussycat," in which a she-cat and a male owl set out to sea in a boat, fall in love, buy a ring from a pig, get married, dine on mince and quince, and finally "they danced by the light of the moon." Interestingly, this little poem contains most of Varo's favorite themes: voyages, love and eroticism, waiting, transformation, eating fruit (as in Carrington's work), the moon of femininity, and the occult.

The owl is an ambivalent bird: for the Greeks it was a symbol of sadness, solitary retreat, and darkness. For the Egyptians it brought night, cold, and death. Like the cat, it accompanies sorcerers, brings thunder and lightning, and is also the positive bearer of wisdom and clairvoyance.

Varo's most famous and significant owl-picture is *The Creation of the Birds* (1958) (Fig. 6). Here an androgynous owl figure, with human arms, feet and lower face, represents the artist as alchemist, painter and musician, with multiple sources of creative energy. The painter's palette is connected to an alchemist's still, and the artist is filtering the light of a star through a magnifying glass held in his/her left hand, while the right hand is drawing with an extended string of the musical instrument hanging

Fig. 6 Remedios Varo, *The Creation of the Birds*, 1958. Oil on masonite. Private collection, Mexico City.

from his/her neck. This serenely performed activity is producing live birds, one still attached to the sheet of paper in front of the creator, others flying off toward the window. The colors, as in most of Varo's work, are those of alchemy: a reddish-golden brown, black, and white. The wise owl represents Varo's ideal vision of herself as an artist, and the birds her vicarious escape from the world through painting (Chadwick 202–3; Kaplan 181–82).

Several of Varo's owls are more disquieting and tend to indicate a split personality. *Skier* (1960) portrays a useless-looking magician, standing in a strange floating contraption amid clouds and barren trees, with a double face (one upside down) beneath his pointed hat, an empty crystal ball inside his coat. The two owls on either side of him merely reflect his impotence. The woman at the center of *The Encounter* (1962) is cloaked in blue, the unreal color. A small bird is peeping out of her leafy gossamer garment; the woman is holding a replica of her face in one hand and opening a door with the other. On the other side of the door, she encounters an owl, whose face is yet another version of her own, with a calmer expression, and whose human legs seem to belong to a very young man. Here Varo, looking like a *femme fleur,* meets her creative animus and/or potential lover. In Varo's work, as in Fini's, men and women are barely differentiated.

In *Nocturnal Hunt* (1958), an angry, pregnant-looking owl draped in gold cloth is grotesquely tiptoeing forward on long thin human legs and feet.

172

She is being observed from behind by two normal all-bird owls, flying about the Chirico-style building. The childlike humor in this picture also appears in several of the cat-paintings. It seems to indicate animals' "normality" as opposed to the complex, fundamentally hybrid nature of human beings.

The cat, like the owl, can signify clairvoyance, on the one hand, and darkness or death on the other; this opposition is a constant in Varo's world. The cat has a more paradoxical symbology than any other animal. In world mythology it ranges from goddess and sacred animal to evil omen and dangerous pest; it can also be a comical creature. Varo exploits this last aspect when she creates a cross-looking green *Fern-Cat* (1957), or an odd, somewhat reptilian cat constituted by falling dead leaves in *Unexpected Visit* (1958). In such pictures, Varo appears to be making good-natured fun of her own creative process.

In Varo's world, the cat is the owl/artist's ideal silent companion and usually a friendly, touching creature. Such a cat looks on with anxious empathy in *Mimesis* (1960) as his mistress melts into her Magritte-like surroundings. He is looking up through a hole in the floorboards, exactly like the woman protagonist's second face in *Emerging Light* (1962); the cat can therefore be an alter ego. Small decorative cat companions or doubles often appear, like the one curled up at the feet of the *Vagabond* (1958), in his strange little house on wheels, or the one imperturbably sitting under the window in *The Revelation or the Clockmaker* (1955), while a ball of light comes whirling in. The oneiric subject of *Enchanted Gentleman* (1961) is actually disguised as a cat, probably indicating human envy of a cat's simpler existence.

There are only two pictures in which cats are given more importance than the human figures. *Cats' Paradise* (1955) is atypical of Varo. As in Carrington's *Horses,* no humans are present: cats have taken over the world. Two towers (an obsessional motif with Varo) blend into the landscape: extensions of large tree-roots on one side, they are connected to a strange windmill on the other, in an interesting nature-culture configuration. Various happy-looking cats are sitting, standing or lying about. The one gazing out of the first tower window is no Rapunzel: he has the large square head of a tom, and we know he can climb down at will. The cats convey the "ritual fascination" advocated by Baudrillard and a form of contentment unknown to Varo's human characters.

My favorite of Varo's cats is the one at the center of *Sympathy* (or perhaps *Empathy*) (1955) (Fig. 7). The feline is caught in arrested movement, jumping onto a table and thus forming an alchemical egg-shaped figure with the woman seated there. The animal has rumpled the cloth and spilled a glass (Varo explains in a note that cat-lovers like herself tolerate such behavior! [Paz and Caillois 177]). Woman and cat have similar dilated, bright, astonished eyes. She is watching the cat's rapturous upward gaze a little

Fig. 7   Remedios Varo, *Sympathy,* 1955.

anxiously: above them a complicated geometrical constellation of electric sparks has formed, originating from the cat's fur, the woman's hair, and what looks like the tails of other cats, hidden under the table. The liquid from the glass, like Alice's tears, has spread into a lake. The magic electricity refers to an exclusive complicity between the woman and the cat, like the one Baudelaire jealously describes in his poem "Le Chat" (*Les Fleurs du mal* 51). To Varo's solitary woman alchemist, the owl and the cat seem to provide a slightly reassuring sibling or specular presence which connects her to a receding reality. However, Kaplan suggests that the comforting feline of *Sympathy* may also be paradoxically infecting the woman with madness, like Carroll's Cheshire Cat, and hence generating anguish (122–24). Varo's world is never truly serene.

The Cat That Walks by Herself: Leonor Fini

Like her name, Leonor Fini is de*fini*tively feline: her first name is an essential component of her varying mythical monster, the sphinx, and closely related to her basic totem animal, the cat.

Fini's mother left Argentina and a tyrannical Neapolitan husband for her native Trieste when the child was a year old. Xavière Gauthier reports that Leonor was often disguised as a boy, to avoid being kidnapped by her father: androgyny began early (*Fini* 85–89). She also supposedly had vertical pupils, like a cat's, until she was four! In 1937, at seventeen, Fini moved to Paris, the same year as both Carrington and Varo, but on her own. Fini rejected Breton's authority and always refused to join his group,[12] but became friends with several Surrealists and other rebels, including Ernst, Bataille and later Genet. She spent the summer of 1939 at St. Martin d'Ardèche (Chadwick 80–84), and painted a portrait of Carrington looking like Boadicea, Fini, and herself combined.[13]

If Varo was Oedipa, Fini is Narcissa, forever contemplating her own image and reproducing it on canvas.[14] She told Gauthier:

The painting instinct draws a whole world out of me and that world is me. It is always an ambivalent and contradictory place where I find myself, and that can be an astonishing experience at times. (*Fini* 16)

Baudrillard recalls Pausanias's version of the Narcissus myth: the young man, in mourning for his beloved twin sister, first mistook his image in a stream for hers and later used it as a consolation for her loss (97). In Fini's *Incomparable Narcissus* (1971) (Gauthier, *Fini* 93), Narcissus is sitting, naked, with his feet in the water. Next to his own reflection stands another: a female identical twin, naked and upright. Outside the water, only her legs, which now look masculine, are visible. For Fini, as for Baudrillard, mirrors, like seduction, are always deceptive, and seduction is always self-seduction (Baudrillard 95–100).

While Carrington and Varo were inspired by Renaissance artists and medieval alchemists, Fini acquired an early taste for Klimt, Munch, Beardsley, the Pre-Raphaelites, Art Nouveau and Art Deco. She descends from the Symbolists and Decadents. Fernand Khnopff's famous picture *The Caress* (1896)[15] could be a symbolic portrait of her. It in fact represents Khnopff and his sister, cheek to cheek, she with a woman's head and the body of a large spotted feline lying down, he leaning his naked torso against her; they have almost identical faces, forming an androgynous ensemble. Together they constitute a perverse combination of the Greek sphinx – a woman's head and breasts, a bird's wings and a lion's body – and of the earlier Egyptian version, a reclining lion with a man's head (Borges and Guerrero 84–85). Fini's numerous sphinxes are always female, with the artist's face. As Gauthier suggests, these creatures seem to be sadistic monsters, frequently surrounded by scattered skulls and bones, whose would-be victims are young men (*Fini* 46–47). The *Sphinx Amalburga* (1942) (Fig. 8) has her hands around the neck of a delicate sleeping youth, with the apparent intention of strangling him.

Chthonian Deity Espying the Slumber of a Young Man (1947) (Jelenski 65; Gauthier 9) conveys the usual sexual ambivalence. His naked body looks androgynous and limp. The crouching black sphinx behind him appears

Fig. 8   Leonor Fini, *The Sphinx Amalburga*, 1942.

more threatening than protective. Death always lurks in Fini's work. She creates a surreal antinomy between the worlds of the living and the dead. For her, as for Cocteau's Orpheus, stepping through the looking glass means falling in love with death. Her sphinxes ominously guard the limits between masculine and feminine, human and animal, the world and the underworld.

Cats take the place of sphinxes in real life (Gauthier, *Fini* 53). No animal illustrates Baudrillard's theory of ritual and ornament so well as the cat. Fini is supposed to live in a perfectly arranged Art Nouveau setting, surrounded by Persian cats and beautiful people of both sexes, in "fearful symmetry," in "luxe, calme et volupté."

Fini always portrays cats with a woman (herself), reflecting each other's grace and dangerous beauty (except for one picture of a lone cat, *The Cat Manoul* [1947] [Jelenski 60]). *The Ideal Life* (1950) (Fig. 9) provides the finest example of Leonor as Cat-Goddess, with a sullen expression, enthroned in front of a round striped screen. Five Persian cats and an ocelot are gathered around her in a counterbalancing circle: a white cat to her left, the ocelot to her right, the black witch's cat in the center and the others in front. All the animals (except one) and the woman are staring straight at the spectator with cold, hard eyes.

Although Leonor Fini has never lived in Mexico, as have Carrington and Varo, it seems relevant here that Ocelotl (the ocelot) was one of the god Quetzalcoatl's twins, representing "the passage of sun and planets through the underworld" (Nicholson 52). Quetzalcoatl, Ocelotl and the dog Xolotl were born to the goddess Coatlicue, mother of the gods, sister of the Celtic White Goddess and devourer of sacrificial victims. She wore a skirt of live snakes. The cat, with its double nature, takes on its full significance in

176

Fini's work as a miniature reflection of the mother/monster, earth/hell, life/death goddess Fini wishes to incarnate herself. Cats were sacred animals in ancient Egypt, where a double goddess, Bastet the benevolent cat and Sekhmet the malevolent lioness, was worshipped (De la Rocheterie 67–72).

The last card of the Tarot, The Fool, is represented with a flesh-colored (meaning sexual) cat clawing and biting him in the leg and probably the testicles (De la Rocheterie 67–71; Grillot de Givry 285). Much has been said about Fini's castrating effect (Gauthier, *Fini* 71, 151). Several photographs show her hair provocatively styled to imitate Medusa's snakes. Like Cixous's Medusa, she is beautiful; unlike her, she is not laughing.

Conversely, Fini has expressed the earth and fertility aspect of the Goddess in a series of pictures, each of which represents a white-skinned, white-breasted woman with an egg-shaped shaved head holding a large egg in each of the alchemical colors.[16] The red egg is held at arm's length, the black egg on the woman's lap. In the third painting, titled (like Carrington's story) *The Oval Lady* (1956), the even larger white egg has become the woman's pregnant belly; a winglike cloak draped about her against a black background suggests the presence of death.

Like the Goddess in her macabre aspect, and unlike Carrington's and Varo's fruit-eaters, Fini's protagonists can be murderous, carnivorous and

Fig. 9   Leonor Fini, *The Ideal Life*, 1950.

Fig. 10   Leonor Fini, *The Girl Mutants,* 1971.

even cannibalistic. In *The Strangers* (1968), three women with wooden spoons are bending over a pot containing a "stew" of human limbs (Gauthier, *Fini* 116). Unsavory dissections and operations appear in several pictures, and *The Guests* (1971) depicts two women eating what is supposedly their hostess's face (Gauthier, *Fini* 105). This type of horror recalls fairy tales, some of Carrington's stories (not her painting), and the Red Queen's "Off with their heads!" Witches, ogres, monsters and assassins are natural components of a child's imagination. Fini told Gauthier that she had decided long ago to remain at the stage when a child thinks (s)he is the whole world: "I am the snake that bites its own tail. I am the Moon, Astarte, metaphysically a virgin, an amazon" (*Fini* 72, my translation).

Like Varo, Fini believes in the superiority of cats, and like Carrington, she would prefer humans to be more animal-like. *The Girl Mutants* (1971) (Fig. 10) shows three little girls turning into cats (Gauthier, *Fini* 134–35). Their features seem so feline that one expects them to start purring. Each one is clasping a large cat between her legs, where her "pussy" should be. This humorous picture reads like a perverse adult interpretation of a child's dream.

Fini also writes. Gauthier quotes an astonishing extract of an unpublished text (*Fini* 134–35) describing the woman protagonist's oneiric meeting with a giant, sensual sphinx, Amaouri, who comes close to Carrington's creature in "Quand ils passaient." In the dream-novel *L'Oneiropompe* (1977), the heroine encounters the perfect lover. He is, of course, a cat

(*Obliques* 117). There is an underlying irony and self-irony about Fini's work, creating a distance between her and the world, such as can be perceived in cats, in Baudelaire's idea of Beauty as a stone sphinx (*Les Fleurs du mal* 32), and Baudrillard's fascination for women and animals. Neither Carrington's passionate feminist quest nor Varo's anxious inner peregrinations can be sensed behind Fini's perfect aesthetics: she never removes her mask.

Three artists, three witches,[17] three animal incarnations of the Goddess (winged mare, owl-cat, sphinx-cat), and three symbolic colors, representing the microcosms of three "fantastic" women painters: red for the molten gold of Carrington's feminist life-drive, white for Varo's moonlit dream universe, and black for Fini's chthonian otherworld.

Notes

1. For animal symbology throughout this essay, see Jean Chevalier and Alain Gheerbrant, *Dictionnaire des symboles* (Paris: Robert Laffont/Jupiter, 1982) and Jacques de la Rocheterie, *La Symbologie des rêves* (Paris: Editions Imago, 1986).

2. Both pictures are reproduced in *Leonora Carrington: A Retrospective Exhibition,* catalogue (New York: Center for Inter-American Relations, 1975), unpaginated.

3. For color symbology throughout this essay, see Chevalier and Gheerbrant.

4. French version, "La Maison de la peur," *La Débutante* 26–30.

5. See Orenstein, *Theater* 122–23: "She experienced a 'mental breakdown' or what might be better described . . . as a 'breakthrough' to another dimension, to a world of magical and visionary domains."

6. Reproduced in *A Retrospective Exhibition.*

7. Reproduced in color as the cover of *The Oval Lady.*

8. See also Roger Caillois, "Cases d'un échiquier," *Obliques* 219.

9. For more data on Varo and Pynchon, see Colvile.

10. See also Paz: ". . . non le monde à l'envers, mais l'envers du monde" (70).

11. All paintings referred to in this section are reproduced in Paz and Caillois.

12. See Fini's "Lettre à Roger Borderie," *Obliques* 15.

13. See *The Alcove: An Interior with Three Women* (reproduction no. 72 in Chadwick). Carrington is shown in the foreground wearing a breastplate of armor over her dress.

14. All paintings by Fini referred to in this essay are reproduced in the works by Gauthier, Jelenski and Brion.

15. Reproduced in John Christian, *Symbolists and Decadents* (New York: Park South Books, 1977).

16. *La Gardienne à l'oeuf rouge* (1955), *La Gardienne à l'oeuf noir* (1955), and *La Dame ovale* (1956) are all reproduced in Brion.

17. See Andrade's reference to the "Three Sisters" in *Macbeth* with regard to women Surrealists in Mexico.

References

Andrade, Lourdes. "Le Mythe de l'histoire, l'histoire du mythe. La Femme et le Sur-réalisme au Mexique." *La Femme et le Surréalisme,* catalogue of the exhibition. Lausanne: Musée des Beaux Arts, 1987, 85–89.

Baudelaire, Charles. *Les Fleurs du mal* [1861]. Paris: Librairie Générale Française, 1972.

Baudrillard, Jean. *De la séduction.* Paris: Editions Galilée, 1979.

Bettelheim, Bruno. *Psychanalyse des contes de fées.* Paris: Robert Laffont, 1976.

Borges, Jorge Luis, and Margarita Guerrero. *Manuel de zoologie fantastique.* Paris: Julliard, 1965.

Breton, André. *The First Surrealist Manifesto* [1924]. English translation in Lippard.

Brion, Marcel. *Leonor Fini et son oeuvre.* Paris: Pauvert, 1955.

Carrington, Leonora. "La Débutante." *La Débutante* 21–25.

———. "The Bird Superior, Max Ernst." *View* 2:13.

———. *La Débutante contes et pièces.* Paris: Flammarion, 1978.

———. *En-Bas.* N.p.: Henri Parisot, 1945. Paris: Eric Losfeld, 1973.

———. *The Hearing Trumpet.* New York: St. Martin's Press, 1976.

———. "Histoire du petit Francis." *Pigeon vole* 63–148.

———. Interview with Germaine Rouvre. *Obliques* 14–15: *La Femme surréaliste* (1977) 91–92; English translations by and in Chadwick 105.

———. "Jemima et le loup." *Pigeon vole* 47–62.

———. "La Maison de la peur." *La Débutante* 26–30.

———. "The Oval Lady." *The Oval Lady* 13–18.

———. *The Oval Lady* [1939]. Trans. Rachel Holt. Santa Barbara: Capra Press, 1975.

———. *Pénélope. La Débutante* 114–182.

———. *Pigeon vole: contes retrouvés.* Cognac: Le temps qu'il fait, 1986.

———. "Quand ils passaient." *Pigeon vole* 33–46.

———. "The Royal Command." *The Oval Lady* 41–45.

———. "The Sisters" ("Les Soeurs"). *La Débutante* 48–57.

———. "The White Rabbits." *The Oval Lady* 27–31.

Leonora Carrington: A Retrospective Exhibition, catalogue. New York: Center for Inter-American Relations, 1976.

Carroll, Lewis. *Alice's Adventures in Wonderland* and *Through the Looking Glass* [1832]. New York: Bantam Books, 1981.

Chadwick, Whitney. *Women and the Surrealist Movement.* Boston: Little, Brown and Co., 1985.

Chénieux-Gendron, Jacqueline. Preface. *Pigeon vole: contes retrouvés,* by Leonora Carrington. Cognac: Le temps qu'il fait, 1986. 7–9.

———. *Le Surréalisme et le roman.* Lausanne: L'Age d'Homme, 1983.

Chevalier, Jean, and Alain Gheerbrant. *Dictionnaire des symboles.* Paris: Robert Laffont/Jupiter, 1982.

Colvile, Georgiana. *Beyond and Beneath the Mantle: On Thomas Pynchon's "The Crying of Lot 49."* Amsterdam: Rodopi, 1988.

De la Rocheterie, Jacques. *La Symbologie des rêves.* Paris: Editions Imago, 1986.

Ernst, Max. "Some Data on the Youth of M.E." *View* 2 (1942): 28–30.

La Femme et le Surréalisme, catalogue of the exhibition. Lausanne: Musée des Beaux Arts, 1987.

Freeman, Margaret B. "The Birds and the Beasts of the Tapestries." *The Unicorn Tapestries* [1976]. New York: E. P. Dutton, 1983. 67–90.

Gauthier, Xavière. *Leonor Fini.* Paris: Le Musée de Poche, 1973.

———. *Surréalisme et sexualité.* Paris: Gallimard, 1971.

Graves, Robert. *The White Goddess* [1948]. New York: Farrar, Strauss and Giroux, 1986.

Grillot de Givry. *Witchcraft, Magic and Alchemy* [1931]. New York: Dover Publications, 1971.

Jelenski, Constantin. *Leonor Fini.* New York: Olympia Press, 1968.

Jung, Carl G. *Man and His Symbols.* New York: Doubleday, 1964.

Kaplan, Janet A. *Unexpected Journeys: The Art and Life of Remedios Varo.* New York: Abbeville Press, 1988.

Lascault, Gilbert. *Le Monstre dans l'art occidental.* Paris: Klinksieck, 1973.

Lear, Edward. "The Owl and the Pussycat" [1871]. New York: Golden Press, 1982.

Lippard, Lucy. *Surrealists on Art.* Englewood Cliffs: Prentice Hall, 1970.

Markale, Jean. *Women of the Celts.* London: Gordon Cremonesi, 1975.

Marks, E., and I. de Courtivron, eds. *New French Feminisms.* New York: Schocken Books, 1981.

Nicholson, Irene. *Mexican and Central American Mythology.* New York: Paul Hamlyn, 1967.

Obliques 14–15: *La Femme surréaliste* (1977).

Orenstein, Gloria Feman. "Leonora Carrington's Visionary Art for the New Age." *Chrysalis* 3 (1977): 66–77.

———. *The Theater of the Marvelous.* New York: New York University Press, 1975.

Paz, Octavio. "Apparitions et disparitions de Remedios Varo." *Courant alternatif.* Paris: Gallimard, 1972.

Paz, Octavio, and Roger Caillois. *Remedios Varo.* Mexico City: Ediciones Era, 1972.

Pynchon, Thomas. *The Crying of Lot 49.* New York: Bantam Books, 1966.

Schwarz, Arturo. "La Machine célibataire alchimique." *Les Machines célibataires,* catalogue. Venice: Alfieri, 1976.

Todorov, Tzvetan. *Introduction à la littérature fantastique.* Paris: Editions du Seuil, 1970.

View 2 (1942).

Valentine, André, Paul et les autres, or, the Surrealization of Valentine Hugo

Jean-Pierre Cauvin

Je dis un jour à André Breton – venu voir dans mon atelier le portrait que j'avais imaginé d'Arthur Rimbaud: "Je rêve d'être quelque chose entre les poètes et les peintres" et . . . il me répondit: "Mais vous êtes déjà cela – et vous êtes peintre – aussi."

Je ne t'ai jamais plus aimé qu'au moment même où je mettais tout contre moi.

Tu portes avec toi le merveilleux – un petit peu de ce merveilleux est passé en moi – tout peut arriver puisque tu m'as aimée et puisque je t'admirerai jusqu'à mon dernier battement de coeur.[1]

Valentine Hugo's credentials as a Surrealist rest chiefly on the illustrations she contributed to a number of books authored or published by Eluard, Char, and Breton, and on several remarkable works painted under the direct influence of the surrealist group – the best known being the portrait of the Surrealists, begun in 1932 and completed in 1948, and the portrait of Rimbaud, completed in December 1933. Her admiration for and abiding devotion to Eluard, Breton, Char, Buñuel, Crevel, and Dali are well known. Significant as they are, however, her work and her association with the Surrealists have not received the attention they deserve.[2]

Documents housed in the Harry Ransom Humanities Research Center at the University of Texas shed considerable light on the evolution of Valentine Hugo as an artist and person during the years 1925–35, the most critical decade of her life. Composed of notebooks, journals, scrapbooks, dream transcriptions, photographs, jotted memoranda of her travels, and especially drafts of her letters to André Breton and others,[3] these papers provide an intimate glimpse, almost day by day, into the activities, inner thoughts, and crises of a gifted artist whose involvement with the Surrealists changed her life and who in turn enriched much of their work – most notably Eluard's.

A brief overview of Valentine Hugo's early years as an artist – before her conversion to Surrealism – will help place her evolution in perspective. Born on 16 March 1887, in the Channel town of Boulogne-sur-Mer, Valentine Gross evinced from childhood a love of art and music, no doubt owing to the influence of her father, a pianist and musician who also communicated to her his fondness for the theatre. After moving to Paris in 1907, Valentine enrolled at the Ecole des Beaux-Arts. Her first work, exhibited in 1909, displayed a penchant for blue backgrounds and an impressionist style. Attracted as were many Parisians of the time by the spectacular creations of the Ballets Russes, Valentine drew many sketches of the star of the troupe, Nijinsky, and of the choreography of such successful productions as *The Afternoon of a Faun, Scheherazade, The Spectre of the Rose, Petrouchka, Daphnis and Chloe, The Firebird,* and others. In April 1913, the paintings she exhibited in the foyer of the Théâtre des Champs-Elysées on the occasion of the famous premiere of *The Rite of Spring* received much acclaim. Although she subsequently published several essays and reminiscences on the dance, she never completed her long-projected work on Nijinsky.

Valentine quickly became acquainted with many of the artists, musicians, and young writers of her day, inviting them to her *salon* to discuss their latest and future creations. Nothing seems to have given her more pleasure than to receive her artist friends in her home. The variety and quality of the successive *salons* she held over the years and from home to home is reflected in many of the portraits or sketches she drew of her guests: Satie, Picasso, Radiguet, Cocteau, Stravinsky, Auric, Valéry, Poulenc, Artaud, Tzara, Princess Bibesco and, of course, her later surrealist friends Breton, Eluard, and Ernst. In Valentine Gross's *salon* was first conceived the idea of the ballet *Parade,* which eventually brought together Satie, Cocteau, Picasso, and Diaghilev. In 1917, she became acquainted with a young officer on leave, Jean Hugo, a great-grandson of Victor Hugo. Jean was struck by "ses yeux perçants, mobiles, inquiets parfois, [qui] ne semblaient jamais rêver."[4] (Appearances can be deceiving indeed. . . .) As a result of his acquaintance with her, Jean discovered an environment utterly different from that of his military experience, where *"Parade* was more important than Verdun."[5]

Premiering 18 May 1917, *Parade* cemented the friendship between Valentine and its most articulate co-creator, Jean Cocteau, who often referred to her as "le Cygne de Boulogne" owing to her long and graceful neck. An episode told by Jean Hugo points to late 1917 as the occasion of Valentine's first encounter with André Breton, then in an army medic's uniform, the occasion being a reading by Cocteau of his *Cap de Bonne Espérance.*[6] While the latter hoped to elicit from his audience testimonials of approval and admiration, the young medic said nothing, pointedly retreating into an icy reserve that betrayed what would later become an evident and abiding dislike for Cocteau the person and his work. Valentine's increasing admiration and affection for Cocteau, on the other hand, is exemplified by her choice of him and Satie to be witnesses at her wedding to Jean Hugo on 7 August 1919. Further evidence of her devotion to Cocteau and Satie is to be found in Valentine's creative activities. She contributed to the sets and decor of *Les Mariés de la Tour Eiffel* and to several of Satie's musical farces, *Le Piège de Méduse, Socrate,* and *Mercure.* Until his death in July 1925, the composer, known for his eccentric ways, communicated with Valentine in typically grumpy yet affectionate terms, calling her "ma chère grande fille" and "ma douce petite fille"; she in turn called him her "grand-père."[7] Valentine's later friendship with Paul Eluard, whom she addressed as her brother and confidant, was essentially of the same kind.

Valentine's work habits, indeed her very inspiration as an artist, were very much a reflection of her friendships and loyalties. Her best efforts were born, and sometimes torn, from her enthusiasms, her personal relationships and especially – as will be shown later – her consuming passion for Breton. According to Jean Hugo, though, she was not always disciplined in her work patterns and, at least until the early thirties, the rhythm and pace of her creative output were somewhat irregular. But her work attests to a very genuine talent for costume designs, including disguises, theatre sets with a decidedly nocturnal theme, and certain colors set off against dark backgrounds.[8] A comparison of Valentine's costume and set designs with those of Jean Hugo, himself a noted designer and the better-known of the two during the twenties, strongly suggests that he incorporated many of her ideas, at least in the case of many designs that are credited to him. Where they collaborated jointly and equally, her more visionary and dramatic style stands out with greater relief. Such an observation is borne out by Valentine's post-1930 work, which she created on her own, independently of Jean. A glance at the latter's watercolors, gouaches, paintings, and décors reveals fundamental differences – Jean's manner favors pastels, a lighter touch, and a *naïf* style; Valentine's bears the mark of a more intense and oneiric vision, especially after the beginning of her association with the Surrealists.

From 1925 on, the bright star that had shone in Valentine's artistic firmament began to dim. By 1929, Cocteau had been eclipsed in her affections by Breton, though without any encouragement on the latter's part – indeed, despite his protestations and attempts at avoiding her, as shall be seen later. The ascendancy of the new star became manifest to Valentine as early as June 1926, when she envisioned Breton in a remarkably premonitory dream. In her dream, while going up a stairway with Jean, her attention is drawn to a number of descending faces which she does not recognize. There suddenly emerges a face whiter and more resplendent

André Breton and Valentine Hugo, ca. 1931. Reproduced courtesy of the Harry Ransom Humanities Research Center, The University of Texas at Austin.

than the others – Breton's – around which the other faces progressively gather. She recognizes the profiles of Eluard, Aragon, and Drieu la Rochelle.[9]

Je vois alors que A.B. regarde fixement à côté de moi. Je me demande "pourquoi regarde-t-il à côté de moi et pas moi?" Je suis alors prise de terreur. . . . Ma terreur augmente à mesure que le visage de B. s'approche blanc comme l'ivoire. Au moment où le visage va nous atteindre et disparaître en nous dépassant le regard de B. se fixe sur moi et je me réveille.

She continues:

Ne trouvez-vous pas ce rêve bien étrange – en ce temps-là, pourquoi l'ai-je fait? . . . Pourquoi ai-je justement, moi, été prévenue de cette sorte d'isolement lumineux dans lequel vous êtes volontairement ou non depuis quelque temps et ces cercles de visages autour de vous apparaissent et disparaissent pour reparaître ensuite différents mais toujours suivant le même rythme. Et c'est enfin ce rêve qui m'a donné la force de vaincre un peu de la timidité que me donnait l'admiration que j'avais pour vous et la volonté que j'ai eue de vous connaître et d'avoir votre amitié et votre confiance peut-être un peu malgré que tout semblait en effet contraire. Je voudrais savoir pourquoi je suis hantée depuis si longtemps. . . . C'était pourtant bien simple, bien facile à vous demander, et s'expliquerait alors ma façon d'être avec vous comme si je vous connaissais depuis longtemps, et pourquoi je vous parle souvent comme une soeur, comme un ami de toujours, et cela m'est naturel, et cela vous blesse . . . vous vous doutez bien de mon désespoir profond et inexplicable. Je hais tout ce que je semblais avoir aimé. Je voudrais écorcher vif le monde entier pour savoir rien qu'un peu de vérité sur tout ceci.

Other dreams reveal the coruscating impression left upon her psyche by Breton. Awaking after another such dream, she felt impelled to translate it first into a blue-on-black drawing, then to paint it. "Mais Jean Hugo m'a fait perdre courage en me disant que deux êtres mariés faisant tous deux de la peinture était une chose ridicule – j'ai donc tout abandonné."[10] Such flagrant sexism may help explain why, starting the same year (1926), Valentine and Jean lived increasingly apart, she in her beloved Paris, he at the Mas de Fourques near Lunel, in Languedoc, where he enjoyed greater peace and better health than in the bustling capital. Their separation, an entirely amicable one, was interrupted by visits to each other, "en frère et soeur." In 1927, Jean was hired to design the sets and costumes for Dreyer's La Passion de Jeanne d'Arc. But it soon became clear that the director and his designer did not get along. Valentine, on the other hand, full of admiration for Dreyer, devoted all her energies to the project over several months and completed the bulk of the work begun by Jean.[11]

While Valentine was drawing closer to the Surrealists, as if under a powerful spell or some inexorable gravitational pull, Jean was going through a personal crisis of a different sort. As a child, he had been raised in a resolutely atheistic family environment. Between 1927 and 1929, feeling a spiritual void, he sensed an increasing need for fulfillment which, after a number of retreats and pilgrimages, he found in religious

André Breton, Valentine Hugo, Salvador Dali, ca. 1931. Reproduced courtesy of the Harry Ransom Humanities Research Center, The University of Texas at Austin.

faith. In March 1931, he was baptized. Valentine and Jean were divorced in 1932.

Through Breton and Eluard, Valentine extended her immersion in the surrealist milieu by befriending Gala and Salvador Dali, Max Ernst and Marie-Berthe Aurenche, Char, Tzara, Crevel, Sadoul, and Hugnet. At the behest of Breton who, as is well known, had no appreciation for music, and despite her own very deep love for that art, she sold her piano and her musical library to Marie-Laure de Noailles.[12]

At the very time that Valentine was subjugated by her *amour fou* for Breton (a love of excruciating intensity, judging from her letters and note-books), he was still in the throes of his own passionate affair with Suzanne Musard, the woman evoked in his most famous love poem, *L'Union libre,* and the person referred to as "X" in *Les Vases communicants.* As a consequence of Suzanne's unstable ways, his own financial difficulties, and differences of social environment, Breton alternately experienced, in the words of his friend André Thirion, "le paradis et l'enfer" between 1927 and 1931.[13] As he acknowledged in *Les Vases communicants,* Breton had reached a point where life was more or less completely out of joint and where his sense of reality was impaired. "Sous mes yeux," he wrote in a pithy and vivid sentence, "les arbres, les livres, les gens flottaient, un couteau dans le coeur."[14] It is no doubt because he had felt reality slipping

Paul Eluard, André Breton, X, Valentine Hugo at the Montmartre Fair, ca. July 1932. Reproduced courtesy of the Harry Ransom Humanities Research Center, The University of Texas at Austin.

out from under his feet that he chose to examine, in his 1932 essay-journal, the relationship of dream phenomena to wakeful states and his own recent dream experiences. *Les Vases communicants* – and more generally the realm of dreams – can be interpreted as the means by which Breton sought to regain his psychological bearings and to overcome despair. And of course the turbulent years 1929–31 were for Breton, aside from matters of personal affect, also fraught with ideological conflict and polemical confrontation.

Attracted to the Surrealists in general and to Breton in particular like the proverbial moth to a dazzling flame, Valentine got a decidedly cool reception from the object of her fascination. Still under the sway of his feelings for Suzanne, Breton kept his distance from Valentine until late 1931, as his letters to Valentine make abundantly clear. The very formal, deferential, but always courtly tone he employs does not conceal a refractory intent. In oblique and sometimes contorted ways, he refuses to accede to her offers of friendship and solace, permitting only an occasional conversation, under the pretext that it would be highly improper for a person of his low station to frequent her kind and that he is not at all what he appears to be. "Songez, Madame," he writes, "que je vis presque dans la nuit. Depuis dix ans, c'est vrai, presque tout ce qui subsistait en moi de jour est tombé." He is unable to understand that there is a tomorrow and besides, he gets along only with a few "voyous de mon espèce (et sur le plan du 'mal,' encore!) et quelques êtres, encore une fois, de la rue." In her presence, he could not be "simple." He would feel entirely at a loss.[15] In his next letter to her, nearly a month later, he entreats her not to repeat a statement she recently uttered in his presence – most probably an avowal of her affection. It is, he writes, so serious a matter that it induces paralysis. "L'hostilité même met plus à l'aise."[16] Clearly, then, Breton has other concerns. Valentine is not one of them, except for her assiduousness, which he finds disconcerting. There are many things that stand in the way of their developing a relationship. Chief among them are her social status as a member of the *haute bourgeoisie* (whose values and life style she had by and large already renounced, though not some of its manners),[17] the difference in their ages (she was nine years his senior), and Breton's known partiality for a different type, the *femme-enfant*. To the list one could add the fact that their acquaintanceship was one of relatively long standing, going back to 1917. A serendipitous encounter or *hasard objectif* it was not. Her very persistence and devotion no doubt prompted him to rebuff her. And yet . . .

Her letters, written at an average rate of two a week and an eloquent, if often tormented psychography of her obsession, are evidence of her unrelenting efforts to win Breton's confidence, to earn his friendship, and, after December 1931, to preserve their intimacy.[18] Together with her notebook entries, they constitute a record of her states of mind, from the

189

Castellane le 18 septembre

Valentine je t'aime

André

Bonsoir Valentine

[Explanatory note
in Valentine Hugo's hand]

1931

Le 18 Septembre pendant le déjeuner André fit un essai d'écriture où les lettres étaient pen-
chées tantôt à droite tantôt à
gauche. Il écrivait ainsi presque
couramment. Sadoul et moi écri-
vions ainsi avec beaucoup plus de
difficulté. Le soir après m'avoir dit bonsoir il glissa ce billet sous la porte qui faisait
communiquer nos chambres. (Reproduced courtesy of the Harry Ransom Humanities Research Center, The University of Texas at Austin.)

reflective and the plangent to dizzying flights of exaltation. What they reveal most of all, however, is the congruence of her vision of persons and
things with her artistic work, especially after 1931. Just as her dream transcriptions show a pattern of luminous visions and often swirling motion,
her epistolary style is studded with images of light and color, especially
when she describes her perceptions of Breton. Her pictorial vision clearly
reflects a fundamental inner vision that her love for Breton further stimu-
lated and developed. By a truly remarkable *hasard objectif,* it is Valentine,
the spouse of a direct descendant of Victor Hugo, who evinces the greater
kinship with the imaginative powers and Romantic sensibility of the seer-
poet of *Les Rayons et les ombres, Les Contemplations, Dieu,* and *La Fin de
Satan.* For hers is the creativity and temper of a visionary Romantic (or a
Romantic visionary) turned surrealist.[19] This is of course evident in her
pictorial art. It equally informs her epistolary style, which possesses some
of the characteristics of automatic writing. A very spare, at times nonexistent use of punctuation is noticeable throughout her drafts and notes.
(Dashes are her favored means of separating sentences.) A number of
more consciously worked passages feature the rhythms and imagery of
the prose poem. In those instances (between 1931 and 1932) when she
yields to a *délire d'amour,* her writing becomes at best dithyrambic, at
worst fulsome. Whatever the emotional register, her imagery remains
predominantly luminescent or starkly contrastive.

The following excerpts from her unpublished writings represent the
range of her oneiric and often searing style:

Vous me parlez sans cesse de mon jour, de ma terrible lumière. J'enterrerai avec moi ce jour, cette lumière. Et si ce tombeau où je serai bientôt a des fissures, les rayons qui en sortiront en feront pour vous en phare, lorsque vous serez dans la nuit la plus profonde et la plus désespérante. . . . Je suis emportée sur les ondes puissantes d'un monstre merveilleux. Il vole bien et sait ce qu'il veut dans l'irréalisable. Ni diable ni dieu ne sont rien pour moi. La force dominante qui me guide ou m'aveugle est la seule qu'il me soit possible de tolérer pour que je voie vraiment clair. . . . Pourquoi donc promener au grand jour une apparence qui ne voit plus et n'entend plus, ne parle plus. Parfois je suis une statue d'un autre âge que l'on a fait descendre de sa niche et qu'on oblige à sembler vivre. J'ai hâte de regagner mon socle et de reprendre l'immobilité qui me fera revivre selon ma foi. Ces murailles dont j'aspire à m'entourer depuis si longtemps, elles m'enterreront bientôt. J'ai encore la faiblesse de vouloir constater cette mort. Quelle liberté enfin. M'attendront et me trouveront vivante ceux-là seuls que j'aime et qui savent. Traversent les murailles les corps et les âmes comme la flamme merveilleuse qui dévore tout en recréant les plus précieux trésors.[20]

Parfois je songe à une vie impossible sans doute – pure – transparente et riche d'illusions comme le diamant – à une vie qui serait comme un grand feu dévorant purifiant tout sur son passage et qui ne s'éteindrait jamais – oui c'est bien moi qui rêve à tout cela – moi qui voit [sic] tout de suite la fissure dans le mur d'apparence solide, la tache sordide sur l'étoffe somptueuse, qui entends le son faussé dans la limpidité des cloches et qui sens l'odeur immonde de tout ce qui doit retourner au fumier dans les plus suaves tromperies de parfums. C'est parce que le réel m'atteint violemment et me blesse que je suis toujours perdue dans des songeries presque ininterrompues." (Undated, ca. October 1930)

Her judgments about the contemporary arts are expressed in incendiary terms, reflecting her complete assimilation of surrealist values. She speaks of the difficulty in cleaning up the "great stinking cesspool of contemporary literature and painting": "il faudrait pouvoir faire ce qu'on fait aux marais de Camargue pleins de moustiques et d'herbes pourries et de fièvres – il faudrait tout ravager d'un grand feu – le feu. . . . Comme j'aimerais être . . . le maître du feu" (7 November 1930).

This stance is exacerbated by her involvement in the scandal surrounding L'Age d'or (in which she herself played a minor supporting role) and by the ideological and political wars being waged by, around, and against Breton in connection with surrealist orthodoxy and Communist Party affairs. In January 1931, she inveighs against both the party's maneuverings and "la bourgeoisie française tout rongée jusqu'aux os par la cupidité, l'hypocrisie, l'égoïsme, . . . cette bourgeoisie sournoise corruptrice de l'idéal depuis des siècles."[21] Conversely, she describes the volume of L'Immaculée Conception, authored by the two persons she most admires, as "cet immense oiseau merveilleux plus terriblement oiselé que ne le fut jamais le plus rarissime et célèbre gerfaut des glaces polaires" (10 December 1930).

Light imagery reaches its greatest intensity when she describes Breton, most notably his facial features, his eyes and hair, thereby achieving an apotheosizing effect:

Mon coeur est si plein de joie lorsque vous êtes près de moi que je suis toute illuminée par cette clarté qui vient de votre visage et surtout de ce glacier blanc comme le ravissement qui prend vos tempes vos yeux et se perd dans vos cheveux. (Undated, ca. September 1930)

L'eau si noire est si profonde que ni moi mi toi ni ce qui est dans l'air ni dans la terre et dans la mer ni toi ni moi ne saurions en entrevoir le fond – et le feu mon amour est si violent si éclatant qu'il me dévorera bien un jour tout entière comme il dévore mes pensées sur toi et brûle mon coeur la nuit et le jour et m'aveugle parce que tu brilles toi seul au monde tu brilles et tu m'éclaires plus que tous les soleils et toutes les étoiles et je suis parfois éblouie presque mortellement par toi toi mon astre sombre. (18 December 1931)

Il y a en toi des lumières merveilleuses que tu ignores. . . . Je te vois devant moi et il y a autour de moi sortant de toi des lueurs qui ont ce brillant froid des vers luisants – cet éclat imprenable qui brûle mon coeur. (3 February 1932)

Cette nuit j'ai rêvé de toi – nous étions sur un grand bateau plein de soleil . . . les cheveux étaient entourés de soleil comme des flammes d'éclipse. (11 May 1931)

The following entry in one of her notebooks, a portrait of André, is an exercise in poetic prose:

Ses mains sont plus douces que l'hermine chaude des beaux incendies. Son regard est plus scintillant que ce rayon d'astre avant le lever du jour, que cette comète merveilleuse après le passage de laquelle tout ce qui est ne sera plus.
Ses caresses sont de grands vols d'oiseaux de lune plus précieux et plus éblouissants que les plus belles fleurs de l'air de l'eau et du feu.[22]
Ses pensées sont les miroirs obscurs des mares qui miroitent cruellement la nuit dans les forêts de ses cheveux, flammes noires d'orages accrochés aux montagnes de mon amour qui tourne enchanté dans l'espace du désir de toutes les couleurs où son regard merveilleux me cherche et me trouve et caresse de ses flèches de diamant mon coeur de soie changeante, de cristal blessé par le diamant de son regard magique – irisé – des cheveux de Vénus de ses lèvres qui sont les tubéreuses de plumes de sang. Ses pensées sont des étoiles de neige pure et brûlante brûlante comme la seule flamme dans laquelle je peux vivre.

One day in June 1931, having gone shopping for ferns, Valentine unexpectedly meets Breton and Eluard. (She provided André with ferns on a regular basis.[23]) Their sudden encounter nearly drives her to distraction. What had been a *rêve éveillé* verges on hallucination:

J'étais allée chez trois marchands de fougères sans en trouver une qui soit assez belle pour aller près de vous – je voyais votre visage – plus que toujours – partout – sur les maisons – sur les voitures – sur le ciel sur le sol – et surtout vos yeux très brillants dans les arbres – dans la verdure des arbres – le long des quais avant que le taxi ne s'arrête – j'ai cru rêver en vous voyant – en entrant là – vous aussi en vert comme les fougères et les arbres – Convenez que ce n'était pas naturel – et j'ai continué de ne voir que vous pendant un assez long temps – je n'ai réellement vu Paul Eluard que lorsqu'il fut tout près de moi, me disant bonjour. . . . Pourquoi aviez-vous lundi dernier ce visage – ces yeux – ces cheveux plus brillants que d'habitude? si brillants que vous avez bien vu que je pouvais à peine vous regarder. . . .

J'ai touché ce vêtement vert que vous portiez et qui continuait le vert des fougères et des arbres – je l'ai touché malgré moi . . . parce que je ne pouvais croire à votre présence si soudaine. . . . Vous êtes si loin quand je suis près de vous – vous êtes si près quand vous n'êtes pas là – l'absence est la plus redoutable présence – et l'attente aussi de la fin de cette absence est une angoisse d'une douceur mortelle – je voudrais être cachée – invisible – morte – quand je suis tout à coup près de vous – près de votre visage qui a la dureté et la tendresse des astres. (19 June 1931)

A week later:

Aujourd'hui je vous ai vu en plein soleil pour la première fois – vos yeux et vos cheveux étaient plus brillants que jamais – Je ne vous ai jamais tant reconnu qu'aujourd'hui. . . . Je voudrais vous voir toujours au soleil – cela m'étonne de moi qui aime tant l'ombre. (27 June 1931)

Light, eyes, and *vision:* the pattern is constant. Upon learning that she may be suffering from an eye disease (a false alarm, as she finds out to her relief two weeks later), she writes that her own eyes are her greatest treasure:

Je vois comme personne ne voit. . . . Je souhaite que ma vue – que ma vie – soient d'autant plus précaires que je vous verrai davantage – S'il existe au monde une puissance qui entende – qu'elle m'entende – je ne dis pas cela pour vous apitoyer – je suis l'être le plus orgueilleux qui puisse exister après vous – qui l'êtes encore plus que moi. (5 September 1930)

A manuscript note in her scrapbook is unforgettable in its disturbing simplicity:

Si j'étais aveugle, je ne voudrais recevoir que les êtres les plus beaux du monde.

She repeatedly refers to the power that André's eyes have over her whole being:

Tes yeux . . . sont pour moi les seules fenêtres sur ce qu'il importe seul de connaître les seules fenêtres sur ce que j'aime – tes yeux mènent ma vie entière – ils sont pour moi la vue sur tout ce qui existe au monde pour moi – tu peux tout sur moi avec un regard dans tous le sens – tu ne le sais pas peut-être. (11 May 1932)[24]

His gaze is that of an "étoile de poignard, [regard] merveilleusement doux étincelant et acéré" (13 September 1932).

The portrait of Breton that emerges from her letters is that of a wizard whose supernatural powers affect all those who come into his presence, and who is himself affected by the unseen:

Vous êtes le seul être mystérieux que j'aie jamais connu de ma vie . . . l'être le plus sensible et le plus inattaquable à la fois. . . . Il y a autour de vous un cercle d'atmosphère magique d'une puissance qui échappe à ma défense – quelquefois cette atmosphère est très favorable – elle me fait vivre cent vies en une seconde – quelquefois elle est terriblement oppressante. . . . Vous êtes étrangement lucide vous voyez ce que d'autres ne voient pas – vous êtes bouleversé par des choses qui n'émeuvent presque personne d'autre – les êtres et les choses s'éclairent lorsque vous les regardez – sans que vous vous en doutiez. (25 June 1931)

There is a reverse side to her supernaturalizing perception of Breton, expressed at times through momentary disintoxication and reflection:

Je suis assez terrifiée par certains avertissements qui me font voir plus clairement encore André tel qu'il est avec sa volonté d'acier et sa mollesse obligatoire. Je suis de plus en plus bouleversée par ce mélange non ces intermittences de grandeur et de mesquinerie – je prends la vie qui m'est dure plus qu'à lui car tout est relatif – et je tombe plus haut que lui matériellement s'entend et il me faut une énergie sans égale pour être là encore et ne pas tomber moralement au dessous de tout – en proie que je suis aux pires égarements d'imagination. Il me semble que l'année dernière [1932?] j'ai fait preuve d'une noblesse qu'il ne saura jamais à quel degré. . . . A-t-il donc peur de me revoir – quel orgueil pourrai-je en prendre?[25]

She is very conscious of her feminine self, at times rebelling against the constraints placed upon her or the assumptions made on account of her sex, at others torn between her natural desires as a woman in love and her intuition that the best she can hope for is a desexualized companionship with the object of her affections:

Vous ne voudrez pas comprendre que je suis si peu une femme et tout le mystère de ma terrible vie est là, pris dans un noeud indénouable. (Undated, ca. August 1930)

Je ne suis qu'une femme. Voilà tout mon malheur dévoilé. Si je n'étais pas une femme je serais tous les jours près de vous peut-être comme peut l'être le moins cher de vos amis. Si je n'étais pas une femme tout ce que je veux dire serait mieux dit. Il y a tant de choses que je pourrais faire enfin. Je vaudrais quelque chose si je n'étais pas une femme. Hélas je ne suis rien rien puisque je suis femme. (Notebook)

Je m'en veux à me poignarder de désespoir contre moi lorsque je suis comme hier – avec ce désir si féminin de te voir de te prendre dans mes bras de voir tes yeux tes lèvres et toi – très souvent je te cache cela. . . . Je t'aime et j'ai si peur de te laisser voir à quelle violence et j'ai l'air si calme et glacée. (3 February 1932)

Il y a tant de moments où je voudrais être un garçon pour risquer avec toi beaucoup de choses – ne ris pas de moi – cela n'est qu'imagination – Je suis une femme – André – une femme qui t'aime – toi tu m'as fait découvrir en moi la plus femme des femmes – avec sans doute des réflexes de femme qui n'ont pas encore eu le temps de s'adoucir un peu.[26] (10 May 1932)

Not unexpectedly, Valentine's letters reveal much about the vicissitudes of her relationship with André. They frequently traveled together and in the company of others (especially Eluard) between February 1931 and September 1932, mostly to the South – Lunel, Montpellier, Castellane, the Var and the Ardèche, and occasionally as far as Cadaquès, on the Catalonian coast of Spain, to visit Dali. As the owner of several cars (first a Renault, then a Ford), she was the provider – and driver – of that appurtenance of modern bourgeois society that Breton and many of his friends were never able to afford and therefore lacked – a vehicle. She, Breton, Paul and Nusch drove to Brittany and the island of Sein in July 1931, where they were met by Georges Sadoul. Her photographs documenting some of Breton's and Eluard's antics are well known. Several jottings in an automatic vein seem to be contemporaneous with her visit to the isle of Sein:

L'amour n'est pas devenu la pluie mais de nouveaux oiseaux qui partent vers un passé de feu qu'on ne saura jamais reconnaître et qui dévore tout l'avenir. Quand ce bel oeil de foudre entrera en lutte avec la nuit éphémère et immortelle on me verra convulsive et lente traverser les montagnes les forêts les vallées et les mers et les airs avant de disparaître dans la pupille de vérité qui me conduira au miroir des merveilles.

A l'île de Sein dans l'épave de l'Hélène je me suis promenée avec des grandes traînes d'algues laminaires qui faisaient un bruit de soie en me suivant sur le métal rouillé de l'épave

Des bouquets de coralliaires sont posés sur moi et me blessent de leur neige coupante

Her physical relationship with André was of relatively brief duration, probably from July 1931 through May 1932.[27] Judging from her letters and his, their liaison was not a smooth and uneventful one, at least not after late 1931. The disparity of their social backgrounds partly explains his ambivalent feelings. Valentine's upper-class, salon manners, which remained unaffected by her surrealist persona, annoyed him. In taking Valentine as his mistress he probably yielded much less to his own feelings than to hers. His acceptance of her companionship was ultimately an acknowledgment of, as well as a concession to, the constancy and vehemence of her love for him. A sign of their greater intimacy occurred in early May 1932, when Valentine established her residence at 42, rue Fontaine, in the same building as Breton and Eluard.[28] Almost immediately after she had settled at that address, their relationship suffered a severe crisis. On May 8, she seems to have precipitated a scene that caused Breton much embarrassment and anger. Overwhelmed by feelings of guilt, Valentine attempted suicide, swallowing first a vial of Gardenal (a sleeping potion), then some perfume. Realizing that the consequences of her action would place Breton in a terrible situation, she telephoned Eluard, who arrived in time to save her from harm.[29] Their liaison never quite recovered.

Three months later, on a trip to the Midi and eventually Spain with André and Paul, Valentine observed in a daily log she kept: "Je suis certainement plus heureuse mais déjà c'est comme une maladie passée – et quels doutes sur la vie commune."[30] Things deteriorated further. They quarreled, she had fits of jealousy (not without reason), and, on September 9, in Castellane, struck him with her fist. This time their falling-out was irreversible.[31] André's withdrawal from the relationship was final despite her attempts to revive it. As a number of post-1932 *cadavres exquis* and other documents show, however, they continued to see each other in connection with surrealist group activities and as a consequence of their proximity in the same building for three more years. While never abandoning his well-known courtesy, André maintained a prudent distance. A note written by Valentine at a later time further reveals how sensitive she was to the *merveilleux quotidien:*

Pendant tout le temps où je fus l'amie de A.B. – 30-31-32 – je portais une Hématite en bague énorme et sphérique – très lourde et gênante pour conduire et 3 pareilles au milieu d'une chaîne autour du cou – l'Hématite de la bague au contact d'une alliance d'or qui était là pour l'empêcher de glisser de mon doigt était très ternie d'or et devenue mate en septembre 1932.

Valentine demonstrated her unwavering loyalty to her surrealist friends and their values in some of her most famous works, chiefly in the dream-like *Les Surréalistes* (also known as *Les Constellations*), begun in 1932. A 1935 photograph by Man Ray of Valentine seated on a couch shows the mostly completed top portion of her oil, featuring the faces of Eluard, Breton, and Tzara. The state of the painting as it is reproduced that year in the *Cahiers d'Art* (5–6, 137) with the caption "tableau en cours d'exécution" and the indicated date 4-35 is substantially the same, except that part of Crevel's face can be seen emerging from the lower left-hand corner. In its final state thirteen years later, the bottom half is completed, and the lacelike background has been reduced. The constellation has become a pentad. A fifth face – Char's – has been added. A sinuous golden hairline in the shape of a nearly perfect S delicately binds the five faces together. Most prominent, of course, is Breton's. But a closer examination reveals that the upper left-hand segment of the synthesizing S (obviously standing for the Surrealists) in fact perfectly limns Eluard's spiritualized profile. No doubt this detail must be read as a sign of Eluard's faithful and sustaining presence through the sixteen years of the painting's execution, especially in its final phase when the S was added as a kind of signature. The intermittent but intense attention Valentine lavished on the painting, and the extensive revisions it underwent, bespeak the importance she placed in achieving the ultimate symbolic representation of her surrealist experience. An undated entry in her notebook (probably 1933) expresses the inner turmoil that the realization of the painting caused her to experience:

Me voici comme l'hiver dernier méduse échevelée chatoyante chavirée dans les toiles bleues de la mer mauvaise et malicieuse et magique aussi.
Il faut que je finisse ce portrait ou il me tuera – je suis prise dans des vertiges effrayants lorsque je travaille. J'imagine un peu ainsi le mal de mer que je n'ai jamais eu – un mal de mer qui serait causé par une sorte de mouvement ondulatoire de vague dans le cerveau.

Paul Eluard and Valentine Hugo, ca. 1931. Reproduced courtesy of the Harry Ransom Humanities Research Center, The University of Texas at Austin.

Valentine Hugo, Cover illustration for *Contes bizarres* by Achim d'Arnim, 1933. Reproduced courtesy of Renée Riese Hubert.

There is no more revealing a sign of Valentine's relationship with Breton than the cover she created for the 1933 French edition of Achim von Arnim's *Contes bizarres*.[32] Her design for that piece is foreshadowed by a wish she had expressed earlier:

Je voudrais faire un livre d'images sur l'amour. Je voudrais qu'il soit tellement magique que l'on puisse arriver à se tuer en le regardant, ou *revivre* – qu'on ne puisse le regarder sans frémir, être très exalté. Je le ferai d'après tout ce que vous avez écrit sur l'amour – avec un peu de ce que j'en pense.

In a 1982 interview, André Pieyre de Mandiargues states his opinion that Valentine's illustrations for Arnim's *Contes bizarres* represent the most extreme figuration of love in the fantastic mode, and that Valentine and André intended the book to be a monument to their love.[33] Valentine's front cover illustration represents an archangel pointing a flaming sword downward. Lying convulsively with her back to the ground, arms outstretched behind her head, her eyes in a trance, her bosom almost bared in a wide and plunging décolleté, Esther-Valentine is wholly under the sway of the archangel that hovers above her, his fire-sword directed at her face. A close look at the angel's facial features, surrounded by flamelike hair and a swirling robe, reveals an evident likeness to Breton, who is thus depicted in a position of supernatural domination. There can be no doubt that the female figure's state of convulsive and reverse prostration represents not only Arnim's Esther, but the woman who like Valentine gives herself paroxysmally, body and soul, to the godlike being whom she idolizes.

By 1935, Valentine's surrealist orthodoxy was complete, at least as she professed it in a statement she gave in response to a survey conducted among painters and illustrators:

Je voudrais qu'une femme entreprît ce qui n'a jamais été osé et témoignât par l'image de toute sa vie depuis les heures les plus graves de son enfance. Voilà qui permettrait d'y voir clair. Il ne s'agirait pas de mille anecdotes en couleurs. Il importerait de rendre sensibles les réactions les plus secrètes. Pas un seul repli de l'inconscient ne pourrait jouer à la zone interdite. Tous les voyages imaginaires seraient à raconter car le rêve ne vaut pas seulement pour les évasions qu'il permet. Il peut être à la base même d'une réalité nouvelle et toujours en voie de devenir.[34]

All of Valentine's graphic works, paintings, and writings after 1931 bear witness to the obsessive presence of André Breton and her association with the Surrealists. Jean-Charles Gateau rightly suggests that it was in fact Eluard who best appreciated her art. His perceptive assessment of her work is right on the mark: "[Eluard] appréciait le dessin délicat de Valentine, dont l'académisme très sûr et l'élégance sophistiquée servaient un sens très rare de la féerie. Ce maniérisme proposait une version 'esthète' de l'inconscient, et fuyait la violence, la cruauté et le grotesque qui s'étalaient parfois dans les oeuvres des peintres masculins du Mouvement."[35] Though never giving in to some of the more untamed modes of expression favored by the male Surrealists, Valentine derived from her association with them a darker, more intense style. Central to her art and writing in its surrealist phase is the motif of vision, of sight, of light, backgrounded against a nightlike blackness, as if her work made visible the "infracassable noyau de *nuit*" that Breton refers to in his introductory essay to Arnim's *Contes bizarres*. Set against this background, astral presences commingle with an oneiric flora and fauna, which in turn serve as emblematic or contrastive settings for the human disembodied and idealized quality. Breton, who never mentions her in *Le Surréalisme et la peinture*, is noticeably discreet about her work. One can surmise that he judged it to be incompatible with the surrealist principles of pictorial automatism and convulsiveness because of its vestigial academicism.

Valentine lived until 1968. Hardships, both pecuniary and physical, befell her in her last years. The loss of Paul Eluard proved especially painful. For the most part, she maintained her artistic and social activities thanks to the assistance of her friends and fellow artists.[36]

Epilogue: There is an item in Valentine's papers that appears to be a *portrait caractérologique* or a graphological analysis. Written in a fine handwriting (not Valentine's), it sums up everything that her art, her writings, and her life lead us to know about her as a person:

Une extraordinaire impressionalité une sensibilité extrêmement accessible et vulnérable, mais par ailleurs une certaine dose consciente d'ambition et de ténacité. Les représentants achevés de ce type sont des personnalités compliquées. Très intelligents d'une haute valeur, des êtres à la sensibilité fine et profonde d'une éthique scrupuleuse et dont la vie du coeur est d'une délicatesse excessive et d'une ardeur tout intériorisée; ils sont des victimes prédestinées de toutes les duretés de la vie. Ils renferment profondément en eux-mêmes la constance et la tension de leurs sentiments. Ils ont des capacités raffinées d'introspection et d'autocritique. Ils sont très susceptibles et opiniâtres, mais avec cela particulièrement capables d'amour et de confiance. Ils ont pour eux-mêmes une forte estime et sont pourtant timides et pleins d'insécurité quand il s'agit de se produire. Tournés vers eux-mêmes et pourtant ouverts et philanthropiques, modestes mais d'une volonté ambitieuse, et ont au reste de hautes vertus sociales.

Such was indeed the person about whom André Pieyre de Mandiargues said, "Admirable et terrible Valentine, l'une des plus ardentes des femmes surréalistes. . . ."[37]

Notes

1.   Response given by Valentine Hugo to a question on the occasion of a radio interview, 22 December 1950. ("Couleurs de ce temps: Valentine Hugo," Poste National, produced by G. Charbonnier and A. Trutat). Draft letter to André Breton, 10 May 1932. Draft letter to André Breton, 10 September 1932. All of Valentine

Hugo's draft letters, notebook entries, drafts, and autobiographical notes referred to are in the Carlton Lake Collection, Harry Ransom Humanities Research Center, the University of Texas at Austin.

2.   Henri Béhar, *André Breton: le grand indésirable* (Paris: Calmann-Lévy, 1990), 246–51. Whitney Chadwick, *Women Artists and the Surrealist Movement* (Boston: Little, Brown, 1985). Jean-Charles Gateau, *Paul Eluard et la peinture surréaliste, 1910–1939* (Geneva: Droz, 1982), 307–15. Anne de Margerie, *Valentine Hugo, 1887–1968* (Paris: J. Damase, 1983). *Eluard et ses amis peintres* (Paris: Centre Georges Pompidou, 1982), 126–27.

3.   The drafts of Valentine's letters to André Breton held in the Lake Collection (71 in number) were written between July 1930 and February 1934. These draft letters as well as her notebooks and other jottings clearly reflect her desire to keep a scrupulously faithful record of her relationship with Breton, not only as a means of documenting what was to be the most meaningful experience of her life, but enshrining it in her memory and, as it were, in her heart of hearts. A question arises as to the faithfulness of the draft letters with respect to the final letters actually sent to Breton. Those letters that reached their addressee – and there is no reason to doubt that Valentine did in fact send her letters – are of course sealed for many more years to come, in accordance with Breton's testamentary wishes. Until such time as they can be compared with the definitive text of the letters actually received by Breton, the draft copies in the Lake Collection must be presumed to be accurate for the most part.

4.   Jean Hugo, *Le Regard de la mémoire* (Le Paradou: Hubert Nyssen, 1983), 122.

5.   Hugo, 123.

6.   Hugo, 123, 125, 173. Cocteau was first introduced to Valentine in May 1914.

7.   See her testimonial article, "Le Socrate qui j'ai connu," in *La Revue musicale* 214 (June 1952), 139–45. She describes how she became "peu à peu, son enfant, son amie, sa soeur." Typical of Satie's gnomic, self-deprecating banter is the following excerpt from a letter of February 1917 written to Valentine, who was then in the South of France: "Vous rentrez? Contente? Bonne santé? Toujours jolie? Moi, toujours laid; toujours aussi méchant: une teigne!"

8.   Her costume designs for the masquerade balls of the Count and Countess de Beaumont and of the Count and Countess de Noailles during the twenties were particularly original. See Margerie, 37–38.

9.   Draft of letter dated 25 August 1930. In the letter, Valentine assigns to her dream the date of 8 or 9 June 1925. Jean Hugo refers to it as having taken place in 1926. Inasmuch as Valentine first met Paul Eluard in March 1926, the later date is clearly the preferred one.

10.   Scrapbook note, Lake Coll. Jean Hugo refers to a number of his wife's dreams in which Breton appeared: "Ses yeux brillaient dans un ciel de nuit, ou bien, de son visage, croissant de lune aux cornes tournées vers la terre, un rayon de lumière sortait et allait se perdre dans les nuées" (318).

11.   Margerie, 43. In November 1929, Valentine worked on another film directed by Dreyer, probably *Vampyr*.

12.   Margerie, 53. The full extent of Valentine's earlier sacrifice can be gauged from her radio interview of 22 December 1950 (see n. 1): "Et puis, enfin, il y a la musique, que j'écoute au concert, au théâtre, à la radio, ou que je joue pour moi-même. Oui, il y a la musique. Et je crois bien que c'est elle que j'aime le plus, car je l'aime depuis que je suis au monde." Breton's self-acknowledged antimusical bias stemmed to a great extent from his tone-deafness.

13. Thirion, *Révolutionnaires sans révolution* (Paris: Laffont, 1972), 139. See also 231–32, 277–78.

14. *Les Vases communicants* (Paris: Gallimard, "Idées," 1955), 84. The state of mind he describes in chap. 2 partly explains, not only his resisting Valentine's offers of friendship and her pleas for his confidence, but his concomitant efforts to steel himself into some sort of equanimity, as the tone of the text itself attests. In this regard, see Thirion, 278.

15. Letter of 29 June 1930 (Lake Coll.). Breton returns to the night-and-day antithesis in a letter dated 11 August 1930: "Commencez-vous à apercevoir à quelle nuit j'appartiens et comme elle est gardée, que je le veuille ou non, de votre *jour?*"

16. Letter of 24 July 1930 (Lake Coll.). The earliest of Valentine's draft letters to Breton in the Lake Collection is dated 28 July 1930 (see n. 3). Several months later, Valentine protests her good faith: "Je n'ai jamais voulu apporter aucune guérison malfaisante à cette merveilleuse maladie qui est la vôtre" (draft letter, 7 December 1930). Thirion describes Breton's response to Valentine's advances as being "la sympathie émue, un peu agacée, de l'homme qui pense encore à quelqu'un d'autre et qui sait, lui, que celle qui est à ses côtés a perdu d'avance" (322).

17. "Je sais bien ce que représente pour vous l'acte de venir chez moi – que vous persistez à voir en moi la représentation du monde, de ce qu'on appelle le monde – vous ne voulez pas croire que j'en ai volontairement une fois pour toutes fini avec ce monde" (draft letter, 17 September 1930).

18. From July 1930 through July 1931, she addresses Breton in the *vous* form. There is a break in their correspondence between July and December 1931. From December 1931 through September 1932 she addresses him in the familiar *tu* form, reverting to *vous* in all subsequent letters.

19. See Renée Riese Hubert, *Surrealism and the Book* (Berkeley: University of California Press, 1989), 11.

20. Undated notebook entry, probably the draft of a letter sent to Breton, whose own letters of 29 June and 11 August 1930 to Valentine seem to refer quite explicitly to hers. The entry can thus safely be assumed to have been written prior to late June 1930.

21. Draft letter of 14 January 1931.

22. The elemental imagery is reminiscent of the concluding line of Breton's famous love poem *L'Union libre*, published in 1930 and inspired by Suzanne Musard.

23. "Fougère – j'ai confiance en vous" (handwritten note, Lake Coll.). Valentine also sent Breton stalks of rosemary from the Hugos' country home in the South of France, the Mas de Fourques ("Romarin – votre présence me ranime, me rend à la vie").

24. In May–August 1932 Breton suffered from eye pain for which he sought medical advice.

25. Drafts and autobiographical notes, Lake Coll.

26. Cf. Thirion, 322: "Cette femme adorable, intelligente, d'une inépuisable douceur."

27. The apparent gap in her letters to Breton from July to December 1931, together with other evidence, justifies the supposition that the intimate phase of their relationship started during this time.

28. From April 1928 until late October 1931, Valentine resided at 8, rue Vignon (8^{e}); thence she moved to 30, rue Montpensier (1er) until May 1932. She left the

rue Fontaine in 1935. Eluard resided at the rue Fontaine from early 1932 until April 1933.

29. Note of 8 May and draft letter of 10 May 1932. No details about Eluard's exact actions are given.

30. Note of 4 August 1932.

31. "La jalousie est un mal affreux que j'ai connu moi aussi entre 30 et 40 ans. J'essayais déjà de lutter contre cette abomination qui coupe, mord, arrache le coeur, à partir de 1932 j'en fus totalement guérie" (undated note). In a letter of 13 September 1932 to Eluard, now in the Lake Collection, Breton relates the incident in unusually caustic terms. His patience and tolerance are at an end. Already in July, Eluard had written to Gala: "Breton a *définitivement* rompu avec Valentine, qui essaie de prendre patience, dans l'espoir d'être un jour avec lui sur le plan de l'amitié " (Eluard, *Lettres à Gala* [Paris: Gallimard, 1984], 176).

32. Paris: Les Cahiers libres. Besides the book's cover, Valentine contributed a frontispiece and three plates. Breton wrote the preface, which he later incorporated into *Point du jour*. His admiring comments on Valentine's illustrations are quoted in Margerie, 58.

33. A. Pieyre de Mandiargues, *Un Saturne gai (entretiens avec Yvonne Caroutch)*, (Paris: Gallimard, 1982), 170.

34. Typescript (drafts and autobiographical notes). I have not ascertained whether the piece appeared in print and, if so, in what publication.

35. Gateau, 308.

36. See Margerie, 93–102.

37. Pieyre de Mandiargues, 170.

Refashioning the World to the Image of Female Desire: The Collages of Aube Elléouët

Gloria Feman Orenstein

To study the collage oeuvre of Aube Elléouët, the daughter of André Breton and Jacqueline Lamba, is to experience firsthand the vision of a woman of Surrealism who was raised with the Marvelous as an integral part of her everyday life.

When I first met Aube in the late seventies, and she explained to me the nature of the events she had created as a social worker in Saché, the small village in the Touraine where she lives, I understood in a flash exactly what was meant by "the poetry of ordinary life." For at that time Aube was organizing special expeditions to the sea for those who had never seen the ocean, and special expeditions to the mountains for those who had never seen the heights. She has even staged village fairs (kermesses) of the medieval genre for those modern villagers who have never experienced them in their original form. With their many elaborate feasts, processions, and days of dancing, they are somewhat akin to an explosion of the Marvelous within the context of everyday rural life. Yes, Aube has redefined what it means to be deprived, and in her world it is the alienation from nature and the absence of beauty that create a real spiritual impoverishment, not just a deficit of money.

My own initiation to the experience of the Marvelous in Aube's art occurred when the poster for her recent exhibit, "Flagrant Délices," arrived in the mail. It came as a packet containing sixteen pieces of a puzzle, each piece the size of a single postcard, which when correctly assembled would flesh out the full-sized poster announcing her show.

As I carefully pasted the puzzle postcards into their proper places, I began to realize that I was being gently tutored in the art of collage as well as in the perception of the Marvelous, for it had just erupted within the context of my own daily life, there on my living room floor. As I struggled to make the seams joining the two parts of each image disappear, I began to understand the real difficulties involved in the process of creating collage. But then, as soon as the new image sprang forth into life, I became conscious of the spark that is produced by the juxtaposition of two heteroclite subjects, and of the thrill that one experiences in the creation of the Marvelous. Indeed, when I had succeeded in matching the hands of a floating woman to the Eiffel Tower, and a male torso to a neck, upon which sat a globe that soon revealed itself to be a head-in-the-clouds shared by a male cyclist and a woman-in-the-sky, I felt an immediate surge of liberation and the desire to explore still further the mysterious process of making surrealist art. For Aube's art invites us to muse upon how we too might rearrange the real in order to envision a more poetic, expanded reality, as well as to explode all conventions, banalities, and clichés about what it is that we refer to when we use the word "real."

Aube's artistic vision has a coherence that, not surprisingly, resonates with the poetic and painted worlds of many of the other women of Surrealism. Her aligning of women with the order of the natural world, rather than with that of technological civilization, is not a form of biological destiny, but a redefinition of woman with a mission to rescue the Marvelous, to defend the life force, and to protect the earth from the cataclysmic destruction that has been wrought upon it by the excesses of modern science.

In Aube's universe an underwater realm (reminiscent perhaps of the Celtic underworld) symbolizes the unconscious, the land of the heart's suppressed desire. As a woman of Surrealism, Aube speaks primarily to woman's relationship to the subterranean depths, and to the nature of female dreams and female desires. Whereas we might have expected to find the object of a woman's desire to be represented by the image of a human lover (either male or female), in Aube's universe the object of desire is often a sea creature.

In *Le Secret* (Fig. 1) a woman is depicted in an ecstatic, amorous embrace with her fish lover. The image reconciles us to our instinctual passion for all forms of life, both human and nonhuman. It transgresses many taboos in its cross-species eroticism, but instead of provoking feelings of violence in breaking the conventions and social codes, it inspires feelings of beatitude and peace. In this work the woman is not simply the "object" of the beloved's desire. She is the "subject" of desire, and the fish lover is her chosen partner. What is remarkable is that in Aube's transgression, there is no pain and no sadism, as so often appears in the works of male Surrealists when breaking erotic taboos and transgressing moral codes.

Moreover, the liberation of desire in Aube's artistic universe involves a merging with the natural world rather than a conquest of it. However, Aube's vision is neither androcentric nor anthropomorphic. It is what we have come to call "ecofeminist," for in her work humans are no longer at the center of creation, but are rather seen as a part of nature, and interconnected with all species of life.

In *Au péril de la bonne habitude* (Fig. 2) a storm at sea causes such turbu-

Fig. 1 Elléouët, *Le Secret*. Collage.
Photo, Michel Courant.

Fig. 2 Elléouët, *Au péril de la bonne habitude*. Collage. Photo, Michel Carbacheff.

lence that two large ocean liners come perilously close to sinking. Then, from the depths of these storm-swept waters a female figure draped in black emerges, and sets free a dolphin. While the earth and its waters undergo disastrous upheaval, the woman-on-a-spiritual-path (wearing a black habit) surfaces just in time to rescue the animals. Foregrounded against an enormous globe suspended in the sky, the woman might be the Spirit of the Earth, a mythic savior materializing from the underwater realm where the tribes who once worshipped the Goddess now reside on the submerged island of Y's, according to Celtic legend.

In *N'avouez jamais* (Fig. 3) a man and a woman are alone in an aquatic underworld. Fish, fruit, and vegetables are placed in erotic relationships to them, all suggestive of female sexuality. The woman is highlighted, and it seems to be implied that she is the one under constraint not to confess her passion for the aquatic and terrestrial life-forms depicted in larger-than-life proportions in her oneiric environment. In Aube's world, birds, fish, fruits, and vegetables become mysterious personae and active participants in the mysterious intrigues and dramas usually associated with humans alone. The animal and vegetal realms in her work are not metaphors for the human, nor are they used in a purely symbolic manner. Instead, they are real, vibrant, actual, and as viable as catalysts of desire as humans. Each living thing has its own poetry, its own secret life, its own dream world.

Fig. 3 Elléouët, *N'avouez jamais*. Collage. Photo, Michel Carbacheff.

Fig. 4   Elléouët, *Adèle H.* Collage.

In *Adèle H* (Fig. 4) a woman is saving as many fish as possible from an octopus embattled with a deep-sea diver. In this subaquatic environment the cloaked woman looms larger than life; she breathes naturally, without any need for underwater equipment. The male diver, on the contrary, is engaged in mortal combat with an octopus, and is felt to be an alien invader in this marine world. However, the woman is in her natural habitat, and she protects the fish as if they were her own offspring. This Sea

Fig. 5 Elléouët, *En Espagne devant le conseil de guerre*. Collage.

Mother is twice as large as the diver, and while he struggles with the creatures on the ocean's floor, she rescues them in her ample cape.

Birds of liberty also swoop unexpectedly down upon scenes such as the council of war in *En Espagne devant le conseil de guerre* (Fig. 5). In the chamber of the council of war, seagulls drift in from the open window and materialize from a painting on the wall (which may also be a window). They perch upon the shoulders of soldiers, and they seem to have been invoked by the dream of a sleeping woman whose face appears lying on the floor in the lower right. Sometimes, however, the flying presence is that of a human rather than a bird. In the poster for "Flagrants Délices," a tight-laced woman of the turn of the century is swept off her feet and flies horizontally through the sky to join a young cyclist. Both heads meet in the clouds.

Globes and maps also appear frequently in Aube's collage world. In *Les Congés payés* (Fig. 6) globe-headed people appear on the road in front of a car driven by two men who seem to be taking off on their paid vacation. The vacationers feel menaced by the globe-headed beings. A cloaked man holding a globe flies in overhead like Superman. The meaning of the work is mysterious, but a concern for the earth seems to be evident. Is Aube suggesting that the world of the *congé payé* is too narrow, and that a more

Fig. 6 Elléouët, *Les Congés payés.* Collage. Photo, Jean Dubout.

global mentality is required? Or are the globe-headed men the ones on paid holiday, and does she imply that once released from the pressures of the routinized work-world, thoughts about liberty and the life of the planet begin to take wing?

The earth is being rescued by women from the onslaught of the technological era in *Dans un silence d'enfer* (Fig 7) where a locomotive speeding down the track knocks over two women – one saving a part of the map of South America that includes Brazil, Bolivia, and Venezuela, the other saving a portion of the map of Africa that includes Mauretania, Ghana, Libya, Nigeria, and Zaire. Although the women are rescuing the endangered earth, their lives are also threatened by the oncoming train, which relentlessly wipes out everything in its path.

Through her collages, Aube has taken us on an expedition to the Marvelous, only to reveal its precarious state of immanent danger. For in her universe, the Marvelous is composed of elements from the organic, natural world with which women have been closely identified. Since both women and nature have been victims of scientific "progress," the Marvelous itself is also in jeopardy. Aube seems to be suggesting that women, in rescuing the earth, are metaphorically rescuing the Marvelous as well. Ultimately, her subterranean desire is to foster the rebirth of a vision similar to that of the Celtic Elysium, where all creatures, human and non-human, would live together in a natural state of peace and harmony.

Fig. 7 Elléouët, *Dans un silence d'enfer*. Collage.

Thus, the image of female desire in the collage world crafted by Aube Elléouët, while transgressing taboos and breaking boundaries, does not do so in order to provoke a scandal or shock the viewer, nor in order to produce a state of trance; rather it does so in order to recall us to our longings for an ecstasy-in-living, so that we may rescue the wounded planet, and thus revive the Marvelous. Her surrealist vision of beauty is less "convulsive" than that of her father. Rather, it seems to me that Aube's surrealist vision seeks to bring about a healing to a world that is already in "convulsion" of another kind, one in which the natural world has been violated by technology and is, as the title of one of her collages suggests, *in peril.*

Eileen Agar
Judith Young Mallin

Eileen Agar in her London apartment in 1988. She is seated in her favorite wing chair in front of her worktable. Photo by JYM.

"My life is a collage, with time cutting and arranging the materials and laying them down, overlapping and contrasting, sometimes with the fresh shock of a surrealist painting. You see the shape of a tree, the way a pebble falls or is formed, and are astounded to discover that dumb nature makes an effort to speak to you, to give you a sign, to warn you, to symbolize your innermost thoughts. Chance is not a neutral but a distinctly positive force; the Surrealists believe that you can get on good terms with chance by adopting a lyrical mode of behavior and an open attitude."[1]

A lyrical mode of behavior, an open attitude, and chance were all forces in Eileen Agar's life in the winter of 1927, when she and her lover, Hungarian writer Joseph Bard, rented a small villa in Portofino, near the small sea resort of Rapallo. Although married to others,[2] they had been lovers for over a year. Rapallo was a favorite off-season gathering place for poets and writers attracted by the cheap cost of living and proximity to the sea. A pause at a small Rapallo café for a cup of cappuccino and a game of chess led to a meeting with a "red-bearded Apollo," who pulled up a chair and began to advise Eileen on her moves. He introduced himself as American poet Ezra Pound. By the time the afternoon was over, a friendship began that was to last until Pound's death forty-five years later. Pound was forty-two, Eileen twenty-eight, and Bard thirty-five. The three soon became inseparable. Pound showed them the back streets and artistic life of Rapallo and introduced them to his friend W. B. Yeats. When Pound's parents arrived for a visit, they met his new friends and asked Bard to keep an eye on their son, "the first white child born in the state of Idaho" (77).

The un-English atmosphere and surroundings began to affect Eileen's use of color in her paintings. It seemed "as if the sea was showing its brown petticoat, while tall palms waved their fronds in soft south winds" (75).

"Don't be a wobbly vagina, not that I think you are," said Pound (77). Eileen didn't think she was either. She decided that "Eileen" was too frothy and feminine a name for a serious artist; after consulting with Bard and Pound, she settled on "Allegra" as more interesting and complex. She remained "Allegra" until her return to London in 1928. "Allegra" belonged to the Mediterranean; "Eileen" was more appropriate to London. "But Eileen's trick sunlight softens London's November."[3]

In 1929, Eileen arrived in Paris with a letter of introduction from Pound to his friend Paul Eluard.[4] She soon met Eluard and André Breton, and when Pound himself came to visit he introduced her to Brancusi. Tristan Tzara was out of town, but Pound gave her a letter of introduction before he returned to London. She took a studio in the Rue Schoelcher (Bard took his own apartment on the Ile St. Louis) and began to study painting. She discovered the Jardin des Plantes with its collection of prehistoric fossils and bones and spent hours there studying the skeletons of prehistoric birds. Archaeopteryx in particular fascinated her.

Eileen returned to London (to be joined later by Bard) in order to formally divorce her husband, Robin Bartlett. Her work was evolving. "Surrealism was in the air, for painters and poets in France, and later in England, were kissing that sleeping beauty troubled by nightmares; and it was the kiss of life that they gave" (93).

It was during this time that Eileen created her first surreal object out of a skull her former husband had used in his medical studies. She first painted the skull gold and then began to decorate it with small shells she had picked up on her beach explorations. Perhaps Eileen was also combining the separate elements of her personal life by integrating the shells she and Joseph had discovered with Robin's anatomy skull. The object is kept today in a small trunk that belonged to Dorothy Thompson, Joseph Bard's first wife.

Eileen first met artist Paul Nash in 1935 in Swanage, a small sea resort where she and Bard had rented a house. Nash suffered from chronic asthma, and along with his wife Margaret, a former nurse, had come to the area for the healthy sea air. Eileen was familiar with Nash's work and liked it; when she met the artist himself she was immediately intrigued by his "allure and dark triangular looks" (109).

Nash began to bring Eileen curious and interesting stones that he found during his walks along the beach. As Pound had shown her his Rapallo, Nash showed her his Swanage. They spent hours together looking for interesting washed-up objects on the beach. When the two scavengers first discovered a large, sand-submerged object deeply imbedded with stones, shells, and various forms of sea life, Eileen thought it was a true sea monster. Eileen painted it and Nash photographed it; he eventually used the photographs in a collage, *Swanage*, now hanging in the Tate Gallery. Unfortunately, the object itself, in reality an old anchor, did not survive the blitz of London in the mid-forties.[5]

"One day I was an artist exploring highly personal combinations of form and content, and the next day I was calmly informed I was a Surrealist!" (115). Surrealism officially entered Eileen's life with the International Surrealist Exhibition, held in London in 1936. The idea for the exhibition had grown out of a chance meeting in Paris between two enthusiastic Englishmen, poet-writer David Gascoyne and painter-writer-collector Roland Penrose. Gascoyne was twenty and Penrose thirty-six; both had been living and working in France and felt a deep affinity for the group around André Breton. Gascoyne was finishing his study of the surrealist movement, *A Short Survey of Surrealism*, the first in-depth study of the movement to be published in English. The exhibition was scheduled to be held at the New Burlington Galleries in June and July of 1936. The English exhibition committee, with Rupert Lee as chairman, soon included Hugh Sykes Davies, McKnight Kauffer, Paul Nash, Herbert Read, Henry Moore, and Humphrey Jennings. Artists from fourteen countries were to be included. Herbert Read wrote the introduction for the catalogue, while the preface was by André Breton.[6] In the spring of 1936, Penrose and Herbert Read came to Eileen's studio; they chose three paintings and five objects for the show. Eileen Agar was the only woman included in the English group of artists. "I was proud to be among them" (18).

One of the paintings the committee included was *Quadriga* (Fig. 1), a work she had completed in 1935. The piece evolved out of a photograph Eileen

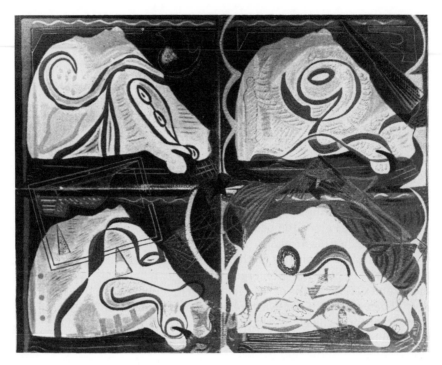

Fig. 1   Agar, *Quadriga,* 1935. Oil on canvas. Private collection.

had of a stone horse's head from the Acropolis. "I wondered what strange way I could make it into a painting which would fit into the twentieth century, which could bridge the gap between the centuries. I knew that there was a fountain in Boetia sacred to the muses, which first rose from the ground when struck by the feet of the flying horse Pegasus. Then there was Selene, the pre-Greek goddess of the moon who was given horses to drive across the sky. And I had ridden a lot as a child, in that exalted innocence the Surrealists so admired. In other words, the fountain sacred to the muses was also the horse's fountain which in turn reflected the moon, so I said a private prayer, invoked the childhood drumbeat of hooves, and started on my painting" (121–22).

As she studied the image the painting began to take form. "One horse's face became four ghost heads, agitated, beating rhythmic cabalistic convoluted signs expressing movement and anxiety, each square a different mood. Were they the four horses of the Apocalypse? War was encroaching on the selfish peace of England: the Spanish Civil War acted as a kind of distant prelude to the Second World War, and it was to be many years before the Four Horsemen allowed their steeds to return to my frame."[7]

The exhibition received an enormous amount of publicity. The Surrealists had a natural flair for publicity and they made themselves highly visible. Breton officially opened the proceedings, and Sheila Legge paraded around the streets with her head and features completely covered by a hood of roses. Large crowds flocked to the gallery. "The respectables acted as people usually act when observed in an 'immoral place.' They tried to be invisible." T. S. Eliot, with Herbert Read, stood rooted in front of Meret Oppenheim's fur teacup and saucer. Across the room Dali's watch was melting (117).

A series of lectures by the visiting Surrealists were scheduled. On June 24, Eluard spoke on the Marquis de Sade. When the poet referred to Sade as a "holy martyr of freedom," Eileen saw Augustus John abruptly get up and leave.[8] Breton lectured on "The Limits Not Frontiers of Surrealism" and Herbert Read on "Art and the Unconscious." It was a particularly brutal summer, and on one of the hottest days, Salvador Dali was scheduled to speak on "Authentic Paranoiac Phantoms." Always a showman, he entered the lecture hall leading two white Russian wolfhounds and carrying a billiard cue. Since he planned to plunge the audience into the unconscious, he was wearing a deep-sea diving suit complete with a round, hard diving helmet. As the audience watched, Dali began to wave his arms in a strange fashion; through the glass face-piece in the helmet they could see his face turning redder and redder. As they laughed and applauded, Dali struggled for air. It was only when Gala Dali and Edward James rushed to the stage to assist in removing the helmet that had been inadvertently bolted from the outside, that they realized they had almost witnessed the ultimate surreal act.

The London press had a field day with the cooperative and outrageous artists. Within the group itself, however, things did not always go smoothly. A good deal of political maneuvering and vanity was involved in the taking of what was to become the official group photograph documenting the exhibition. The French group made the arrangements for the photograph; it was Eluard who telephoned Eileen and told her to be in the gallery that afternoon for a group picture of people who were involved with the show. Eileen mentioned the call to Paul Nash, who was furious. Not only was he on the English committee, he was deeply involved in the movement and no one had called him. He refused to accompany Eileen to the photo session, and does not appear in the official picture (Fig. 2). Henry Moore and Graham Sutherland were never called either, and the photograph became, according to Eileen, "curiously selective."[9]

It was not only the art, but the individuals in the surrealist circle that attracted Eileen. Their presence was like a group of exotic birds landing in a square filled with sparrows. The striking good looks and bold attitude of both the men and the women made them stand out from the usual groups of English artists that the public had been exposed to. The women spent a

Fig. 2   The exhibitors photographed at the International Surrealist Exhibition at the New Burlington Galleries, London, in 1936. Standing (left to right): Rupert Lee, Ruthven Todd, Salvador Dali, Paul Eluard, Roland Penrose, Herbert Read, E. L. T. Mesens, George Reavey, and George Sykes Davies. Sitting: Diana Brinton Lee, Nusch Eluard, Eileen Agar, Sheila Legge, and "a friend of Dali."

great deal of time and effort "inventing" themselves and their surroundings in offbeat and startling ways. Their attire was unusual and outrageous, and they had flair and style coupled with a zest for life that struck a responsive chord.

"Our concern with appearance was not a result of pandering to masculine demands, but rather a common attitude to life and style, a striking contrast to other professional woman painters of the time, those who were not Surrealists, who if seen at all, tended to flaunt their art like a badge, appearing in deliberately paint-spotted clothing. Juxtaposition by us of a Schiaparelli dress with outrageous behavior or conversation simply carried the beliefs of Surrealism into public existence."[10]

That year, nineteen-year-old English beauty Leonora Carrington was in London studying art with Amédée Ozenfant, when her mother gave her a copy of Herbert Read's *Surrealism*. Her response to surrealist art echoes that of Eileen Agar's. It was "like a burning, inside; you know how when something really touches you, it feels like burning."[11] Read presented a free society governed by love rather than law.[12]

However, the double standards of the European Surrealists infuriated Eileen; she felt the women "came off worst."[13] Jacqueline Lamba, in particular, was a victim of this dual attitude. Eileen felt that Lamba had been cast in the role of the great man's muse, and was therefore denied an active, creative existence of her own. "Breton never mentioned her work. Surreal men expected to be very free sexually, but when Lee Miller had the same attitude while with Man Ray, the hypocritical upset was tremendous" (120–21). To be an appendage, even a petted and pampered one, was not at all acceptable or agreeable to Eileen. She saw clearly the good-natured acceptance of Nusch Eluard, the strong-willed determination of Lee Miller, the mysterious aura around Valentine Boué,[14] the striking, young, and bold good looks of Leonora Carrington and Leonor Fini, both involved in the web spun by Max Ernst.

In the summer of 1936 Franco marched into Spain; the Spanish Civil War had begun. As a humanist, Eileen supported the fight against fascism by joining demonstrations and signing petitions. "The Spanish Civil War was shamefully ignored in England. Roland and Valentine and David Gascoyne went to Barcelona to support the Popular Front and speak against fascism" (123). Eileen argued with her mother, who thought Franco was a wonderful person. Her mother knew nothing about the real situation; whenever she went to Spain after the fighting was over, she talked only to friends who supported Franco. Besides, she told Eileen, the "minor Spanish upheavals" were so far away, she shouldn't care so much, and shouldn't become involved.[15] The Surrealists tried to make people think, but "the English turn everything into a social gathering."

She and Bard left London for a holiday in Ploumanach, an area in Brittany famous for its unusual huge and ancient rock formations. The enormous stones reminded her of giant prehistoric monsters emerging from the sea. They captivated her so that she and Joseph made a special trip to the nearby town of Brest to buy a camera. It was her first Rolleiflex. It was then that she began a lifetime habit of documenting the important events around her. Those first images are hanging in her London apartment today.

The following July, Eileen and Bard joined a surrealist house party in Cornwall at the home of Beacus[16] Penrose, Roland's brother. Lee Miller, Nusch and Paul Eluard, and Roland were already there. Roland was the leader, and the high-spirited group followed his lead. They enjoyed changing partners. "Roland was always ready to turn the house party into an orgy."[17] On one occasion they all attempted to join Lee Miller, who was taking a bubble bath.

Bard enjoyed the charms of Nusch, while Eileen found a special fulfillment with Paul Eluard. It was not just a physical attraction, but a spiritual one for her. She never had the same sort of attraction for Roland, but she and Eluard forged a special bond. She understood, she told me, the basic polygamous nature of French men, and besides, she felt, if love came your way from someone you were attracted to, it was foolish to deny it.[18]

At Eluard's suggestion, the group arranged to meet in September at the hotel Vaste Horizon in Mougins in the South of France. Picasso and Man Ray would be there. Before leaving Cornwall, Eluard gave Eileen a copy of Edward Lear's *Book of Nonsense*. He inscribed the book with the following poem that he had written for her:

Le "non-sense"
de la prononciation française

Les poules du convent
Avec candeur convent
Les oeufs sacrés du Fils
Et tissent les longs fils
De la Vièrge qui parent
Leur déplorable parent

(Convent tarts
Hatch with candor
The sacred eggs of the Son
And weave the long threads
Of the Virgin and avoid
Their deplorable parent)[19]

When the group reconvened in September, they exchanged not only bedmates, but identities. It was Picasso who first came up with the idea of name-swapping. Eileen Agar became Dora Agar, Pablo Picasso became Don José Picasso, Joseph Bard became Pablo Bard, Man Ray became Roland Ray. If you forgot what your name was for the day, you were fined one or two francs.

It was interesting, Eileen told me, to see the difference between Picasso and the other men. After lunch, Mesens would always say, "To bed, to bed,"[20] looking in particular at Lee and Eileen, who always declined. Picasso on the other hand would end lunch with "au travail, au travail!" (138).

By now, the Rolleiflex had become such a permanent part of Eileen's persona that Lee Miller photographed Eileen's shadow/profile with the distinct outline of a camera snout protruding from her belly. Picasso was so delighted with the image of an Eileen impregnated with a Rolleiflex that he asked Lee for a copy of the print.

In 1988, Eileen showed me a sunny back hall in her flat, covered with her photographs of fascinating rocks and objects as well as of friends, now all dead, from the happy summer of 1937. Larger photographs of a muscular, semi-reclining, nude Joseph Bard and a beautiful, vibrant Eileen Agar, prancing joyfully in a diaphanous robe after a night of too much drinking in the South of France, hang by themselves (Fig. 3). Eileen paused with a smile and a little pat each time we passed these two photographs, saying, "Isn't he a *beautiful* man?"

Picasso kept a small black trunk he had purchased in Cannes in his rooms. It was filled with small pieces of wood, pebbles, shells, and in-

Fig. 3 Eileen Agar, dancing after an all-night party with friends Paul Eluard, Nusch Eluard, Picasso, Man Ray, Ady, Roland Penrose, Lee Miller, and Joseph Barr. Mougins, 1937.

teresting stones that he had picked up on the beach. He began carving images on some of the most interesting pieces, transforming them into pieces of jewelry. Dora Maar proudly wore a heavy, wide African bracelet on which Picasso had carved a minotaur and maenads.[21] Nusch Eluard, a particular favorite of the painter, wore a bone shard that he had engraved especially for her; the others knew it was a special mark of acceptance and approval, Eileen said. Eluard kept offering his wife to Picasso as a gift of friendship, but Eileen would not comment on whether or not the gift was accepted. She did say that she thought that his portrait of Nusch reflected his special affection and caring. After the Eluards returned to Paris, Picasso told Eileen he could still hear Nusch's voice on the stairs (142). After Picasso left, Eileen took down the thumbtacks that he had used to impale his drawings on the walls of his room; she kept them as souvenirs of a special summer.[22]

That same year, Eluard arrived in London for a short visit. He confided to Eileen that he thought Bard resembled André Breton, "mais mieux proportionné" (130). They agreed, Eileen told me with a conspiratorial twinkle, that Breton was too short; Joseph was indeed better proportioned. Eluard wanted to telephone Belgian expatriate E. L. T. Mesens, one of the leaders of the British surrealist movement. It was not to be just a telephone call, but a surreal telephone call. To make this possible, Eluard needed some help from his host and hostess. Did they possibly have some old chains about, any old chains would do? The success of the call, from a surrealistic point of view, would depend on his ability to rattle the chains as noisily as possible during the telephone conversation. It seems that Mesens had a phobia to loud and alarming noises. Unfortunately, a hurried search of the apartment yielded no chains.[23]

The two men left for lunch at Bard's club, the Savage Club, an all-male, very British bastion. Although the quality of the furnishings did not excite Eluard, his enthusiasm for the club's special dessert was unmistakable. The waiter carefully served two plates of a quivering orange mass of jelly that resembled nothing more than an undulating, miniature, nubile breast. Eluard was delighted and with enjoyment began prodding, poking, and playing with the new toy, using his spoon like an inquisitive finger. He did this for quite a while while Bard and the other members watched. Then he devoured it.[24]

By the fall of 1937, war with Germany appeared certain. London became a temporary stop for a number of refugees en route to the United States. With the spirit of Surrealism still in the air, Eileen and Bard planned a farewell dinner for a small group of friends about to leave for New York. During the First World War Eluard and Max Ernst were in the same sector on the western front, but on opposite sides; they discovered later that they were shooting at each other. It was a story that Eluard had told Eileen and Bard; what could be more fitting than a surreal meal held with the lunacy of war so close? The guests included Walter Gropius, Marcel Breuer, Moholy-Nagy, Roland Penrose, and Lee Miller. In a world gone mad, "toasted soprano savoury," "wayzy goose," and "creme passionelle" washed down with "red chianti" were just right.[25] One of the gustatory highlights was the bright pink potatoes. The memorable surreal meal was served on a ping-pong table covered with enormous linen napkins Eileen had inherited from her mother's family. The centerpiece was a pedal-operated fretsaw covered with fruit and flowers. From time to time the host or hostess would press the pedal of the centerpiece, which would noisily begin to move. Eileen wore the same dress that she had worn to the opening of the International Surrealist Exhibition the year before. It was a long, pleated Fortuny, "much like a nightgown," in bright blue, with flesh-colored leather elbow-length gloves (the nails of the glove fingers were bright red).

The surrealist way of looking at familiar objects and using them in a completely unexpected and new way appealed to Eileen. Always interested in fashion, she incorporated the unusual with humor, flair, and style. "The Surrealists made objects out of whatever turned up, believing that they came at the behest of chance and went that way also. . . . The object is an even more typically Surrealist creation than the collage, and at once comes into competition with sculpture. . . . The found object had a special significance for me, for the choice of one particular thing from amongst a host of others, whether stones or bones, has often provided the solution to a creative problem, or provoked its own separate inspiration" (140–41).

Eileen's best-known use of a found object in an unusual and personal way developed during a visit to the small fishing village of Saint-Tropez. Eileen discovered a vendor selling the cork dishes traditionally used in the region for serving bouillabaisse. The texture and the shape of the bark bowls intrigued her, but not as a serving piece. She returned to the small hotel, where Bard was napping, wearing a new hat! (Fig. 4) The next step in the transformation was to change the color of this marvelous object: yellow and blue were the colors of the South of France, and so *The Ceremonial Hat for Eating Bouillabaisse* became yellow and blue. To top off the decorations, she added some of the objects she had picked up along the beach: a starfish, seashells, a lobster tail, and a bit of fishnet. The object caused an immediate sensation and soon became her trademark. "It was a

Fig. 4 Eileen Agar, wearing her original *Ceremonial Hat for Eating Bouillabaisse*, shown with *Hand of Fate*, ca. 1936.

223

sort of Arcimboldo headgear for the fashion-conscious, and received a lot of rather startled publicity" (168).

In 1948, Eileen appeared on an English television program called "Eye of the Artist." The narrator, Halam Fordham, asked her to discuss and demonstrate her exploration of fantastic art, in the surrealist manner. She obliged by creating an object on camera, from gourds, sponges, seashells, and branches. She called the piece *Phantom of the Sea.* Two months later, she was back. This time it was a program on hats, hosted by fashion historian-writer James Laver. She naturally wore the *Ceremonial Hat.*

"I like what Picabia said: 'Our heads are round so that thoughts can change direction.'"[26] Eileen has her own method for encouraging the creative process: "I sit about for a quarter of an hour or more, wondering what on earth I am doing, and then get an idea for something. Either it is the beginning of a title, or just the germ of a visual image. Later on, if I'm stuck with a half-finished painting, I might take a snooze and after that it comes together quite simply. It may well be that we hunt too much when we are completely on the alert. Too much awareness can be as inhibiting as too little" (125).

A surreal chain of events in Eileen's life began shortly after World War II was over. Eileen's sister surprised her with an amusing object she'd found in a small shop. The object was a beer bottle embellished with a voluptuous woman painted on its curved surface. Eileen immediately recognized the object as the whimsy of a fellow Surrealist, Belgian René Magritte. She and Joseph had recently bought two small Magritte sketches from the Redfern Gallery in London for about fifteen pounds each. Thanks to sister Winifred, the couple now owned three examples of Magritte's work.

When art dealer Jimmy McMullen, owner of the Obelisk Gallery in London, came to look at Eileen's work in 1957, he spotted the three Magrittes. Surrealism was out of fashion, but McMullen had always liked the unusual; he had the reputation for having a good eye and supporting the art that he liked. Eileen got her show but McMullen got the Magrittes; she was delighted when the exhibition sold out in two days. When William Seitz organized a show at the Museum of Modern Art in New York in 1957, he included a piece of Eileen's. The exhibition was called "The Art of Assemblage" and as a contributor, Eileen received a catalogue. To her dismay, there was her Magritte bottle, but with a small addition (Fig. 5). In a moment of playfulness, Eileen had inserted a small African wooden cork, carved in the shape of buttocks, into the neck of the bottle. It fit perfectly, and although she had told McMullen that the cork was her own private joke, he had sold it along with the bottle to a private collector.

Eileen immediately wrote to William Seitz, outlining the chain of events. When Seitz replied, he thanked her for solving a mystery. He had received an annoyed letter from a worried Magritte who said he had never, under any circumstances, put a cork in a bottle. Eileen next received a pained letter from Magritte himself, explaining that what he thought of as valuable in his work was that which set it apart; by adding an African cork she had made it her work. It had been transformed from a Magritte into an Agar. "At the time, I thought so too, and that I had improved it!" (196).

Fig. 5 Magritte, *Bottle,* with Eileen Agar addition, as it appeared in the "Fantastic Art, Dada, Surrealism" catalogue, 1936.

In an essay from the catalogue of that show, the following statement appears: "We still have to touch upon Surrealist objects, the importance of which cannot be sufficiently emphasized. Nothing that the movement has produced is more authentic, more varied, more personal and at the same time so anonymous. They have realized Lautréamont's saying 'poetry must be made by all. Not by one.' Related in appearance to Dada sculptopaintings Surrealist objects are essentially different for they are the automatic, reasonless and yet material expression of inhibited wishes, anthropomorphic vegetations of the permanently unpredictable in man. Made in secret, symbolical in their function, images for the hand, they are among the most singular subjects for the study of psychoanalysis. These objects, endowed with a minimum of mechanical function, are based on ghostly fancies and are representations provoked by unconscious acts. . . .

The incarnation of these desires, the manner of their embodiment by metaphor, their symbolical realization constitute a process of erotic substitution which resembles at every point the process of poetry' (Dali)."[27]

Eileen Agar has always believed in "womb-sense": "Women's state of mind encompasses more the possibility of a mixed world – a survival and fortune world, not the male world of absolute values, which cannot stand for long without strife and war. . . . The opening up of the instinctive self is also essential. . . . The true poem is not the work of the individual artist, it is the universe itself, in which the artist is a sort of somnambulist."[28] Eileen always remained a bit like Alice in Wonderland, eager to explore the terrain of the new, the fantastic, the magical, the forbidden, but always finding her own way back through the looking glass.

Notes

The above text is drawn in part from a series of conversations I had with Eileen Agar in 1988 while in London doing research for a book on the surrealist artists in New York during World War II, and looking for documentaries for a PBS television series about the surrealist artists. Among the topics we discussed were the most influential friendships in her life and their role in the development of a personal creative pattern. Andrew Lambirth, her friend and collaborator on her autobiography, joined us for many of these sessions, and was a great help in confirming specific dates and information; it was Andrew who discovered the collaged menu for the surreal dinner party.

1. Eileen Agar, in collaboration with Andrew Lambirth, *A Look at My Life* (London: Methuen, 1988), 3 and 121. Hereafter, page numbers in parentheses in the text refer to this book; citations below are indicated by AGR.

2. Eileen was married to Robin Bartlett, a doctor, and Joseph Bard to Dorothy Thompson, an American writer.

3. AGR, 169, and Ezra Pound, *Pisan Cantos*, Canto LXXXI.

4. Conversation with author.

5. Eileen and Nash remained lovers and friends until his death in 1946. Eileen told me that they had no wish to cause pain to either Joseph or Nash's wife, Margaret. She still has all of his letters, but has given the Tate copies of them.

6. Marcel Jean, *The Autobiography of Surrealism* (New York: Viking Press, 1980), 362.

7. Shortly after the exhibition was over, Roland Penrose, who had purchased the canvas, informed Eileen that the Museum of Modern Art in New York wanted to include it in their December exhibition, "Fantastic Art, Dada, Surrealism." For Eileen, who had hardly received any notice before, inclusion as a Surrealist assured her reputation. The painting is now in the permanent collection of the Tate Gallery in London (AGR, 122, 124–25).

8. AGR, 118, and conversation with author.

9. AGR, 122. Included in the photo are Sheila Legge, "the legendary surrealist phantom who walked around Trafalgar Square with her head covered in rose petals and ladybirds," and a friend of Dali.

10. AGR, 120, and conversation with author.

11. Leonora Carrington, *The House of Fear* (New York: E. P. Dutton, 1988), 5.

12. Roland Penrose, *Roland Penrose Scrapbook* (New York: Rizzoli, 1981), 75.

13. AGR, 120, and conversation with author.

14. French poet and first wife of Roland Penrose.

15. AGR, 123–24, and conversation with author.

16. Spellings of Bernard Penrose's nickname seem to differ, and include "Beakus" and "Becus," but "Beacus" is used by his brother Roland, *Roland Penrose Scrapbook.*

17. Conversation with author.

18. It was during this period that Eluard told Eileen about a trip he had taken to the Far East to try to free himself of the influence of his first wife, Gala, who was now living with Dali. Eileen showed me the recently published French edition of Eluard's love letters to Gala, and said he never did succeed in ridding himself of her. Letter 232 in the book is a postcard dated July 1937. The brief message of love and fidelity to Gala from Eluard is signed: Paul; Lee Miller; Amitiés, Roland Penrose; baisers, Nusch; Eileen Agar; Affect., Man Ray (Paul Eluard, *Lettres à Gala 1924–1948* [Paris: Gallimard, 1984], 281–82).

19. AGR, 134. Mary Ann Caws pointed out to me that "fils" is a pun here in the sense of weaving the sons to get to the parents, and that "parer" can also mean "to decorate," which the weaving does.

20. AGR, 126, and conversation with author.

21. Dora gave Eileen a beautiful ivory necklace, with tiny languid folded hands. Eileen wore it to lunch one afternoon during my visit with her.

22. A few days after we talked about that summer, I was going through the Lee Miller-Roland Penrose Archives outside of London. They were all there; everyone was young, high-spirited, and playful. I saw Man Ray and Ady making monkey faces; Eileen, Eluard, Nusch, and Lee Miller soaking up the sun; a playful E. L. T. Mesens giving a beneficent blessing to a blissful Max Ernst and Leonora Carrington; Picasso and Nusch sitting side by side before a lunch table; and, finally, a postcard from Eileen Agar to Roland Penrose and Lee Miller. Written in block letters beneath a photograph of Lee Miller and Roland Penrose sitting on the beach, it said: "DEAROLANDLEE / WE ARE STILL SITTING PRETTY ON THE MOUNTAIN TOP AT MOUGINS. ONE SLEEPS SO SOUNDLY IN PICASSO'S BED. THE WEATHER'S WUNDERBAR. BARD SENDS LOVE AND KISSES. AGAR." Lee Miller and Roland Penrose Archives, England.

23. AGR, 131, and conversation with author.

24. Ibid.

25. The menu was displayed on a varnished three-foot board collaged by Eileen with a reproduction of Picasso's *Three Musicians* as a warm reminder of the previous summer. The collaged menu had been lost for years, and Eileen rediscovered it during my visit – we decided that was a surreally good omen.

26. Conversation with author.

27. Georges Hugnet, essay in Alfred H. Barr, ed., *Fantastic Art, Dada, Surrealism* (New York: Arno Press, 1968), 49.

28. Conversation with author; AGR, 174–75.

Statement
Dorothea Tanning

My warmest thanks to Dorothea Tanning for her kindness in sending me, for this publication, the following statement which, as she says, defines her position.
—Mary Ann Caws

If you lose a loved one does it matter if it is a brother or a sister? If you become a parent does it matter if it is to a boy or a girl? If you fall in love does it matter (to that love) if it is for a man or a woman? And if you pray does it matter, God or Goddess?

During the spaces of time between great events, human beings have created their various cultures. They have learned to give breath to their life with art, to give (a kind of) hope to that life with science. Art, science. We are notoriously free to choose. If you consciously choose you may be said to win a battle against nothingness, a battle as momentous as anything in the mythologies of the world. But it is only the first battle. Like the phalanxes of an enemy, myriad assailants converge to bedevil your purpose and bewilder your vision. So, as someone, a human someone, who has chosen art, the making of it, the dedication to it, the breathing of it, this artist has pursued with a high heart that great aim; and has utterly failed to understand the pigeonholing (or dove-coterie) of gender, convinced that it has nothing to do with qualifications or goals.

December 3, 1989

Chronologies of Women Surrealists

In compiling the chronologies, I used the following sources: Jacques Baron, *Anthologie plastique du surréalisme* (Paris: Editions Filipacchi, 1980); Adam Biro and René Passeron, *Dictionnaire général du surréalisme* (Fribourg: Office du Livre, 1982); Whitney Chadwick, *Women Artists and the Surrealist Movement* (Boston: Little, Brown, 1985); Erika Billeter and Chantal Michetti, eds., *La Femme et le surréalisme* (Lausanne: Musée cantonal des Beaux-Arts, 1987); and Roger Broderie, ed., *La Femme surréaliste, Obliques* 14–15 (Paris: Editions Broderie, 1977).

Judith Young Mallin

EILEEN AGAR

1899   Born in Buenos Aires to a wealthy British family.

1911   Family returns to England. Studies briefly at Byam Shaw School of Art.

1920   Studies at the school of Leon Underwood at Hammersmith, where she meets Henry Moore.

1925–26 Studies at the Slade School of Art in London. Marries Robin Bartlett, a classmate, and moves to the country.

1927   First trip to Paris.

1928–30 Studies in Paris with Cubist painter Frantisek Foltyn.

1929   First contact with surrealist works.

1931   Returns to London, collaborates on *The Island* magazine, edited by future husband Joseph Bard, writer and prominent collector of antiquities.

1933   Joins the "London Group."

1935   Begins creating surrealist objects under the influence of Paul Nash. Begins to incorporate elements from animal and vegetable world in paintings.

1936	Joins British surrealist group. Creates collages and surrealistic objects (*The Angel of Anarchy*). Begins photographing on beaches of England and France.
1940	Marries Joseph Bard.
1941–45	Remains in London during war, which interrupts her artistic activity.
1946	Returns to painting and assemblage.
1989	Lives in England, where she continues to work.

LEONORA CARRINGTON

1917	Born in Clayton Green, England. Father a rich industrialist in textiles, mother a daughter of an Irish country doctor.
1932–34	Finishing school, Florence, Italy; begins to paint.
1934	Debut at court of George V.
1936	Studies art with Amédée Ozenfant, London; meets Max Ernst at his London exhibition. Moves to Paris with Ernst.
1937–39	Lives in Saint-Martin d'Ardèche with Ernst. Visitors include Leonor Fini. First surrealist paintings shown by Breton in Paris and Amsterdam (1937). First short stories published, illustrated by Ernst.
1939	Ernst imprisoned as enemy alien. Leonora follows him to camp at Largentière, then to Paris, obtains his release.
1940	Ernst again imprisoned, with Hans Bellmer, near Aix. Leonora travels to Paris, cannot obtain his release, returns to Saint-Martin, breaks down.
1940	Sent by her parents to an asylum at Santander, Spain.
1941	Escapes and marries Renato le Duc in Lisbon.
1941	Flees to New York with le Duc.
1941	Rejoins group of surrealist exiles; writes "Down Below," a memoir of her breakdown, and "Waiting," on the theme of jealous women, which is published in *View*.
1942	Moves to Mexico, divorces le Duc.
1943	Meets Emerico (Chiqui) Weisz, Hungarian photographer.
1944	"Down Below" is published in *VVV*.
1945–46	Writes two pieces for theatre.
1946	Marries Chiqui Weisz, with whom she will have two sons: Pablo and Gabriel.
1948	First solo exhibition, Pierre Matisse Gallery, New York City.

1950s	Her work is influenced by theories and philosophy of Gurdjieff and Ouspensky.
1963	Paints *El Mundo mágico de los Mayas* for the National Museum of Anthropology of Mexico.
1974–76	Publishes earlier novels.
1984	Moves to New York.
1988	Moves to Chicago, where she lives and works.

AUBE ELLEOUET

1936	Born in Paris to Jacqueline Lamba and André Breton.
1940–41	Family emigrates to New York via Marseilles and Martinique.
1942	Parents separate, Lamba begins to exhibit her work and moves in with artist David Hare.
1944	Visits Mexico with her mother.
1945	Parents divorce.
late '40s	Returns to Paris with her mother, who is now married to Hare, whom she will later divorce.
1955	Meets Yves Elléouët, Breton poet and painter (1932–75), when he joins surrealist circle.
1956	Marries Elléouët. Couple adopts a six-year-old Korean girl.
1966	After her father's death, Aube begins to make collages. Couple lives in Saché with group surrounding Alexander Calder.
1974	First exhibition, collages, in Tours.
1975	Yves Elléouët dies.
1989	Lives and works in Saché.

LEONOR FINI

1918	Born in Buenos Aires. Mother of Venetian-German-Slovenian origin, father Argentinian. Raised in Trieste.
1932	Begins to draw and paint, studying art in museums and her uncle's library but never attending art school.
1935	First exhibition, in Trieste. Invited to Milan to paint first portrait commission. Meets artists Funi, Carrà, Tosi.
1936	Moves to Paris. Befriends Eluard, Ernst, Dali, Man Ray, and Bataille. Exhibits with the Surrealists in London (1936), New York (1936) and Tokyo (1937) but never becomes a member of the group.

1939	First solo exhibition, Julien Levy Gallery, New York City. Spends war years in Rome and Monte Carlo.
1945	Illustrates *Juliette* by de Sade.
1946	Returns to Paris. Befriends Jean Genet.
1952	Works on costumes for the film *Romeo and Juliet* by Renato Castellani.
1954	Begins the series "Guardians": hieratic women with shaved heads.
1956	Makes a series of drawings on the theme of the sorceress. Befriends Victor Brauner.
1966	With *Le Fait accompli,* she arrives at the theme of the revolt of the sorceress against the power of men.
1989	Lives and works in Paris as a painter, theatre designer, and illustrator.

VALENTINE HUGO

1887	Born in Capécure, France (suburb of Boulogne-sur-Mer). Only daughter of schoolteacher mother and musician father.
1903	Father dies by drowning.
1892– 1907	Studies in Boulogne at school for English girls.
1907	Enrolls in the Ecole des Beaux-Arts in Paris, in the atelier Humbert.
1909–14	Befriends Cocteau and Satie. Inspired by the Ballets Russes, makes numerous drawings and paintings, which are noticed and sell well. Works for fashion magazines.
1914	Becomes engaged to arts patron Charles Stern.
1917	Meets painter Jean Hugo, great-grandson of Victor Hugo.
1919	Marries Hugo, collaborates with him on designs for ballet, including Cocteau's *Mariés de la Tour Eiffel* (1921).
1926	Befriends Eluard and falls out with Cocteau. Begins to engrave.
1929	Separates from Hugo. Brief liaison with Eluard.
1930–36	Participates in the surrealist movement, illustrating works by Eluard, Breton, Char, Crevel, Lautréamont, d'Arnim, and Rimbaud (1939). First exhibits in Salon des Surindépendants, 1933. Gives financial aid to surrealist friends.
1930–32	Tumultuous relationship with Breton.
1931	Begins *Portrait of the Surrealists.*

1932	Divorces Jean Hugo.
1935	Exhibits in Copenhagen and Tenerife. Her mother moves in with her on a permanent basis.
1936	Exhibits in New York.
1937	Exhibits in Tokyo.
1940–45	Has difficult years, with narrowing circle of friends.
1944–47	Becomes president of the Syndicat des décorateurs, working mostly in theatre.
1947	Writes and illustrates *Les Aventures de Fido Caniche,* for children.
1950s	Lives in solitude and misery. Gets few commissions for book covers or illustrations. Paints portraits and sells her valuables.
1963	An auction, organized by a group of artists, earns her enough to provide a regular pension.
1968	Dies in Paris.

JOYCE MANSOUR

1928	Born in Bowden, England, of Egyptian origin.
1953	Living in Paris. Publishes first collection of poetry, *Cris,* which attracts the attention of André Breton, who becomes a close friend.
1958	*Les Gisants satisfaits,* J. J. Pauvert, Paris.
1959	J. Benoît's famous surreal fête, "L'Exécution du testament du marquis de Sade," takes place in her home.
1965	*Carré blanc,* Le Soleil Noir, Paris.
1976	*Orsa Maggiore, La nuova folio,* illustrated by Wilfredo Lam.
1977	*Faire signe au machiniste,* Le Soleil Noir, illustrated by Camacho. (Other publications with Le Soleil Noir illustrated by Matta, Svanberg, Baj, and Alechinsky.)
1987	Dies in Paris.

MERET OPPENHEIM

| 1913 | Born in Berlin-Charlottenburg. Her father, a German-Jewish country doctor, is interested in psychology and later attends the seminars of Jung in Zurich. Her mother, Swiss, comes from a family of painters and writers. |
| 1914–18 | Lives with her grandparents in the Jura, Switzerland. |

1918	Her family lives in a village in the Black Forest. Studies in Germany and in Basel. Begins to draw at the age of seven.
1930	Leaves school without graduating.
1931	Takes a few weeks of classes at the Kunstgewerbeschule in Basel.
1932	Moves to Paris, occasionally attends free life classes at the Académie de la Grande Chaumière.
1933	Meets Alberto Giacometti and Hans Arp, who introduce her to the Surrealists. Exhibits in the Salon des Surindépendants. Poses nude for Man Ray's series of photos "érotiques voilées."
1935	Exhibits in Copenhagen and Tenerife.
1936	Creates *Le Déjeuner en fourrure*, the famous fur-lined teacup. To support herself, she designs jewelry and accessories for Schiaparelli and Rochas. Exhibits in London and New York. Has affair with Ernst, who writes the invitation for her first solo exhibition in Basel.
1937	Leaves Paris for Basel. Enters a period of psychological and artistic crisis that will last 18 years. Reads Jung.
1938-39	Studies academic drawing at the Kunstgewerbeschule in Basel. Makes *Table with Bird Feet*, exhibits fantastic furniture with Leonor Fini, Max Ernst, and others, Galerie René Druin and Leo Castelli, Paris.
1940-48	Restores paintings for a living. Exhibits in Mexico City and New York.
1944-56	Little artistic production. Consults a Jungian analyst.
1949	Marries Wolfgang La Roche, whom she met in 1945. Lives in Bern.
1954	Rediscovers the pleasure of painting.
1956	Creates the object *The Couple*, of coupling shoes.
1959	Conceives and organizes a "Feast on the Body of a Naked Woman" for a dinner party, which she repeats for the exhibition "EROS" in Paris.
1967	Retrospective, Moderna Museet, Stockholm.
1981	Publishes *Sansibar*, a collection of poems (1933–57) and serigraphs.
1985	Dies in Bern.

GISELE PRASSINOS

1920   Born in Istanbul. Father a Greek professor of French, mother of Italian origin.

1922   Family moves to Paris. Studies at the communal school of Nanterre, the lycèe Racine, and the lycée of Saint-Germain-en-Laye.

1934   Draws the attention of the Surrealists for her poetry and her personality as *femme-enfant*. Publishes poems in *Minotaure* and *Documents 34*.

1935   Publishes *La Souterelle arthritique,* first book of stories. Makes first surrealist objects.

1937–54   Works successively as stenographer, kindergarten teacher in Saint-Cloud, and secretary at an art gallery. Resumes literary activity after the war.

1958–66   Publishes several novels, including *Le Temps n'est rien* in 1958 and *Le Visage effleuré de peine* in 1964.

1962–85   Publishes several collections of poetry, including *L'Homme au chagrin* (1962), *La Vie, la voix* (1971), and *L'Instant qui va* (1985).

1974   Begins to make figures from wood and hand-sewn tapestries.

1976   Publishes *Trouver sans chercher,* stories and poems on the theme of femininity and communication, written from 1934 to 1944.

1980   Lives in Paris. Writes poetry and novels.

KAY SAGE

1898   Born Katherine Linn Sage in Albany, New York. Father a wealthy and conservative senator from New York and trustee of Cornell University. Mother unstable and dependent on morphine.

1900   Parents separate. Lives with mother in Europe.

1914–18   Takes courses at the Corcoran Art School in Washington, D.C. Works as translator for Censorship Bureau in New York.

1920   Studies drawing and painting in Rome at the British Academy and the Scuola Libera delle Belle Arti.

1922   Meets Prince Ranieri di San Faustino.

1925   Marries Prince Ranieri. Lives for ten years in Rome and Rapallo. Meets T. S. Eliot and Ezra Pound. Paints, inspired by Vorticism.

1935	Divorces Prince Ranieri.
1936	First solo exhibition, Galeria del Milione, Milan.
1937	Moves to Paris. Paints, inspired by De Chirico. Publishes first volume of illustrated poetry for children. Exhibits one painting in the Salon des Surindépendants and is discovered by the Surrealists.
1939	Meets Tanguy.
1940	Returns to New York, organizes exhibitions of Parisian artists with the French Ministry of Education and helps a number of Surrealists to escape the war in Europe. Marries Tanguy. Has first American exhibition.
1941	Moves to Woodbury, Connecticut.
1950	Begins exhibiting at the Catherine Viviano Gallery, New York.
1954	Joint exhibition with Tanguy, Wadsworth Atheneum, Hartford, Connecticut.
1955	Death of Tanguy. Depressed and starting to go blind, Sage continues to paint and write. Finishes her autobiography, "China Eggs."
1956	Paints *Passage,* her last self-portrait.
1957–62	Publishes four books of poetry.
1958	Stops painting, undergoes several eye operations.
1960	Retrospective, Catherine Viviano Gallery, New York City.
1963	Completes a catalogue raisonné of the work of Tanguy. Commits suicide in Woodbury by shooting herself.

REMEDIOS VARO

1913	Born in Anglés, Spain. Travels as a child in Spain and North Africa with father, a hydraulics engineer who sparks interest in mathematics, mechanical drawing, and locomotives. Mother very devout. Varo attends convent schools.
1924	Studies painting at the Academia de San Fernando in Madrid.
1930	Marries painter Gerardo Lizarraga.
1932	Studies at the Ecole des Beaux-Arts in Barcelona.
1935	Frequents the "Logicophobiste" group, including Esteban Francis.
1936	Meets poet Benjamin Péret, just come to Spain to fight in the ranks of the anarchists. Leaves her husband.

1937	Marries Péret, accompanies him to Paris, joins Surrealists. Meets Leonora Carrington. Exhibition in Tokyo.
1938	Her drawings, inspired by the early work of Oscar Dominguez, Ernst, and Magritte, are published in *Minotaure* and *Trajectoire du rêve.* Exhibits in Amsterdam and Paris.
1942	Forced to flee France for political reasons. Settles in Mexico with Péret. Writes "Lady Milagra," a story on the theme of the magical ability of women, but does not paint for her first years in Mexico. Becomes close friend of Leonora Carrington and Natalia Trotsky. Active in the group of Trotskyites.
1947	Separates from Péret, who returns to Paris.
1949	Visits Caracas, works several months for the Ministerio de Salud Público, where her brother, a doctor, occupies an important post.
1953	Marries Walter Gruen, successful businessman, who encourages her to resume painting.
1955	Her first solo exhibition is a huge success.
1961	Struggles with depression, paints the humorous and ominous *Woman Leaving the Psychoanalyst's.*
1963	Paints her last picture, and first without a single human figure, *Nature morte ressuscitant.* Dies in Mexico City.

NOTES ON CONTRIBUTORS

ROBERT JAMES BELTON teaches art history, theory, and criticism at McMaster University in Hamilton, Canada. He is currently preparing a book on the image of woman in Surrealist art.

JEAN-PIERRE CAUVIN teaches French literature at the University of Texas at Austin. He is the author of *Henri Bosco et la pensée du sacré,* and coeditor of *Poems of André Breton.*

MARY ANN CAWS teaches French and Comparative Literature at the Graduate Center of the City University of New York. Her publications include *The Poetry of Dada and Surrealism, André Breton, The Eye in the Text, Reading Frames in Modern Fiction, The Art of Interference,* and *The Women of Bloomsbury.*

PETER G. CHRISTENSEN teaches in the English Department at Marquette University. He has published numerous articles on twentieth-century literature and film.

GEORGIANA COLVILE teaches French, Film, and Comparative Literature at the University of Colorado. She is the author of *Vers un langage des arts autour des années vingt* and *Beyond and Beneath the Mantle: On Thomas Pynchon's "The Crying of Lot 49."* She is currently coediting a book, *Women Writing In and Out of the Americas.*

MADELEINE COTTENET-HAGE teaches French at the University of Maryland, College Park. She has written on Gisèle Prassinos and published articles on francophone women writers, including Marguerite Duras and the Haitian Marie Chauvet, in various American and European journals.

MARYANN DE JULIO teaches French at Kent State University. Her research interests include modern poetry, film, literary criticism, and translation. She has just completed a full-length study of the contemporary French poet and art critic Jacques Dupin.

INEZ HEDGES teaches French and coordinates the Program in Cinema Studies at Northeastern University. She is the author of *Languages of Revolt: Dada and Surrealist Literature and Film* and of the forthcoming *Breaking the Frame: Film Language and the Experience of Limits.*

RENEE RIESE HUBERT teaches Comparative Literature at the University of California, Irvine. She is the author of *Surrealism and the Book* and is currently working on *Women, Partnership and Surrealism.*

RUDOLF KUENZLI teaches Comparative Literature and English and directs the International Dada Archive at the University of Iowa. He is the coauthor of *Dada Artifacts* and *Dada Spectrum: The Dialectics of Revolt,* editor of *New York Dada, Dada and Surrealist Film,* and coeditor of *Marcel Duchamp: Artist of the Century* and *André Breton Today.*

JUDITH YOUNG MALLIN is working on a book, *Stars, Stripes and Surrealists.* Her series *The Surreal Eye* was aired on Channel 13 in New York. She is currently a consultant for two new PBS projects as well as several upcoming exhibitions relating to the Surrealists.

239

STEPHEN ROBESON MILLER has lectured and written about Kay Sage extensively. His archive on her and other Surrealists in Connecticut in the 1940s is in the Archives of American Art, Smithsonian Institution.

GLORIA FEMAN ORENSTEIN teaches in Comparative Literature and the Program for the Study of Women and Men in Society at the University of Southern California. She is the author of *The Theater of the Marvelous: Surrealism and the Contemporary Stage*, and of *The Reflowering of the Goddess*, forthcoming from Pergamon Press. Currently she is coediting an anthology, *Ecofeminist Perspectives: Culture, Nature, Theory*.

JUDITH PRECKSHOT teaches French at the University of Minnesota–Twin Cities. She has published esssays on twentieth-century French poets and is currently working on the intertextual presence of Valéry in Tournier's fiction.

GWEN RAABERG directs the Center for Women's Resources and Research and teaches English at Western Michigan University. She is author of a number of articles on Surrealism, the interrelations of art and literature, and issues in contemporary critical theory. At present she is completing a book titled *The Poetics of Collage*.